FOLLOW
THE STORM

A LONG WAY HOME

David Dick

First Edition, November 1, 2002

Copyright 2002
By
Plum Lick Publishing, Incorporated
P. O. Box 68
North Middletown, KY 40357-0068

Dust jacket design and book production
by Stacey Freibert Design
756 South First Street, Suite 208
Louisville, Kentucky 40202

Front cover photo by Dale Hancock

Other books by David Dick

The View from Plum Lick
Follow the Storm (Original Edition)
Peace at the Center
A Conversation with Peter P. Pence
The Quiet Kentuckians
The Scourges of Heaven

Other books by David and Lalie Dick

Home Sweet Kentucky
Rivers of Kentucky

ISBN: 0-9632886-9-5

Library of Congress Catalog Card Number
2002107954

For

Congressman Leo Ryan,
Don Harris, Robert Brown,
Greg Robinson, Patricia Parks,
and
Bill Stewart
who died

and for

Lalie and Rose
who lived through it

and for

Cathy, Debbie, Nell,
Ravy, and Sam
whose legacy it becomes

I cannot praise a fugitive and cloistered virtue, unexercised and unbreathed, that never sallies out and sees her adversary, but slinks out of the race, where that immortal garland is to be run for, not without dust and heat. Assuredly we bring not innocence into the world, we bring impurity much rather: that which purifies us is trial, and trial is by what is contrary.

John Milton
Areopagitica, 1644

CHAPTER ONE

Storms shaped me from the beginning—the first force striking in the month of my conception—May 1929—one of those "mistakes" my mother, Lucile, revealed to me several winters before she died in 1975. The year of my birth, 1930, was no time for a young mother and father to be adding another child to a struggling, threadbare family with scarcely enough food on the table. She would remember those days as if it had been yesterday.

Lucile Crouch, born at Plum Lick, Kentucky, near the start of the twentieth century, had once thrown caution to the wild wind and run off to become the teenage bride of a Disciples of Christ minister's son, Samuel, youngest child of Nellie and the Rev. Coleman Woodford Dick. They wanted the best for their last born, their baby boy—they worried about him because he was such a beguiling, unpredictable risk taker. Lucile's mother and father, Laura and Bill, wedded to the land, bound and taking their breath from it, could not abide New Age shenanigans. They could smell summer storms coming.

Lucile and Samuel were luckless almost from the start—she with her restless laughter and fiery temper, he with his seductive tenor voice and devil-may-care dreaming. Why, he just wanted to patch up the world of scraped knees and faltering hearts. He'd become a loyal medic serving in the respected Barrow Unit—Base Hospital No. 40—in World War I. The

Lexington, Kentucky, group was headed by "old" Dr. David Barrow, whose son, "Young David," had been my father's best friend. They'd played together as children, conspired to fathom the mysteries of creation, seeking the Grail of the fullness of the Good Life. They must have thought they were invincible.

In 1914, young David, filled with wanderlust, drowned when his small craft capsized in a storm on Lake Michigan—he was nineteen years old. My father, unexplainably not on David's odyssey to the Northland, became a grieving nineteen-year-old pallbearer who, through his tears, vowed to have a son and to name him for his friend. That's how I came to be David Barrow Dick.

When Samuel was twenty-four years old, after the Armistice was signed, the Barrow Unit returned to Lexington, April 15, 1919. There's no record or recounting of how he hastily courted seventeen-year-old Lucile, but they were married that same year after obtaining a license across the Ohio River in southern Indiana. For a time he tried to sell insurance in Hopkinsville, and he failed. In Winchester, Samuel assembled enough pre-med credits at Kentucky Wesleyan College and began to hobo to the University of Cincinnati School of Medicine, where he stitched together a medical degree.

The first roof over Samuel and Lucile's head was on Fleming Road just off Springfield Road in Greater Cincinnati. The small house with the arched front door was the question mark of a curving line drawn northward from U.S. 27 from Bourbon County, Kentucky. Grandparents had warned against the dangers of leaving the richness of the soil on the farm alongside Plum Lick Creek, but Lucile and Dr. Sam were in no mood to listen. They were in love, and he dared to go on dreaming of being a truly fine physician and surgeon.

In the romantic nights of the Queen City, Samuel did not foresee that the years of "the Roaring 20s" were dancing in a mindless frenzy toward the brink of destruction—the Jazz Age had not quite disintegrated into the Great Depression. My older sister, Jane, was born in 1922, two years after Prohibition became the law of the land, and Florence was born in 1926, the year Congress heard testimony that Prohibition was responsible for an *increase* in alcoholism.

In the midst of a financial plague spreading to every nook and cranny of the nation, Dr. Samuel Stephens Dick loved his medical profession, loved his wife and his daughters. But he had an unfulfilled dream—a son—to perpetuate the memory of a friend lost in that storm off the port village of Ludington, Michigan.

With the passage of time my mother confessed to me how she'd "acted badly" at the time of my birth, February 18, 1930. She didn't tell me exactly what that meant, but she must have been remembering bitter frustration and foreboding about my father and what she could clearly see and feel happening all around her. Wall Street's "Black Thursday" came crashing down when she was five months pregnant, there were dresses and shoes to be bought for eight-year-old Jane and four-year-old Florence, my father's new medical practice had barely begun—and Prohibition had driven him and many others to pure grain alcohol.

"If you wanta have a good party, be sure to invite a medical student!" was a rallying cry of the Thou Shalt Not Drink time. "If a medical student throws a party, be sure to go, because that's where you'll find "Purple Jesus"—grape juice graced with "laboratory gin."

When I was one year old, bread lines were forming in cities throughout the land, four to five million people were unemployed. Dr. Sam would soon enough learn that most who were sick were unable to pay their doctors' bills. In a Model A Ford, my mother drove my father to make his house calls, since he could barely find his way in and out of the houses. Nights were especially fearful when violent storms rolled up the Ohio Valley and Lucile became frantic, wondering how much longer she could endure these infuriating circumstances. Many times she considered leaving Samuel and returning to the home of her mother and father on the "other side" of the Ohio River, back home on the farm. She stuck it out as long as Samuel lived. The Purple Jesus was a balm of Gilead, and Samuel was quickly swept down into its whirlpool.

My father was buried in the North Middletown, Kentucky, cemetery in September of 1931—just thirty-six years old—his dream of becoming a physician and surgeon finished. The son he always wanted was eighteen months old. As soon as possible after the funeral, my mother,

her thinness wracked with grief, packed my two sisters and me into the Model A and without looking back drove one more time south out of Cincinnati, heading home at last toward Plum Lick. I was placed in a foster home because Lucile at twenty-eight years of age was too distraught to manage two young daughters and an infant son too. They moved in with my grandparents, and I went to the home of a childless couple, Bob and Lida ("E") Hughes on South Main Street in Paris, Kentucky. Even though they called me that "puny little thing," they loved me with a devotion that spelled safe haven in a world of unending storms.

Each evening, Bob and "E" sat close by the upright *Philco* to hear through the static the trusted reports of NBC's Lowell Thomas—the 1931 coal field war in Harlan County, Kentucky, the 1932 Japanese invasion of Manchuria, and the 1933 rise of Adolph Hitler. I was too young to understand the meaning of the words, but I remember peeking through the lighted dial opening and imagining that, inside, there was a chair upon which a grownup sat and talked. I had a fancy to sit in that chair, if only I could figure a way to squeeze through the tiny window to the world of *Let's Pretend*. As time went along, I believed I saw Amos and Andy, Fibber McGee and Molly, and Our Gal Sal.

The place where I slept each night was on a cozy pallet on the floor of an upstairs closet a few feet away from Bob and E's bed. Bob and I never failed to say our bedtime prayers together: "Now I lay me down to sleep, I pray the Lord my soul to keep. If I should die before I wake, I pray the Lord my soul to take." E didn't say prayers with us, and she didn't go to Sunday School with Bob and me. She may have gone once or twice but decided that the other women were too stuck up and that the whole Heaven and Hell thing was a bit much. E never went back, but she'd have Sunday dinner waiting for Bob and me when we returned. Her specialties were chicken and dumplings and hot rhubarb pie.

When I was four years old, Mother remarried, and I rejoined her and Jane and Florence at a large nearby farm called Mt. Auburn. The owner, William H. Rogers, a widower, became my no-nonsense stepfather. He had two sons, Warren and Billy, older, bigger, and a lot tougher than I was. They treated me all right as long as I didn't get in the way, and I figured out how to do that. My sisters tolerated me, although several times they threatened to throw me over the banister of the graceful, winding staircase. On the other side of the curved wall there was a secret space where, we were proudly told, Confederate soldiers once hid. Jane and Florence also told me a little bit about how it was back in Cincinnati when they'd prayed for another sister and had vowed that if I turned out to be a boy they were going to shovel me into the furnace. I was never totally sure how much they were kidding—everybody smiled whenever the story was retold.

I was sick a lot—I had to learn to walk all over again after a close call with polio. I survived pneumonia three years out of four, and each time I'd go to get well at Bob and E's. I spent my summers with them. Had my whooping cough there, my measles, and another close call—scarlet fever. Bob and E, who seemed ancient but were about middle aged, took me on a train ride in 1936 to California, where we visited with E's sister in Pasadena. I loved the smell of the flowers, and the beach at Santa Monica fascinated me: I was drawn by sight of the incoming waves and the gathering clouds, and I began to wonder about the world "out there" beyond the horizon. Whenever there was a storm, I'd see it as something to be gone through so as to come out better on the other side. The first book I read was *Tom Sawyer* and the second was *The Adventures of Huckleberry Finn*. I wanted to write like that, but not until I'd had a girlfriend like Becky and had smoked a pipe and floated down the Mississippi River with a good man like Nigger Jim.

Jane and Florence went to college and quickly married. Warren went to war in Europe, and Billy, who fell victim to spinal meningitis, attended the Pennsylvania School for the Deaf. I inherited the enveloping loneliness of a big house with little pieces of doubtful love left scattered around. The wind made the windowpanes to whine and the floors to creak, and I had a lot of nightmares, including the one about the man in the white coat who'd show up to make capons out of bantam roosters. Lord, how that man scared me!—always smiling as he took me by my collar and pulled me beneath the winding staircase. I'd wake up in a cold sweat about the time he was running his finger along the edge of his straight razor.

There were many days when I'd play alone along Little Brush Creek on the eastern side of the old house. It was there that I discovered the curious flow of water—Little Brush to join Big Brush near Flat Rock, then emptying into Hinkston Creek joining Stoner Creek to become South Fork of Licking River. In time, I'd understand that the Licking would empty into the Ohio at Cincinnati, then roll on to the Mississippi and the Gulf of Mexico. Much later, after I'd grown up, I'd know that the water in which I'd waded as a child would return to the atmosphere, arch back up the Ohio Valley, and fall again in newness.

Back in the late '30s I played at steamboat races. Little sticks became paddle wheelers—I'd start them side by side allowing the current to carry them to a finish line, which I called Victory Island. I imagined conniving captains and pilots, sweating deckhands, and pulchritudinous ladies waving kerchiefs and blowing kisses. When each race was over, I in my all-knowing would return to the beginning and start another contest. I did it repeatedly until I was bone tired or until the flash of lightning and the rumble of thunder became so close together that I knew it was time to hightail it to the house. My stepfather had warned me about touching wire fences or standing under trees in a storm, and I listened to everything he said—most of the time.

On one hot summer day, my mother and stepfather were away from the farm, and I was out back in the big barn, where there was a shed with plenty of room for sheep, a long line of pens for newborn lambs, ample stalls for horses and mules, a warm corner stall in which to milk the Jersey cow, and a spacious loft for hay by the wagon load. My stepfather's mare, Lady, was in her stall. I moseyed over, stroked the blaze on her forehead, and straightened her mane. Before I hardly knew what I was doing, I maneuvered the bit into her mouth and slipped the bridle over her ears. Nobody had told me not to ride Lady. She wasn't what you'd call green or raw, but she had plenty of spunk. My stepfather, Mr. Bill, loved that mare as much as he did his birddogs Nip and Tuck.

I led Lady out into the center of the barn and heaved up the saddle. I tried to make sure that the girth was cinched tight, because I had been warned about slipping saddles. Not good, they said. Could get you caught and dragged to death. Could get you stepped on for sure.

Up till then, when I was ten or eleven years old, I'd not gone much farther than to harness up the team of mules—Minnie and Maggie—to harrow the little piece of corn ground that I thought of as my own. I just decided that the time had come for me to take a ride on a good looking, high-stepping Standardbred, and Lady filled the bill. So out of the barn we went at a pleasant trot.

I had a good grip on the reins, and my knees and inner thighs felt the goodness of the polished saddle. When we went by the sheep huddled in the thicket on the long ridge, I was prideful and awfully full of myself. I stuck out my tongue at the maa-maas. "Boogie-de-boo and how are you, damn stupid sheep?"

A few minutes after my being so ugly, a wind arose and rustled the leaves of the locust trees. The limbs bent backwards and whipped like cats-o-nine-tails. White blossoms scattered like ashes. Lightning ran in long, thin, jagged lines on the horizon and thunder sounded closer each time there was a flash. Suddenly the sky was deep purple and rain came over us like a waterfall. A voice inside of me said to get the hell to the barn. The same voice must have spoken inside Lady, because she reared and almost lost me. She commenced to gallop and before you could say Good God Almighty, three gaits turned into five, so that by the time we reached the first fence corner, I didn't know whether she was going to go over it or through it. She went down on her left side, catching my leg and bruising it from my foot to my thigh. It hurt like thunderin' blazes but nothing was broken, so far as I could tell. Then she jumped with me having a death grip on her neck, and she headed straight down the fencerow in the direction of the barn. I wanted to jump off, and I called myself trying to boot out, but gravity held me tight in the saddle like a rock in a deep quarry. I'd been told that if a horse ever tries to run away with you, grab one rein with both hands and pull as hard as you can. I tried that but it didn't work, not even a little bit. Wherever Lady was going I was going with her. When she came up on the next fence corner she went down again, but this time I slid out from under her, still holding on for dear life to the reins. Lady must've heard her voice say, enough is enough, because she didn't run again but stood there trembling, shaking herself from head to tail.

I was limping, but I managed to lead her scary highness into the barn. I didn't turn loose until I had her safely in the stall, and only then did I take off the saddle and remove the bridle. I walked to the house, looked for nobody, and went straight to my bed and said a little thank you prayer. Then I pulled the covers over my head. When my mother and stepfather came home, I didn't tell them anything about what had happened. They were too busy with their own troubles. Mr. Bill didn't ask how Lady had gotten so muddy.

It wasn't too long after that, on a mid-summer Sunday morning, that another storm rolled across Harrod's Creek Road. I was looking out through the bedroom window and saw a bright, almost blinding flash of lightning and a simultaneous crash of thunder. At the top of the hill just to the south of the old house that was spooky enough without any storms, a tall black walnut tree was split down the middle. Lady had been standing there, up close. She was killed instantly. On that day, it seemed as if something died in my stepfather too.

My mother and Mr. Bill's marriage lasted ten years. Maybe they started out being lonely and needing each other after the losses of their young spouses. Maybe my mother was too stubborn and easy to anger; maybe my stepfather was impatient and sometimes goaty. Whatever it was, they just weren't cut out for each other—they were doomed and destined for divorce.

I was fourteen years old when Mr. Bill picked me up after school, October 16, 1944, and said, "Today's a day you'll never forget." I waited for the rest: "As you know, your mother and I haven't been getting along too well." I shook my head, as if to say I wasn't aware of it, but I'd sensed something had been going on that was painful, because it was full of my mother crying almost every night. "Your mother and I are going to separate." It was then I bawled. Mr. Bill put his hand on my shoulder, which I believe was the only time he ever touched me.

That evening, I was called into the parlor where there was a meeting with my mother, Mr. Bill, and a banker. They wanted to know how interested I might be one day to have the farm on Plum Lick, about five miles away as the crow flies. It was sixty-seven acres that my mother had inherited from her parents, and I had a small flock of sheep there along with a shorthorn cow. Without hesitation, I said I was definitely interested. How could I not be? With that I was told I could go back to my room—I don't ever remember being more alone. I finally fell asleep, thinking about separation and divorce and how it might be if I were unhappy with or unsuited for my wife, or she with me. I suppose I thought there's got to be some good in everything.

The next morning, I climbed up a sugar maple at Mt. Auburn and cut my initials on one of the limbs. I wrote a message and put it into a shoebox—"I'm glad to have lived here these ten years"—and I buried it in the side yard. It was my idea for a time capsule, but by the time I returned in my middle years to see if it might still be there, all traces of it had vanished. That was the same day I looked up into the sugar maple and knew that it was now too tall to climb. The initials had most likely healed.

On the morning that my mother, sisters, and I walked with our suitcases off the long side porch at Mt. Auburn, I had some pretty strong feelings seething inside of me. I was going to finish high school and go to college to study literature, starting with Mark Twain, then going on from there. As soon as possible I was going to see the world outside Bourbon County—mountaintops and meadowlands, sunsets and sunrises, hurricanes and tornadoes—and, by damn, I was going to make a name for myself. But when I'd had enough of all that I was coming home to Kentucky.

CHAPTER TWO

"You going to get a job or go to college?" was the question frequently heard in the summer of '48, the year I graduated from high school. Hardly anybody thought of college as a clearing-house for jobs—wasn't it a golden opportunity to enhance the mind? I knew I could work full-time as a groom in a Bluegrass Thoroughbred establishment. At 112 pounds, I might slim farther down to jockey weight.

I could join the regular Navy, because I was a member of the Naval Reserve and by the time I was eighteen years old I had two cruises under my thirteen buttons. One voyage was from Norfolk to New York City, the other began in New Orleans, put in at Key West, and docked in Panama. In Colón, a nightclub act portrayed a raggedy guerrilla tromping across the stage with a scantily clad damsel who at last disentangled herself from the "guerrilla" and performed a striptease to the merriment of hundreds of howling sailors.

An inner voice said, "Go to college…read books…write stories… learn to think…then go back into the world of dancing bears." In the English department at the University of Kentucky, I met Hollis Summers, a kind and sensitive man who taught creative writing and a survey of English and American literature. He awakened in me a desire to be a chronicler of the humanities. Another professor, Wally Briggs, taught me the value of the spoken word, stagecraft, and the importance of comedy and tragedy.

A funny thing happened on the way to the middle of my junior year in college: the selective service, the Korean Conflict, and no more money from my father's little insurance policy. I opted to join the Navy and found myself in the waters of the Far East—Japan, Korea, China, and the Philippines. I served four years as an enlisted man in communications aboard the light cruiser U.S.S. *Manchester* and at Subic Bay in the Philippine Islands. I wrote the *Manchester*'s "cruise book" and worked part-time for the Armed Forces Radio and Television Service. I lusted to be a commissioned officer, but without a college degree it was out of the question. I managed to become a second class petty officer. On one of my returns to California, I attended a ship's party and found myself dancing with Rose Ann Casale, a beautiful USO volunteer formerly of Centerville, Iowa. After a brief courtship, we were married on January 24, 1953, in St. Anthony's Catholic Church in Long Beach. I was a sailor who thought at age twenty-two it was time to start a family. I was discharged from the Navy in 1955, and with the G.I. Bill we headed to the University of Kentucky so that I could finish my English literature studies. Our son, Samuel, was born in 1956, and he was followed by three daughters—Deborah, Catherine, and Nell.

Hungering for a job after college graduation, I tried retailing on an executive training program at Shillito's in Cincinnati—fired. Tried selling nonelectrical typewriters the year IBM came to Lexington— embarrassing failure. Tried being an announcer at WVLK when it was located on the top floor of the old Phoenix Hotel in Lexington—fired. So I retreated to graduate school at UK and earned a master's degree in English literature. It was my first encounter with Cervantes and *Don Quixote*, Theodore Dreiser and *Sister Carrie*, Stephen Crane and *The Red Badge of Courage*, and a young unsung student named Wendell Berry. Those four and many others helped me to recognize that what I needed to do in order to become a writer was first to become a journalist.

In 1959, after I'd won a broadcast journalism scholarship, I began working the early morning shift at WHAS Radio and Television in Louisville. For seven years I woke up at 2:00 a.m. and was in the newsroom by 3:30 every day except Sunday. I was an editor and eventually an anchorman. Bill Small, who hired me, moved on to the Washington Bureau of CBS News. I knew that was where I wanted to be.

In 1966 I dreamed I couldn't go to my grave a fulfilled man unless I was working at CBS network news. I wanted to follow national and international storms. I'd burned out on dead-on-arrivals at General Hospital, house fires started by children playing with matches, and musical chairs at the mayor's office in Louisville and the governor's office in Frankfort. I often thought of myself as Don Quixote, tilting against larger windmills, longing to report more prominent dead-on-arrivals at hospitals from Walter Reed Army to Bethesda Naval, bigger fires started by bigger children, and musical chairs in the Oval Office.

The inner voice said, "Remember the little chair on the other side of the radio dial? Well, it's either now or never." If I stayed in Louisville, I might retire as a news director and live out my days in doddering misery—waging war on crabgrass and dandelions, helping the Holy Name Society with the battle against pornography, playing poker and bingo with the Knights of Columbus, eventually retiring to shuffleboard in St. Petersburg. Instead, the family and I piled into a red 1963 Mustang convertible and headed east to the nation's capital. CBS News had hired me, and I was off to see more of the world than I'd ever dreamed possible when I was fourteen years old walking away from Mt. Auburn. I knew that one day I'd come back to Kentucky to live out my years, but not until I'd tasted some glory as far south as Cape Horn and as far east as Jerusalem.

When it came to the flow of adrenaline through the human body, there was hardly anything to compare with presidential campaigns and other savage storms. Sitting like birds of prey atop the kidneys, the two adrenal glands are the culprits responsible for the secretion of steroid hormones and epinephrine—the good stuff that enters the bloodstream, makes the heart pound, and makes the mind believe it can pole-vault mountains and brave if not deflect bullets. They made a country boy from Kentucky dream of one day becoming a foreign correspondent.

The first four years with the network, 1966-1970, are now a blur of images: the assassinations of Martin Luther King Jr. and Robert F.

Kennedy, racial riots in American cities, days and nights of H. Rap Brown and Stokely Carmichael, the Johnson and Nixon administrations, Timothy Leary and LSD, the Beatles in America, the House UnAmerican Activities Committee hearings, and my first presidential campaigns. Each one—Lyndon Johnson, Eugene McCarthy, Robert Kennedy, Richard Nixon, and George Wallace—a storm of its own making complete with killer sharks, a world apart from proper manners and stable morality. It was crazy.

I had wanted to do softer feature stories, but I quickly found out there was little appetite for them among network television news producers, champions of "hard news." The Charles Kuralts were rare and seen as oddities. From time to time I sneaked pieces through—"Kudzu on the Yazoo," "Maynard the Golf Cart," "Life in a Prairie Dog Town," and "Spring Comes to the Big Bend"—but you could have counted them on the fingers of one hand. A good storm story would at all times beat out a good feature story. Ed Fouhy of CBS News once told me after I had proposed a story about young urban people being rehabilitated on an ocean-going vessel operating out of the nation's capital: "We're not in the market for do-good stories."

The first four years had me constantly on the brink in Washington, D.C. I was close to being fired on more than one occasion, the most memorable being the day in the summer of '68 when I made an ethical decision *not* to have my camera crew take a close-up picture of Ethel Kennedy when she came to Arlington National Cemetery. She was making her first visit to the grave of her assassinated husband, Robert. The decision so angered CBS Washington Bureau chief Bill Small that he told me to get a picture one way or another and whether I was arrested was beside the point. The cameraman made an unsteady "long shot," and I was not arrested, but I was severely lectured for missing an in-her-face close-up.

My first major assignment was Alabama's Gov. George C. Wallace, and I had the dubious distinction of covering three of his presidential campaigns—1968, 1972, and 1976. I first laid eyes on the pugnacious governor on a stormy night in that stormy year, 1968. CBS News had decided I'd had more than enough chateaubriand and lobster tail aboard the Eugene McCarthy presidential campaign jet, a sleek 727 dog. And so it was that the election year news producers sentenced me to the netherworld of George Wallace. Too soon he became my specialty of specialties, my warp and my woof. It's not supposed to be that way. I liked him and he liked me. But he couldn't resist counterpunching with an occasional, private "David's gonna dick us again."

"LBJ"—Liddle Bitty Jedge—was a slur he detested, and I didn't blame him. The storms of those days wobbled my liberal apple cart or, worse, perverted my conservative psyche. But I hung tight with it, and if it hadn't been for George Wallace, there wouldn't be an Emmy perched today on my mantelpiece. He taught me a thing or two about courage and a thing or two about expediency. Most remember him as the racist who "stood in the schoolhouse door." Few would let him forget his inaugural address as governor, when he declared, "Segregation today, segregation tomorrow, segregation forever." Few recall or care that it was the same George Wallace who, seated in a wheelchair, crowned the first black homecoming queen at the University of Alabama. Many would be amused that in the final days he would say to Jesse Jackson, "I'm sorry."

Governor Wallace and I met in a driving rain thirty-four years ago. On that fateful night, Baltimore, Maryland, was drowning in a horizontally slanted downpour with gale force winds whipping the water. Wallace had blown in on a prayer and a creaking, oil-spitting DC3 that had somehow managed to survive another white-knuckled flight. The governor usually stared through the front starboard window of the lurching antique flying machine, muttering to himself and anybody else if they'd listen:

"See those clouds ovah thah? Now, he-yuh! Bettah go 'round those clouds, y'all he-yuh!" These were the days before political correctness, but even then, in 1968, it was all right to point out and make phonetic fun of the way George Wallace talked, while it was not all right to make Martin Luther King Jr. sound like anything other than a Harvard graduate. In print, "Ah hava dream" would be unthinkable and John F. Kennedy's "Cuber" came out spelled "Cuba."

15

One of the first reporters to stomp off Wallace's plane that night was Sam Donaldson, who'd just begun charging hard for ABC News. Other reporters had come to know him affectionately as "Crazy Sam." Wallace's bodyguards on the last stop had seized Sam's television crew's footage of the governor shaking hands with none other than the Imperial Wizard of the Ku Klux Klan. Sam considered the event to be of major importance, which it definitely was, in its own focused way. Wallace accused Donaldson and his crew of waiting doggedly for only one shot of one handshake in a long line of handshakes, and the governor said he had ordered the footage seized to prevent a civil disturbance. Donaldson may have been old crackers, but he wasn't that stale. He was smart enough to know censorship when he saw it, squarely and fiercely in the eye.

Over the years from 1968 through 1976, I followed George Wallace from one end of the country to the other and, if anything, I became much too close to him. On more than one private occasion I heard him use the "Big N" word but didn't report it because he would simply have denied it, and then where would I have been? That was my shallow rationalization. Was it incomplete, unethical journalism? Of course it was.

One dark and foreboding night in the Miami area, I was the only network correspondent with the governor when he showed up at a huge crowd of Republicans. He was so popular they almost ate him for dessert. Later, in the back seat of the campaign limousine, Wallace turned to me and said:

"David, what will ah do if ah win the pres'ency?"

"Well, Govnah, ah guess you'll jes run the country," were the only words I could think to blurt back at him.

The air conditioner wasn't working right in the car, and I thought Wallace asked his driver if a "nigguh" had been working on it. Was it *the* test to see if I could be trusted? Was I just another one of those carpetbag reporters? Or did he say "nigruh?" Possibly, he said "Negro" with more emphasis on the consonants than the vowels. Was I supposed to say, "Now, Guvnah, let's get this thing straight: did you say 'nigger' or not? And if you did, don't ever say it again in my presence, because if you do

I'm going to report it." Even in private he would have said, "Now, heah! What you tryin' to do heah? You know I said 'Nee-gro' and what's wrong with thet?" This was before "black," "persons of color," and African American, and I could have come back with, "Hold on Guvnah, it came out "nigger" as far as I could tell, and at the next stop I'm gonna call up Mr. Walter Cronkite, and I'm gonna tell him *xactly* what you said." And Wallace would have said, "Thet's rite, David *Dickus*, you just tell Mr. Walter Cronkite *xactly* what I said. Why don'tjew jes git outtada car right here and now, take a walk and call him up. Or use the telephone right here *in* the car. Go ahead. Do it. If Walter wants to speak to me 'bout it, I'll jes git onto the telephone and tell him that I said, 'Nee-gro.'"

Marshall Frady, who wrote *Wallace*, a popular and scathing biography of the governor, claimed that Wallace said after a loss in a gubernatorial race that he was "not goin' be out-nigguhed again." The quotation is disputed In Stephan Lesher's biography, *George Wallace, American Populist*: "That harsh, cynical line, in one form or another, clung to Wallace like a sweat-soaked shirt throughout his career." I was present on a podium in San Francisco when Mike Wallace with *60 Minutes* tried to hang the shirt on the governor, but he repeatedly denied having said it. As bulldoggish an interviewer as Mike Wallace is, he could not shake George Wallace.

Every so often, late at night, the governor would invite me up to his hotel room on the campaign trail, or I'd invite myself, and he'd let me come in. I began to realize that some of the things I said to him were beginning to come back to me in his speeches. That was a clear warning that I was too close, yet I never complained about it. George Corley Wallace knew how to give a stem-winding, stump-thumping, slung-twice speech way back before our paths first crossed.

There'd be those clever moments when I would calculate in advance what the governor might say or do:

"Governor, if I were to say that CBS News has learned that Gov. George Wallace will announce his candidacy by, say, next week, would that make me look foolish?"

The governor might simply smile, or he might say, "Nooooo, I don' think that would make you look foolish, David."

And I would go straight as an arrow to a public phone and fire a one-minute exclusive piece for the radio hourlies, built around the line, "CBS News has learned from a reliable source that Gov. George Wallace will announce his candidacy for president. The announcement will probably be made next week." At subsequent news conferences, Wallace would be asked to confirm the report, and he'd reply, "It's too early to say."

Cameraman Laurens Pierce and I, on our own, made a calculated decision that we would cover George Wallace in 1972 as if he *were* the president of the United States, ridiculous as that might have seemed to the news brokers in New York and Washington, D.C. To them he was a bad joke at best—"crumb bums," as one senior CBS News executive called the governor and his entourage. Although we frequently didn't agree with Wallace, we'd treat him with presidential respect, and we would seldom let him out of our sight. We were there on his doorstep when he turned in for the night, and we were there when he stepped through the door first thing in the morning. We were on him like, as they say down South, white on rice.

We were with Wallace in the Laurel, Maryland, shopping center on May 15, 1972, the day Arthur Bremer fired five bullets into him at close range, tearing up the governor's insides and leaving him paralyzed for life. The governor had had his favorite hamburger with lots of catsup and French fries at lunch just before the shooting, which would cause the surgeons at Holy Cross Hospital in Silver Spring to feel as if they were gathering pebbles on the moon.

I had looked Arthur Bremer in the eye at the preceding rally in Wheaton, Maryland. He had a swimmingly vacant, faraway look about him. Some unfathomable impulse told me not to attempt to interview him because, I thought, he looked *too* weird, too unrepresentative of the day-in, day-out Wallacites. Besides that, I was tired of being accused of talking only to weird-looking people. There were weirdoes du jour following all of the candidates, but Bremer really looked like a fruitcake. He was plastered with Wallace campaign stickers, buttons, and anything else he could find, so I elected to interview other, more "respectable-looking" disciples. Not in my wildest, stormiest imagination did I imagine that Bremer was carrying a loaded gun and would empty it into

George Wallace's belly at the next stop.

I remember how bizarre a man-child Bremer seemed to be at an earlier rally in Hagerstown, Maryland—Bremer down front, applauding with his arms fully outstretched, his hands coming together with sweeping, quick, hard claps, like Fourth of July fireworks. Bremer had cheered while state police were dragging out African American McGovern supporters, who had shouted, "Bullshit, bullshit" during the opening prayer for Liddle Bitty Jedge. Hardly anything infuriated Wallace's bodyguards more than for somebody to yell "Bullshit" while the governor was being prayed over.

It was Laurens Pierce of Montgomery, Alabama, and Atlanta, Georgia, who actually won the Emmy for the coverage of the shooting of Governor Wallace. That footage also resulted in Emmys for Walter Cronkite, Dan Rather, Roger Mudd, and myself. We were called the "Team of Correspondents" who reported the story on the *CBS Evening News with Walter Cronkite* on May 15, 1972, but without Pierce's footage there would have been no Emmy for anybody. Pierce had prided himself on being at the eye of storms, first and foremost the civil rights movement, which swept the South in the wrenching '60s, a crusade that would revolutionize the region. Pierce and his Bell & Howell silent camera were covering Martin Luther King Jr. before the editors at CBS had the vaguest notion who he was. On one occasion Pierce used his Bell & Howell to hit a Klansman up the side of the head.

Pierce and I both loved Dixie, but we knew the time for change was considerably overdue, and I believe George Wallace knew it too. He may have been a crumb bum in the minds of the Eastern establishment, but he knew how to win election three times to the governor's office of Alabama—actually four times if you count the administration of his first wife, Lurleen.

Laurens Pierce, the quintessential southern gentleman with a flair for hyperbole and the dramatic confrontation, reveled in describing himself as being "constructively truculent." Through it all he taught me to be calm in the midst of disaster. If I had been Pierce I could not have remained calm when he of all people was not invited to be a part of the live, nationally televised "Emmys" night in New York. Pierce appeared earlier with the "technical" staff, while the "Team of Correspondents" enjoyed the "live" spotlight. When I returned to my table, I presented my Emmy to my wife, Rose, and said, "You earned it." She beamed with pride, and when she mailed it back to me after the divorce, I wept.

Four years before the Emmy Awards night, I was in Los Angeles with the Eugene McCarthy presidential campaign when Robert Kennedy was assassinated. I had been sent out to the hospital where the only bridge over troubled waters was the silver bird sent by the Almighty to bring a son to shelter. Yes, I was enraptured by the Kennedy mystique. I was almost as liberal as they were without knowing exactly why. Liberalism was the middle ground, and maybe we journalists thought of ourselves as guardians of what we believed in our infinite wisdom to be the high ground. None of the Kennedy clan was a "crumb bum," no matter what they did or said or in what dialect any of them spoke it. At all times, in the newspapers, "Cuber" came out "Cuba."

At the hospital in Los Angeles, in the early morning hours, I tried to do an on-camera standupper, but I failed miserably because the simple fact was that I had nothing to say. The inside of my mouth from my tongue to my palate turned to great big wads of cotton, and I was on the verge of choking. Not even two well-functioning adrenal glands could make my mouth work. I froze. Live. On camera. Like a hyperventilating deer caught in the headlights of a speeding eighteen-wheeler. To this day, I've never understood why I wasn't fired on the spot. Nobody ever asked about it, and I made real sure I never talked about it to anybody. Everybody was in such a state of shock that the network executives may have thought I was understandably and forgivably bereaved at the passing of another of our liberal own. The fact was that I had been with the network for only two years. I had not been properly polished at a locally affiliated station, nor had I attended a broadcast school that gave degrees in "Talking on Your Feet." I was caught in a storm I didn't understand and no amount of groping or coaching would cause connected words to come out of my mouth. I just made a solemn promise to myself that if ever "my guy" (racist crumb bum or the finest sliced liberal bread) were assassinated I would try to be more professional next time. More than that, I would be *inside* the hospital. I wouldn't be wandering around outside with my mouth stuffed with cotton balls.

On May 15, 1972, I was standing about ten feet from Arthur Bremer in the Laurel, Maryland, shopping center. I had already written him off, had become accustomed to his face, as the song goes. I decided I'd better go to the telephone and advise the CBS Washington Bureau at 2020 M Street that if the *CBS Evening News* wanted a piece from me, I'd better head in that direction. At the previous rally, protesters had thrown apple cores and chicken eggs at the governor.

"How quiet is the rally where you are?" News producer Ed Fouhy was low-key with few seconds to spare.

"Very quiet, " were two words to haunt me for the rest of my life.

"Then come on in, *if* everything is quiet."

"Everything's quiet. I'm on my way."

I brushed past Arthur Bremer again with that silly smile on his face, and I spoke with Pierce, who was rolling his sound camera on the last of Wallace's "The Speech," the one we'd heard so many times we just about had it memorized.

"Cover for me, Pierce." I whispered softly, "I'm going in to put together a piece for the broadcast."

"Yes, suh." Pierce spoke in his finest *noblesse oblige* southern drawl, his eyeglasses parked high upon his forehead. He had a reputation for holding his camera together with toothpicks, spit, and chewing gum. But God help anybody who doubted his ability to deliver when the chips were down.

I squeezed past Bremer one more time, found my Monte Carlo car rental on the edge of the rally, and calmly and smoothly headed toward 2020 M Street. I relived memories of going back to the news bureau where I'd served from 1966 to 1970. Those had been intoxicating years for a Kentucky boy—covering the White House, Capitol Hill, State Department, and Pentagon. It had included trips with Rose and the children to the California White House during the Nixon years, and the Texas White House with Lyndon Johnson, the real LBJ. Back then, I never imagined that the initials could have a totally different meaning and that instead of rising to the top of the heap in CBS Newsdom, I would sink to the Deep South and one day be hunched over a table in a backroom eating sardines and crackers with Liddle Biddy Jedge, a bottle of hot sauce on the table, our answer to the two martini lunch.

As I made the turn from Washington Circle near the CBS bureau, an announcer broke in on WTOP radio.

"Gov. George Wallace...Laurel, Maryland, shopping center...shots fired...the governor went down...police have arrested the gunman...Wallace's wife, Cornelia, fell on the governor to try to protect him from being hit again...we'll have more details."

We'll have more details...we'll have more details...we'll have more details" ricocheted through my brain as I parked the car and jumped out and ran for the front door of the building at 2020 M Street. As I was entering the elevator, Marvin Kalb, the State Department correspondent for CBS News, also stepped in.

"They've shot Governor Wallace." I was sputtering through little pieces of gristly cotton.

Marvin's reaction was a blank expression that said, "Not again."

Laurens Pierce was the only television cameraman rolling on the attempted assassination, and there was blood splattered on Pierce's white trousers. If I had been there, at least one of the bullets probably would have hit me, because on such occasions I walked in tight behind Wallace's right shoulder. My right arm was usually extended in front of the governor just below his chin, because I tried to record every public word he uttered. Any one of the five different parts of the footage could have qualified for an Emmy: the hand extended before the silly smile, the hand with the gun, the "pop, pop, pop, pop, pop" of the pistol; the governor crumpling to the ground, Cornelia falling on top of him, her black hair glistening; a bullet grazing the neck of Secret Service agent Nick Zarvos; another bullet striking Alabama state trooper Capt. E.C. Dothard; police wrestling to the ground the young man with all the campaign buttons and the silly smile; the body guards loading the governor into a station wagon. It was Sy Wolen, Pierce's soundman, who captured the audio of the "pop, pop, pop, pop, pop," and it was Sy who went to a public telephone and filed a report to CBS Radio. It was

Laurens Pierce who commandeered a Singer Sewing Machine delivery truck and hand carried the priceless footage to the CBS Washington Bureau. He instructed the driver to drive on sidewalks if necessary. To encourage cooperation, Pierce proffered a crisp, new fifty-dollar bill.

While the film was developing in the chemical "soup" and everybody prayed to the God of all reportage that the pictures would come out clean (that there'd be no "hair in the gate"), Roger Mudd interviewed Pierce live on the network.

On the way to Holy Cross Hospital, Quixote beat his fist on the dashboard. "My guy" had gone down, and I wasn't there to report it. I didn't know how I was going to get inside that hospital, but I was going to die trying. I jumped out of the car and began running straight for the front door. I would be "a friend of the family." The wife of the Baptist minister who usually began the rallies with the "bullshit" prayer for the governor, was standing in the entrance with three Maryland state troopers.

"Where have you been, David?"

"I'm here," I replied, as if I were a mourning, long lost cousin. As far as the Maryland State police knew, I might have been a country singer from Tennessee.

"Friend of the family." The woman nodded to the state troopers. Authorities, hospital administrators, even the Secret Service, didn't catch on for several days, and it drove to distraction Cassie Mackin of NBC. Often when I would flounce through the lobby, Cassie would have her face buried against the glass door. One time she waved to me to come closer to the front entrance. She wanted to whisper something to me.

"Ethics, David." Her breath steamed the glass between us.

Pierce had also gained entrance to the hospital using the same ruse. So had Steve Bell of ABC News, and it was about then that we knew the house of cards was falling. One day Pierce and I were in the conference room where "Big Ruby," Governor Wallace's mother-in-law, was stage-managing incoming floral arrangements. We were up to our patoots in flowers. The telephones on the conference table rang repeatedly.

"Is this Holy Cross Hospital?"

"Yes, it is," Miz Ruby , Pierce, or I would reply.

"I'd like to get a word to Governor Wallace."

"Why, sure thing. What would you like to tell him?"

"Tell him we're praying for him."

"Ah'll be sure he gets thet message. Thank you very much for cawlin."

Miz Ruby knew Pierce and me like she did the palm of her aging hand. She knew we wanted one thing more than a weekend with a centerfold or a shopping spree at Fort Knox, and that was to be the first cameraman and reporter to gain entrance to Governor Wallace's hospital room. One day Miz Ruby slyly smiled from ear to ear and said, "Boys, how'djewall like to help me 'liver these here flairers up to the govnuh's room?"

Pierce and I didn't waste time even looking at one another, much less saying anything. We started reching fer flairers, big bunches of heavenly, sweet-smellin', God lovin' flairers, and with grieving looks on our faces, we held these bouquets close to our hearts. Pierce hid his loaded Bell & Howell behind one assortment of snapdragons. We were off to see the Wizard. We had to cross the lobby directly in front of Cassie and all the others who were not "friends of the family." I looked at them like the rabbit in the battery commercial on television twenty years later.

When we passed Steve Bell, who was seated talking to an FBI agent, Steve looked up and what he saw he didn't want to believe. Pierce and I pushed the "Up" button on the elevator, and he, Miz Ruby, and I stepped inside. Before the door could close, Steve's frantic face appeared briefly.

"Wh—wh—where are you-you-you all go—go—going?"

I said, "Steve, we jes goin' upta 'livah these heah flairers to the Guvnah. If you wanna go, you bettah git some too."

With that the elevator doors closed. When we stepped out onto the governor's floor a Secret Service agent who knew us looked like a schoolteacher with a freshly cut switch. "Where do you think you're going?"

"We gonna 'livah these heah flairers to the guvnah's room, ain't thet rite, Miz Ruby?"

"Why sho nuff." Miz Ruby could chirp like a meadowlark defending her children.

"No they're not." The agent's squint was like the eye of an archer pulling back his bow. "You're going to sit over there in that waiting room until we figure out what to do about this." The agent started talking through his skin-colored microphone nested in the palm of his hand. Reporters called it "talking up their sleeves."

Pierce and I sat down. The jig was up. In about one minute, the elevator door opened again and out stepped Steve Bell. He had a pitiful little single carnation in his hand and a sheepish look on his face. The Secret Service agent motioned for Steve to join us, about the way a state trooper would flag down a car that had come upon a head-on collision.

"Set down'n res' yoself, Steve," I said.

Alabama State Trooper David Golden, who had traveled with us for two presidential campaigns, put on a show for the Secret Service agent.

"Gimme thet gawddamned camra, Pierce!" Golden snarled, then winked at Pierce so the Secret Service agent couldn't see.

That same afternoon three friends of the family—Laurens Pierce, Steve Bell, and David Dick—were ordered out of the hospital. Peacefully we faded away, but not until after Pierce had tried to persuade David Golden to keep the camera and use it to take some pictures for CBS.

"Ah cain't do thet, Pierce, gawddamn," Golden moaned.

So, we went outside where Cassie and all the other ethical folks were, and there we stayed for weeks.

Months later, at the mansion in Montgomery, George Wallace was in his wheelchair, and I asked to go along with him and Cornelia down to Barbour County. It was election day, and they were going to vote. The governor's favorite and most trusted mansion servant, one of the black paroled prisoners serving time for murder, carefully and lovingly, it seemed, made sure that the "Boss" was safely down the stairs, into the wheelchair, out the door, and into the limousine. It wasn't as easy as it looked. As we pulled away, I remarked to the governor about the dedication of the man. George Corley Wallace replied, "Remember this, David—a nigguh is a nigguh."

I felt as if a mountain had fallen on me. Do I ask to be let out of the car to make *the* phone call? And if I make *the* phone call, do I say he said "nigger" or "nigguh," "nigra" or "negrah" or "Negro?" I had not recorded it. What was the exact pronunciation? What was the context? Did context even matter? A racist is a racist is a racist. Then there's freedom of speech. Were some words so verboten that they should never be uttered? What about the Big F word? The Big MF word? The AH word? Was there time to describe the Big N word in a forty-second voice report? Would they give me two minutes to explain it? Is there such a thing as a private remark? Is anything private anymore?

I made a command decision. As long as Gov. George Corley Wallace was alive, I would not even try to say what I believe he said. If I was an unethical, irresponsible, racist reporter, then I was an unethical, irresponsible, racist reporter. Years later, after my marriage to Lalie, we went to see Governor Wallace in his residence in Montgomery. His three marriages a cluster of good and bad dreams, he was alone, propped up in bed, virtually stone-deaf. We talked about one of his recent visitors, Jesse Jackson, and one more time George Wallace repeated what he had said so many times in public and private: "I don't hate anybody because of their race or who they happen to be." I didn't try to remind him of what he had said to me more than once in the limousine.

When Wallace died in 1998, Lalie and I should have gone to the funeral, but we didn't. We were busy planting seeds on Plum Lick in Kentucky. When Laurens Pierce died of a heart attack, we didn't attend his memorial service. I was on assignment in Texas. We chose to remember both men as they were in life: courageous and outrageous; hotheaded and cool under fire; as racist as most of those who voted the one into office and put the other on the payroll. Yet still they were brothers of Everyman. They were sons of the South. Few would come even close to understanding them, or their women. Probably not in a million years.

By 1978, there'd been twelve full years of following hurricanes, tornadoes, earthquakes, and volcanic eruptions, plane crashes, mass murders, riots, and assassinations. Quixote had fought for every rung on the ladder on the way up (or down) to the special assignment of opening the new CBS News Latin America Bureau in Caracas. Too many hurricane seasons and hormonal upheavals had made landfall and taken their tolls. The good news was that I had remarried. The bad news was that as Dr. Laurence J. Peter decreed in *The Peter Principle*, I just might have risen to my level of incompetence. The good news was that I knew it. The bad news was that I didn't know when to quit.

The traumas of the 1960s — 1963, the assassination of John F. Kennedy...1965, the assassination of Malcolm X...1968, the assassinations of Robert Kennedy and Martin Luther King Jr....and 1972, the attempted assassination of George C. Wallace — were widening chasms swallowing serenity and security. There was the December 23, 1972, earthquake in Managua, where an estimated 20,000 were killed...the crash of Eastern Airlines 1011 in the Everglades...the crash of the Southern Airlines jet in Georgia...Wayne Henley and the Houston mass murders...the butchering of co-eds at Florida State University...Hurricanes Celia and Agnes, which had taken the life of CBS Southern Bureau reporter Del Vaughan...hurricane Eloise...tornadoes in the Mississippi Delta and throughout the Deep South — each a storm that gave a midlife crisis more rationalizations for being. It was compounded by theatrical boldness, Liza Minnelli in *Cabaret* and *New York, New York,* thick-skulled Archie Bunker coming undone in *All in the Family*, language barrier-breaking *Hair*, and loudly irreverent *Jesus Christ Superstar.*

I'd been in San Francisco with the McCarthy campaign on April 5, 1968, when Dr. Martin Luther King Jr. was assassinated, and wiser heads had kept me out of Memphis. But in 1977, when Elvis died I was covering coalfield strife in West Virginia, and CBS sent me to Memphis to describe the funeral procession as it left Graceland. I was moving from storm to storm, and my own life had become one.

Shortly after twelve noon on March 6, 1978, *Hustler* magazine publisher Larry Flynt was shot on a street in Lawrenceville, Georgia, and I covered it. It was a one-minute piece on the *CBS Evening News with Walter Cronkite*. The only thing I believed I had in common with Larry Flynt was that we were both Kentuckians. There were many more storms to be followed. Nicaragua was only one of them, but it was one of the biggest and most dangerous.

I passionately believed it was the messenger's job to ask questions, to look, to listen, and to write the message, then deliver the message without making judgments. And it was wrong to kill messengers. Even in war it was an injustice to do that, and yet messengers like Bill Stewart were told to lie on the ground so a bullet could be buried in their brains, and it was an evil thing to do that, but it was done. I hated it.

It was fate that caused me to look up that sleepy day in the summer of '73 and see a tall woman walk in front of me at Rosemont in Mississippi. CBS had sent me there to do a story on the first reunion of the descendents of Jefferson Davis, the Kentuckian who became the first and only president of the Confederacy. The woman was Eulalie Anne ("Lalie") Cumbo, born in New Orleans, raised up in Woodville in southwestern Mississippi. Five years later, we would be married. There were years of patient waiting as she moved from being a secretary at Sun Oil Company and Dresser Industries to becoming a marketing executive at Revlon. We began as friends who chanced to meet, stayed in touch, and one day knew in our heart of hearts that we were meant to live out our lives together. My marriage to Rose was destined to last twenty-five years but no longer.

From the mid-fifties through the mid-sixties to the mid-seventies, I had struggled with the rules and expectations of the Roman Catholic Church— confession, no birth control, giving up sex for Lent, and no meat on Fridays. It was a losing battle. I'd converted to Catholicism because of Rose, but there was too much of the Protestant Rev. Coleman W. Dick in my DNA, too much of the adventurer Samuel S. Dick in my independent psyche to keep me in the papal fold.

When the sexual revolution broke open the quasi-Puritan consciousness of America—*Deep Throat* and *I Am Curious Yellow*, *Hustler* and its explicit centerfold cousins—network news reporters were challenged as they'd never been before. The "Big F word" was heard and read as openly as "flower" or "forever." News reporters and their 1950s stay-at-home spouses began to question and sometimes doubt their own sexuality, the foundations of their traditions. The upheaval led to a divorce rate unmatched anywhere in the world. It was only a matter of time until I'd be a statistic.

It became my ritual to keep a journal during the last seven years of my time as a correspondent for CBS News, from 1978 to 1985. I became a daily, minute-by-minute chronicler of events and the mostly hapless people caught up in them—including myself. I wasn't as charmingly candid or as historically important as Samuel Pepys and the other great diarists, but I did my best to lay down unvarnished versions of life, rough little jags and edges of "the truth."

I filled large ledger pages top-to-bottom, side-to-side, often in-between lines. I included flight numbers, departure and arrival times, hotel and motel room numbers, people's names—big people, little people—descriptions reflected from what I saw with my own eyes and heard with my own ears. Often I included my feelings as I related to all these things. You could usually see me carrying the awkward red journal, nursed against my right breast as if it were my baby, running the risk of leaving it in telephone booths or on the back seats of taxis. I valued spontaneity. Since I didn't carry a camera, I took pictures with my mind, because I thought it might be important to make my own detailed record for future generations. Often the words in my journal entries became phrases and paragraphs in the scripts I wrote for broadcast, radio and television. Omissions are often more juicy, salacious, and superior in their own way to commissions and make the better confession, but there ought to be a few self-imposed boundaries. Otherwise, we'd be doing nothing but wallowing in mud. Father confessors would grow weary and become more depressed. They've more important work to do and have no need for such tempting provocations.

My journals strove to become a reasonably complete inside-slaughterhouse glimpse of the realities of making news sausage—occasionally hot, usually mild, seldom cold. Journalism was infrequently pretty, but newsgathering was as truthful as we Quixotes dared to portray reality. It's important to remember that radio and television messengers were expected to be prepared to tell the story of the end of the world in thirty seconds or less. "Hey, tell him to tighten the frigging thing up some more!"

In 1978 I was forty-eight years old, and there was a concurrent storm in my own life, raging in the midst of the upheavals all around me: Jonestown, civil wars in Nicaragua and El Salvador, the Falkland Islands War, Beirut, and George Corley Wallace. My personal storm was both physical and spiritual. I'd had my nips and my rips. Every so often I'd acted in harebrained and downright stupid ways. Mine was a wayward, tattered, hormonally-driven soul thinking about and toying with the idea of redemption but not hungering for it enough to reach out and take it. Some might say it was a bad case of chutzpah.

Humanitarian by nature and formal education, I was struggling, working my way, inch-by-inch, moment-by-moment, toward a closer, more honest, more intelligent and loving relationship with God. Or so I told myself. Inner contentment. Self-control. Something like that. Sinners can never be too sure. The trail is littered with those who are persistently preaching and doggedly climbing on and off their flimsy soapboxes and teetotal wagons. Some will say mine was just another one of those sorry midlife crisis things. I'm not sure.

Most of the time I considered myself fortunate to be a messenger, but it became quite clear to me that people invariably try to "kill the messenger" rather than deal responsibly with the contents of the message. There'll be those who'll read this book and want to kill it rather than follow the storms out there, on their own doorsteps or roaring within themselves. That will be their choice, and they will have to live with it. I wish them well.

I've made selective use of my personal journals in this book, using *italics* to indicate where I've taken from bygone, ink-smeared pages to illustrate the path taken by the book, which I offer as another instance of the role the messenger plays: to observe, to listen, and to record as accurately as possible the fragments of a greater truth. Although I believe ultimate truth, philosophically speaking, is unattainable, the searching and the yearning for a higher fidelity are worth the pain of incompletion.

Emerson's "foolish consistency is the hobgoblin of little minds" might help to explain the deep-seated longing I felt as I came to make

30

better sense of the "magic lady" walking beneath the live oaks and magnolias in Mississippi. In the fullness of time, fancy turned to reality—I reached out and took her hand.

CHAPTER THREE

In the late afternoon of April 8, 1978, Eulalie Anne Cumbo (I sometimes called her Miz Scarlett) and I headed up the road from New Orleans toward Woodville, stopping at a little shack north of Baton Rouge for oysters on the half shell followed by oyster po-boys and more Jax beer. We laughed and held hands and savored each moment on the way north on U.S. 61, where the coastal Bermuda grass was lush and the Brahman cattle grazed among tall pines and stately pecan trees. The years of the civil rights movement were pages in history books. Boycotts had come and gone. Blacks and whites lived in greater proximity and racial accord than in most any community "up North."

I wrote in my journal: *We awakened in separate low-ceilinged bedrooms upstairs, where on both sides of the house, birds were singing near the windows. The azaleas in the front yard and along the streets were in full bloom. We went to church across the street in St. Paul's, built in 1824, the oldest Episcopal Church west of the Alleghenies.*

In 1843, Jane Cook Davis was confirmed at St. Paul's. Her four-year-old son, Jefferson, who worshiped with her, born in Kentucky, would become a favorite son one hundred years later among the white minority of Woodville. His birthday was celebrated on the same day as my Eulalie's mother's, and her name was Eulalie too. Jefferson Davis was her hero until the day she died. She didn't care much for Abraham Lincoln.

The nineteenth-century thousand-pipe organ, on whose bench Eulalie, the younger, and I first kissed on a moonlit midnight, brought broad smiles to our faces. The words in gilded letters, "The Lord Is in His Holy Temple," were in their place on the wall on the pulpit side, and Father Whitney Barnes was his customarily honest, calm, strict, clerical self. He barely deigned to bless our new marriage, which had already received its civil stamp of approval by a judge in Columbus, Ohio.

After greeting and being greeted by our friends in the yard outside St. Paul's, we returned to the little yellow house across the street where Lalie's mother and father, Eulalie ("Betty") and Charles, had raised their mid-twentieth-century family. There was a dinner party in our honor at Rosemont, given by Percival T. Beacroft Jr. and Ernesto Caldeira, who had restored the boyhood home of President Davis. We had drinks on the long, spacious back porch. Our Irish setter, Zoee's Patricia o'Casey, had joined the flourishing dog community at Rosemont, and everybody had a fine time. Ernie cooked, and we ate in the outside kitchen cottage. Kitty Whetstone, archetypal southern lady, and her husband, Glen Ray, quintessential Good Old Boy, were there—Glen Ray promised to take us turkey hunting the following week.

It was another sweet April day in the town considered by many to be the most typically antebellum anywhere in the Deep South. Blacks were winning courthouse elections, but outnumbered whites religiously cherished and assumed their social prerogatives. Vestiges of old plantation habits would probably not be lost as long as mortal man and woman breathed Mississippi air. You wouldn't expect it to become a New Hampshire or a New Jersey. The realities of the New South seemed to a compromising Kentuckian the more powerful of the prevailing winds. Mine was the perception of a Lincolnphile, not openly discussed, above all while hunting turkeys.

It sounded as if all the birds in the world were singing outside our windows this morning—our wedding day, April 15, 1978—the moment for which we have waited so long.

It is now fifteen minutes before it's time for us to be married. I am suited up in my tux, sitting in the upstairs bedroom. I am holding a gold band in my hand, the one I will put on your finger. You will place on mine the gold band bearing the initials "DLC," the ring worn by your grandfather, David Lawrence Cumbo, another turn-of-the-century Sicilian immigrant child. My thoughts at this time can be summed up in three words: "I love you."

Shortly after six o'clock we were standing before a moderately starched Father Whitney Barnes, members of Lalie's family and closest friends standing in their pews as our blessing ceremony began. Geri Ellen Foster played the organ. I had difficulty getting the ring onto Lalie's finger, but other than that the ceremony went smoothly and simply. We went across the street to the little yellow house, where we cut our wedding cake and fed each other the first pieces. Guests began arriving from many directions and the reception lasted long past midnight.

Scott Dunbar, an ancient black man, one of Lalie's dearest friends, slapped his guitar and stomped the patio bricks first with his left foot, then with his right, the patio bricks that had once been a chimney at the Cumbo house when Charles was a boy. Charles, the son of David, would become a man, the father of Lalie, his oldest daughter whom he'd not, before his passing, see married to another David. Several guests became quite drunk. Television electrician John Lunn was last seen falling backwards into the bushes. He did not reappear. Friends Phyllis Deter and Bill Halbert had come over from Houston to help recall the old Timmon's Lane days. We were showered with rice. The good times rolled on into the early hours of Sunday morning, while we retreated to Rosemont to begin our wedding night.

Shortly after we parked at the guest cabin, Ernesto showed up and warned us that a shivaree party was on its way. With all our clothes on, Lalie and I jumped into bed. We gave the shivareers a surprise of our own. About ten people, including Kitty Whetstone, danced around the bedroom, beating spoons against pans in the traditional way. We all moved next door to Ernesto and Percival's cottage and let more good times roll. Ernie played the piano, and some of us who could, and some of us who couldn't, sang the old songs.

About three o'clock in the morning the shivareers packed it in, and

Lalie and I surrendered to our first night of properly blessed married life. It was a new beginning. There was love enveloping us, through us, within us, all around us before we went to sleep and after we awakened. The ghosts of Rosemont spirits weary of the "War Between the States" had found their peace at the center as they slept in the nearby family burial ground. We gave them cause to sing for joy, as in the days of old.

Three days after our wedding, we had a call from Glen Ray Whetstone, who had offered to take us turkey hunting. I had discovered from reading Hodding Carter Sr. that the surest way for a liberal to comprehend and stand any chance of winning the conservative hearts and minds of those who live in the Deep South was to go hunting and fishing with them. I asked Lalie to go with me, and she said she would.

We were up at the gray, ghastly hour of 3:30 in the morning. Glen Ray was on the front porch at 4:00, early by fifteen minutes. We took one of Charles Cumbo's guns, and Glen Ray let us borrow one of his. We climbed into a proud pickup truck and headed out to the Whetstones' 2,800-acre Oakwood Plantation. Our first stop was at the hunting lodge to pick up some camouflage clothing. Glen Ray's brother Charles and the elder Mr. Whetstone were just waking up. They didn't go hunting with us. It had stormed during the night, not a good morning for a turkey hunt, but the three of us decided to go ahead with it anyway.

It was our first time, but for Glen Ray it was a game he'd started playing when he was six years old. By the time he was seventy-three he'd collected three display boards with 150 turkey beards. Using a Lynch Foolproof Box to mimic an almost perfect turkey hen "yelp," Glen Ray blew sequences of three—"Yelp...yelp...yelp." If there's a tom turkey in a range of about 100 to 150 yards he'll let fly a heartless, high-pitch, staccato "Gobble...gobble...gobble" and, according to Glen Ray Whetstone, that's the same thing as beating yourself on a swelled-up chest and trumpeting, "Here I am Baby, come on over here—I'm available and ready for you!"

In the spring breeding season, Mr. Tom Gobbler walks all over the country looking for one more hen to add to his flock. On this day, Mr. Tom was out of range. Either that, or he already had all the females he could handle. Glen Ray wore himself thin blowing those "yelps," and about all he managed to stir up were a few sleepy-eyed crows. We settled for a soft and misty Mississippi early morning, and it was impossible not to love each moment of it. Lalie and I took off our shoes and socks and sloshed across an open plowed field. On our way back to the lodge, a turkey hen passed in front of us, the only bird we'd see all morning. "*Good* mawnin', lady," we yelped. Breakfast at the lodge was hot biscuits, thick slabs of bacon, scrambled eggs, and buttered grits—no turkey.

In the evening, Lalie and I went to Natchez, where we'd been invited to a cocktail party at an antebellum mansion, the Towers. Faulknerian characters floated back and forth through the huge rooms. The last Panama Canal Treaty had passed and, so far I'd been spared the covering of the story. Hardly anybody at the Towers or anywhere in southwestern Mississippi was in favor of giving up the Panama Canal. "Heavens to Betsy, wouldjew wont to turn the country ovah to the comm'nists and be done *widdit*?"

The parties were soon over, the wedding so quickly had been blessed, and it was time to leave. We drove through the live oaks, the Spanish moss, the kudzu, past the riot of azaleas at Rosemont and the sign, "You Are Now Entering the Nineteenth Century." We said goodbye to Woodville, and we drove down Highway 61 to Baton Rouge and Interstate 10 to New Orleans, to Moissant Airport.

Storm clouds were moving closer: revolution in Nicaragua, the Jonestown massacre in Guyana, and in the years to follow, civil war in El Salvador, Argentina's invasion of the Falkland Islands, and anarchy in Beirut would make the sky turn blood-red.

We flew to New York and checked into rooms 2203-4 at the St. Moritz on Central Park South. I called Liz Dribben at CBS, and she invited us to brunch at her place the next day. Marty Burton invited us to come over to his apartment for drinks in the evening. He was a Revlon executive, and he had a sweeping view of a slice of the city—Broadway, and the East River.

Marty took us to dinner at the Russian Tea Room. Since *The Turning Point* was playing next door, Lalie and I went to see it. It was exciting to be in Manhattan. Not, right then, missing turkeys in Mississippi, we picked up a fifth of bourbon for nightcaps together. When we returned to our suite, Sinatra's "New York! New York!" was ringing in our ears.

Brunch with Liz was Bloody Marys, good bread and cheese and lox and sparkling conversation. We strolled from Liz's place in the West Side 70s to John Winslow's apartment in the West Side 90s. A business manager with a publishing firm, he was formerly with CBS. From Winslow's apartment and his insolent Siamese cats we took a cab to the other end of Manhattan, to Twelfth Street and Second Avenue, where we found the last two seats for *Best Little Whorehouse in Texas*. We laughed until we thought we'd collapse. We stopped at a deli and brought our supper back to our room.

Lalie and I took a cab to the CBS Broadcast Center, arriving promptly to keep our 10:30 appointment with Don Hamilton, CBS business manager. He explained the financial details of our relocation to Venezuela, and he told us the terms of my proposed new three-year contract. I was satisfied. I had not had an agent, and there had been no bargaining. Quixote took what he was offered and was grateful. He'd come a long way since his $87.50-a-week salary at WHAS Radio and Television in Louisville. As Charles Kuralt once said, "Don't tell them, but I'd pay *them* to let me work here."

My reassignment to Caracas had come as the result of my request for an opportunity to experience life as a foreign correspondent. I had long admired the courage of Bert Quint in Europe, Randy Daniels in Africa, and David Dow in South America. I told CBS News Senior Vice President Bill Small that I believed I was ready for the chance to show him that I could work in distant cultures, learn a second language, and make the network proud. Small decided my days to come would be in Latin America—the news bureau would be moved from Buenos Aires and re-established in Venezuela, and I would be the bureau chief! I believed I was on my way to stardom, and it was time to celebrate a very fine wedding present.

We recalled the day in Columbus, Ohio, when I had leaped over the snow bank outside a public phone booth after hearing from Small that I'd be going to Caracas. We imagined that all our dreams about South America—a new continent, a new culture, a new language—were about to come true.

The sweethearts went to lunch at Alfredo's on Central Park South, the guests of National Assignment editor Peter Sturtevant. Eulalie fascinated him, possibly because, at six feet two, they could stand toe to toe and look each other in the eye. After lunch, Lalie met Bill Small, the demanding and often cantankerous man who'd hired me in 1959 at WHAS and in 1966 at CBS in Washington. Without Small, there would never have been a CBS News correspondent with the unlikely name of David Dick. When I asked Lalie for her reaction upon leaving, she said, "Intimidating." Small was that and more, but I wouldn't forget the central role he'd played in my career. I had lobbed one over the net, and he had smashed the ball back into my court.

We hand-carried a copy of Lalie's résumé to Revlon International, and in the evening we went to see *On the Twentieth Century* at the St. James Theater. Other than the sets and costumes, I didn't much care for it. I may have seen John Cullum one time too many. We decided to give Broadway a rest. I took Miz Scarlett to Shezan, the Pakistani restaurant where Small had taken me the last time he brought me to New York. Lalie and I ate curried lamb. Our before-dinner drinks were a gin-based fruit concoction. We had a carafe of wine and Mexican coffee to bring down the curtain to our own little show, our own little twentieth-century romance about to move to another continent.

Lalie trembled and told me she was nervous as she left the hotel on her way to her interview with Revlon International. I told her to relax, that everything would be O.K. When she returned, it was about noon, and we went to the Slate around the corner from CBS, where she filled me in on her interview. She was going to Caracas with many blessings from her executives in New York!

In the evening, Diane and Bert Quint and we drove out to Susan and Sid Feders' house in suburban New Jersey for a foreign correspondents' dinner. The food was good, elegantly served, the conversation lively, finally turning to joke telling. Quint won the prize with some classics, including the one about the peasant in Mexico who tells the confused tourist what time it is by lifting the balls of the peasant's donkey high enough to be able to see under them and through the animal's legs to the large clock in plain view on the town square.

Lalie decided she would like to see *Grease,* so she called and made reservations. We had bad seats (front row, extreme left), but it didn't really matter. *Grease* was considered in 1978 to be the longest running musical on Broadway (before *Chorus Line*): the kids in the '50s, full of vitality and innocent vulgarity, forcefully vigorous, sweetly unshakable, sweaty, desperate—as teenage youth mostly were. As we seniors were hoping to be. We finished the evening with the denizens at Wolf's Deli.

We climbed up the steps of St. Patrick's Cathedral and went inside to place our fingers into the holy water, then make the sign of the cross on our foreheads, our lips, and our hearts. After lighting candles, we dropped to our knees and said our prayers. "Oh, God, be with us as we fly off to South America....Watch over our families....Let there be special moments....Sit with us on mountain tops....Point us toward occasions of beauty....Go with us down country roads to see good people....Guard us against warriors and their wickedness....Give us good stories to send back to the United States....Bring us safely home to Kentucky. Amen."

We returned to the Broadcast Center, where I introduced my tall bride to Walter Cronkite, and she suggested that he should come sailing our way. I again thanked Bill Small for the new opportunity as well as the new contract. He wished us well. In the evening we went to a party at Liz Dribben's walkup. The guests included the Quints, a Portuguese banker and journalist, other CBSers, and Liz's two cats.

Cameraman Herbie Schwartz and his wife came to the party, and the four of us went for drinks and the night view of all of New York, New York—from the top of the World Trade Center. The ride up on the elevator was breath-catching. Our hearts were in our throats. When the door opened at the top, we felt another astonishing experience—a world of lights. Herbie insisted to the maitre d' that we be seated next to the windows.

Quixote arose from his chair, went to the glass expanse, and placed the palm of his hand on it to bring him closer to the glow stretching away toward uptown and beyond. The jets taking off from LaGuardia and Kennedy were like fireflies in a swirl of phosphorescence. It was a heavenly sight.

We landed in Venezuela on May 10, 1978, on Pan Am flight 217 nonstop from New York's Kennedy to Caracas's Maiquetía. The in-flight movie had been John Travolta's *Saturday Night Fever*. Quixote fantasized that he was also handsome and irresistibly sexy. I was going to make a name for myself as the new Latin America correspondent and bureau chief, sí Señor! But as it turned out, the first three months were destined to become a lurching, extended honeymoon with on-again, off-again demands from the Foreign Desk at CBS News, culture shock, and dengue fever.

On that fateful Wednesday in May, our driver, Paco Torres, had been waiting for us at Maiquetía. His small black eyes were beaming. He had died and gone to Paradise.

"¿Cómo está, Señor David?"

"Bueno, Paco, muy bueno. Esta es mi esposa, Lalie."

"!Bienvenido a Venezuela!"

"Usted es muy amable, Paco, usted es mi amigo, usted es nuestro amigo." I was reaching at the outer limits of my fractured Spanish, which had not improved since the first time I met Paco in Caracas during a presidential visit by Jimmy Carter.

Lalie leaned down and kissed each side of the smiling face.

Paco treated us to dinner at La Estancia where we feasted on fine carne, aguacate, and arepas (the Venezuelan version of the Kentucky corndodger). The whiskey had character. "Un whiskey, por favor," increased my Spanish vocabulary by four. It underscored an unfolding and deepening travesty: CBS's Latin America correspondent and bureau chief could not speak the local language much beyond "¿Dónde está el baño?" And he didn't have the foggiest notion about Portuguese, spoken by more than 119 million Brazilians. But we had no plans to travel to

41

Brazil unless the Amazon suddenly reversed its course. I would cover the World Cup in Buenos Aires and that would be the extent of my Argentinean experience until the farcical invasion of the Falkland Islands four years later.

May 10, 1978, marked the official uplink of the latest Latin America Bureau's correspondent and its Danish cameraman, Carl Sorensen, an incompatible working relationship doomed from the outset. I'd first met Sorensen in Rome on a George Wallace trip during the 1976 presidential campaign. One of Carl's trademarks was a colorful scarf at the opening of his safari suit. On him, neckties would have looked hideous. The one thing for which he was best remembered by all who ever worked with him was what most reasonable and practical human beings would call his bravery. It was what Dan Rather described in *The Camera Never Blinks* as Sorensen's total absence of fear. Carl simply did not know the meaning of the word. I had made up my mind that I was going to admit fear up and down my quivering spine, and I was going to do everything possible to stay damned well alive, even if it meant turning into the yellowest of cowards. I wanted no red badges of courage, and I was pretty sure Stephen Crane hadn't wanted one either.

Within three months, Sorensen and Quixote would be covering the revolution in Nicaragua, while our private civil war was tearing us nearly to shreds. Rather could not have been more right when he said Sorensen was the kind of cameraman who could get a correspondent killed. Point him toward any storm and Sorensen would be in the middle of it, shooting pictures down the throat of the leviathan. In six months we would be reporting one of the most bizarre stories of the century — Jonestown. The rest of the time we'd be shadowboxing with Venezuelan bureaucracy and what it liked to call "Eternal Spring."

Lalie and I did what we could to make our first evening a good beginning with my new "co-storm master" Sorensen. It was not to be an easy assignment. I explained that Bill Small had said Lalie and I could live in the bureau as long as we wanted. There was thinly disguised disdain oozing from Sorensen's steely body, all of it saying he wished we would get our own apartment as soon as possible. He was right, but I was determined not to allow Sorensen or any other camera general to be my Appomattox — words about as brave as General Lee's.

Carl told me I needed to understand that he would not be my interpreter. He was right again. I shouldn't have needed one. But it continued to be chilling to think that out on the chopping block when just the right word in Spanish might save a situation, possibly my life, Carl might let me discover my own *Oh, Díos mío*. His professional reflex would tell him to take pictures of my head rolling around on the ground.

We could not exit Venezuela until we had a "certificate of solvency," the certificado de solvencia, proof that we had at all times paid national taxes. The solvencia would become the millstone around our necks. Next to my inability to speak the language of the country where I was supposed to be an expert, and the immense incompatibility of the correspondent and the cameraman, the next biggest obstacle to any conceivable success was the inability to leave the country at a moment's notice. I should have known our meat and potatoes were not what we'd prayed for at St. Patrick's. Our specialties were giant mudslides in Peru, assassinations in Bolivia, and earthquakes in Chile. No solvencia, no way out. It worked like a fish trap. Returning to the country was easy; leaving the country was the stumbling block. The transeunte visa meant we were transients, sojourners, passers-by, and possibly thieves in the night. Likely, officials speculated, we were also tax evaders, definitely people to be watched.

Putting the CBS Latin America bureau in Caracas was a screwup, and we would come to understand that reality more with each passing day and each missed story. If there was anything news networks hated more than missing a story, it was admitting a screwup of its own. Quixote was saddled with the complicated business of declaring income and paying Venezuelan taxes for the actual days spent in the country. The solvencia was the main ticket to covering a coup in Bolivia, an epidemic among penguins in southern Argentina, or maybe, if we were lucky, the World Cup in Buenos Aires.

It was the big day, June 21, 1978, and in of most of the crazed world of substitute warfare — the beginning of the XI World Cup.

Lalie shed tears when I departed. I told her I'd be back on Monday or Tuesday. "It's what my life is all about. It's what I strive for, what I live and die for. I give it my best and each time I try harder to do better." As I wrote in my journal, I was at the top of the hill on the roller coaster; it was when I hit the bottom and rounded the curves that I turned to thoughts of Camelot in Kentucky.

Carl met me in a cab at 6:00 a.m., and we headed through the tunnels and over the mountain to Maiquetía. Granted a temporary solvencia the day before (after agreeing to pay Venezuelan taxes), we took Viasa 942, first class, nonstop to Buenos Aires. It was a most pleasant flight. The service was good—better, I thought, than Aerolineas Argentinas. As I worked on my expense accounts, I contemplated the joys of retiring to Plum Lick. It was restful and peaceful to ponder in that way, one of my devices for keeping my head screwed on halfway straight.

Choucino, a stringer cameraman, and his crew, Carlos and José, met us at the airport and took us into the city, where we checked in at the Romanelli. We went to Intel, where it hit the fan with Feders in New York. He claimed he had no idea Sorensen was in Buenos Aries without his equipment and had no idea we had done nothing to have a security bond established with a customs broker there to make possible the importation of the equipment. Acting on my own authority, Sorensen had been designated news producer after he persuaded me that Feders didn't understand Argentinean laws involving foreign camera crews. Sorensen and I figured we'd use local personnel. So much for big decisions.

At that time we thought Brazil had sewed up a spot in the soccer finals, so Feders ruled that I should prepare to go to Rio the next day and that Sorensen should go back to Caracas and cool his heels there. We had not counted on Argentina defeating Peru, 6-0.

Choucino filmed the fútbol mania in the streets, mainly along the 9th of July Avenue. I did an on-the-scene ad-libber for radio and fed it. Sorensen would not be sent anywhere and, of course, I would not be going to Rio. We hurried to Channel 13, where we corralled a color videocassette of the street scene and roped in an editor to put together a 1:15 piece for us that *Morning News* said it would take on the satellite. Sorensen and I were behaving like a pair of draft horses who knew they had a wagon to pull. It was a long night in Buenos Aires, but I did manage to catch a few winks on the top of a desk in the Channel 13 newsroom. All to no avail. We had thought we might be feeding Eurovision, the European syndication service, to London and then back to the United States. But Eurovision rejected it, and *Morning News* finally decided it didn't want to pay for it. I fed a spot to the *World News Roundup* and did a live Q and A with the radio editor. I returned to the Romanelli and slept until about 1:00 in the afternoon.

I reached CBS in New York and was told that the Cronkiters were interested in a "bird," a satellite transmission, that evening. Choucino and his crew had gone alone to the airport for the return of the Argentine team from Rosario to Buenos Aires. Carl and I went to Channel 13, and with little time to spare re-edited the tape. While Carl pulled that wheel, I rewrote a 1:15 piece we had thought we would be able to feed the bird from Channel 13, but at the last moment we were told we could not. Carl and I galloped hell-for-leather across town to the Buenos Aires '78 television production center. The guard allowed us in even though we didn't have credentials. Our stomping and snorting must've frightened him.

Along about this time, it came to my attention that by using phony receipts, a correspondent in South America could tweak the expense account and siphon some easy money. Tales abounded of expense account funny business ranging from inflated tips to invented bribes. Hanky-panky had been known to extend to numerical hocus-pocus. I liked to think that I was basically an honest man— lustful, maybe, but honest. I said no to the thought of outright stealing, even if I spun off a tithe for the God of all expense accounts.

After the daylight hours had passed, Sherrie Moore called from New York to say everything was A.O.K. We had scored again!—a 2:45 piece on the air, which I hoped included my standup bridge. I went to dinner with Carl at the apartment of friends he had known in the days of Juan Perón. The host played Gershwin gloriously on a grand piano, the hostess was witty and sexy, and the Paraguayan servants were smoothly dutiful. The days of Perón had been Hell for CBS correspondent David Dow, but for his successor David Dick, this night in Buenos Aires was Heaven. To my room I returned absolutely stuffed. It was such a joy to shuck off my clothes and slip naked beneath clean sheets. God had repaid me for not mondo cheating on my expense account.

I slept soundly, awoke to take a steaming hot bath, and studied Spanish. Our driver, José, met us at 10 a.m. and took Carl and me to San Telmo, where I bought a maté set. It was silver plated: a tray, two small bowls with tops for sugar and maté, a pitcher for hot water, the maté container, and the mouthpiece. The asking price was 90,000 pesos ($115). I bought it for $105. Maté is a sensuous tea-like beverage derived from the dried leaves of a South American evergreen tree. The green brew was called Paraguay tea or yerba maté. I wrote in my journal, *I would like for our third child to have this, or if there is not to be a third, then the first.*

I called the Foreign Desk in New York and discussed with Kate and Joan and Jennifer what was expected of us for the satellite feeds, after we knew who'd won the World Cup. Several hours before the game began, the horn blowing had begun in downtown B.A. At 3:00 p.m. the match that *was* began. When time ran out, Argentina defeated Holland 3-1 to win its first World Cup!

Wild-eyed people instantly hit the streets. The 9th of July Avenue became a cauldron of human flesh. José took Carl and me to Intel, where I quickly filed a radio report for the next hourly and ad-libbed a description for Wynn Elliott on his sports broadcast. I was told a narration for early *Sunday Night News* was not needed. But one was requested for *Late Sunday News* and *Morning News* the following day, plus a Roundupper and another reaction piece for Wynn Elliott. I was on an ever-loving *roll*! And I hadn't even prayed for it. It paled in comparison to David Dow's serious reporting of the days of Perón and Evita, but a foreign correspondent can't afford to be choosy. Take the glory as it comes and never look back!

Buenos Aires had come unzipped, crazed. It was dangerous just to be standing and breathing on a street corner. We fought our way to Channel 13, where we edited an electronic cassette, then fought our way to the '78 Broadcast Center to feed the bird. We almost blew it, but ABC saved our patoots. We fed the bird by the barest. I unwound at Locos Años. Everybody had gone loony tunes. Sexy women flashed through the night like showers of meteors. They danced with bottles of fine wine balanced on their heads. They smiled the special smile. God might forgive me. He just might. At times such as these, delirium has its own demands. I decided to be true to Lalie, sleeping in Caracas.

When I closed the door of my room at the Romanelli, there was a telex from Kate in New York: "The piece made air with seconds to spare and it looked fine." Words such as these are more precious to a foreign correspondent than a winning lottery ticket or a night of ecstasy surpassing normal fantasy. Sodom never seemed more excusable, Gomorrah more tempting. In his dreams, Quixote toasted the sparkling ladies of the night, wished them happiness, and said a prayer for Argentina as it continued its slide into financial chaos.

We celebrated the next day by going to a livestock exposition in Buenos Aires, where there were magnificent animals on display, row on row, backs combed and shining, perfectly aligned—Santa Maria (a cross with Santa Gertrudis), Shorthorn, Charolais, and Flecklay. The craftsmanship in dehorning chutes, head gates, and holding pens was fine, truly first-class. Hemingway would have approved, surely would have said, "Splendid!

We ate there in the midst of the cattle, the guests of the crew, and Naum and Nicoa. The carne was superb. Sides of beef were hung on iron spikes set at angles into burning coals. Gauchos strode up to the meat, sliced through chunks of it, and placed them on our plates.

"¡*Salúd*, Papa!"

There was no discouraging word but, beneath the surface, the dragon seeds of economic stress and military flimflam were ready to emerge. It would have been the folly of the spoilsport to remind championship soccer players and sensuous dancers of the consequences of Sodom and Gomorrah. Quixote could no more prevent another devaluation of the peso than he could later denounce the yearnings to take back the Falkland Islands.

The crew autographed a bottle of World Cup wine and a table napkin for me. I would treasure them and the irreplaceable memories that went with them. I would grant absolution to Carl, and I would set aside all our awkwardness. For I had tasted glory, had savored it. Sorensen was all right. He was remarkable!

The crew took Carl and me to the airport where, after goodbye abrazos, we boarded Aerolineas Argentinas on the 5:30 flight northward to Caracas. It would be the last time I'd ever see Chouciño, Carlos, José, Naum, and Nicoa. For them, there would be for all time a warm spot in my heart. On the flight climbing up from Buenos Aires, passengers were jammed in like whitebait, but it didn't matter. My mind was swimming with joy. It was too long a flight to go tourist, but I did it, and whatever the discomfort, it all vanished when I looked and saw Lalie waving from the waiting lounge at Maiquetía.

The World Cup was seventh heaven humbug. The real world of Central America was about to demonstrate how the Third World historically lives and tragically dies.

CHAPTER FOUR

August 22, 1978. While Eden Pastora (Commander Zero), was leading his raggedy band of Sandinista rebels to storm the National Palace in Managua, Nicaragua, I was returning from a hand-in-hand walk with Lalie over the long footbridge to the other side of the autopista in Caracas. It was a dirty bridge over troubled waters—flash floods of smoking combustion engines, a reasonable facsimile of Hell on earth. The ugly, creaking, crowded footbridge provided pedestrians in the Parque Centrál area with the only way to move across the super-highway, with its hordes of fuming cars, trucks, buses, and motorcycles. The leather-jacketed cyclists zoomed in swarms so thick that drivers in cars dared not rest their arms on open windows nor allow any part of their bodies to protrude even a fraction of an inch for fear of losing an elbow to motorcycle handlebars. The reason there were so many motorcycles in Caracas was because businesses had no confidence in the postal system.

Each day, Lalie and a colleague commuted to their jobs at Revlon de Venezuela, a company trying to make part of the human race a little more kissable. Cosmetic beauty, *sí*, but difficult to fault. Life throughout the city was dreary and could use a touch of color.

I had fixed myself a little breakfast in the pocket-size kitchen of the CBS Latin America Bureau office/apartment, and had begun writing a two-minute, quick-and-dirty radio script for a profile of Argentina's Cardinal Pironio. He was one of the candidates to succeed Pope Paul VI, who had died two weeks before. I did the best I could with hardly any background material, nothing more than an interview with a local bishop in Caracas. I read up the final draft to Liz at CBS Radio in New York, because her approval was required. After making her recommended changes, I recorded it.

I was in the middle of revising a piece on the Venezuelan presidential election when, about 4:30 p.m., CBS News foreign editor Feders called from New York. Bulletin: Sandinista gunmen led by Commander Zero had not only stormed the National Palace in Managua but seized hundreds of hostages, including Nicaraguan legislators.

Paco, my driver, my confidant, my one and only "fixer," the Venezuelan version of Quixote's Sancho Panza, ordered a jet-prop, and the television crew and I began hauling out our electronic news gear. From the beginning, Paco had made me understand that he did not want to speak English, even if he could, because he wanted me to be forced to speak Spanish. He was on a fool's errand, but our bonding continued with dollar signs racing in Paco's little eyes like cherries in a row at Vegas. He was becoming a true amigo, and in time I came to believe he would lay down his life for me. In good time I'd feel the same about him. Driver Paco and "Mr. David," as he called me, became as tight as Sancho Panza and Don Quixote. The whole idea of my becoming a foreign correspondent was quixotic on the face of it, but Paco was loyal throughout, all five feet two inches of him. When he wore his black leather jacket and drove his dusty green/brown station wagon, he was like Mighty Mouse at the helm of a battleship on the high seas of the Caracas autopista. Paco represented many of the best Venezuelan characteristics—a generous and easy spirit, a sweet fatalism that calmly accepted the harshest of realities.

On the day of the takeover of the National Palace in Managua, we couldn't leave, much to my frustration, until Sorensen and Roberto Moreno, his Venezuelan technician, had gone home for their passports. There were many things to worry about, like having one's passport tattooed on the forehead. Since that was neither feasible nor attractive, the next best thing was to have the passport chained around the neck and waterproofed so it could be worn while showering. One itsy-bitsy inattention to detail could make the difference between accomplishing a mission and falling flat on one's face. The camel's backbreaker on August 22 was a Venezuelan security guard who would not let us take our equipment off the elevator of Edificio Catuche, the building where the CBS News office/apartment was located. We had to produce written permission from the condominium authorities, and it cost us an hour. When we finally extricated ourselves from Parque Centrál in the heart of the city, had gone in the opposite direction from La Carlota, the inner-city airport, to pick up Carl and had turned around and finally had gone back to the airstrip, we were too late to take off. The airport closed at sundown, something the Venezuelan snake oil salesmen had neglected to tell CBS News when it was looking for a new location for its Latin America Bureau.

We limped to Maiquetía, the main airport serving Caracas, but we couldn't find any charter pilots. People looked at us as if we were banditos who'd just robbed the main office of Banco Mercantíl y Agrícola and were trying to escape to Geneva. I called Feders, expecting to be fired. He was at a going-away party for Bill Small who, if he hadn't been moving to NBC, would have sent me back to the farm club in Louisville.

"Please, "Commander Zero", Commandante Céro, por favor, hold on 'til I get there! Don't do anything dotty until I can put a microphone in your darling face and ask you how you feel," I mumbled as I paced back and forth at Simón Bolívar Aeropuerto Internacionál on the edge of nowhere. "You're one sumbitchin' storm, you Commandante Céro."

The front-page story in every newspaper on all the newsstands was Nicaragua. Commander Zero and his revolutionaries were demanding $10 million and a plane to take them to—you guessed it—Venezuela. Holy God! Paco and Don Quixote stayed on alert at the office, popping their knuckles, studiously trying to get their feces consolidated.

In the middle of all this, there was a telephone call from New York that seemed to suggest it might serve a better purpose if we were to get on a charter to Buenos Aires. No big deal—just a little transcontinental flight over the little nation of Brazil, only slightly larger than the forty-eight contiguous states of the United States of America. I alerted Carl and he showed up with "warm clothes."

But then, about 4:30 p.m., Feders called and asked if we could be on the Aero-México flight to Panama at 6:30. No big deal. Cancel the transcontinental flight to Buenos Aires (where it was winter), and head north to Panama City (where it was summer). I told Feders we'd try. Carl whined that he wanted to go home for "cool clothes." I said, No way, Man. I called Candes Travel Agency and asked sweet Delia, the head honcha, to make up tickets. Only then did Roberto poleax me with the news that he had to go home for his bloody passport. He was reverting to his natural Venezolano DNA, and there I was thinking we'd brought him along to being a reasonable facsimile of a damn Yankee.

While Roberto, frustrated and embarrassed, raced across town, we loaded Paco's station wagon and hauled our bare hind ends to the travel agency, picked up the tickets from our smiling, easygoing friend Delia. As we went out the door and swooped away in a swirl of dust, she must have thought, gringos are all the same, they want both yesterday and tomorrow to be today. We barreled out to Maiquetía Airport, making it there in record time, and by the skin of his teeth Roberto made it too. We were on-again, off-again, about like the water in Caracas and the Foreign Desk of *whim du jour* at the Broadcast Center in New York.

Bill Small's new institution, NBC News, was the only network to fly its reporters into Managua before the airport and the Nicaraguan borders were sealed. CBS Cameraman Bernie Nudelman did not make it from Miami the first night. Nor did correspondent Bruce Hall from Atlanta. So, let Commandante Céro *have* the frigging Palacio Nacional! Who needed it worse than he did? Pres. Anastasio Somoza thought *he* did, but he must have been seeing the Peter Principle handwriting on the bunker wall, even if President Carter had given him more money to play out the shortening string of his family's dynasty.

Bill Small was doubtless cheered that the National Biscuit Company was kicking the Communist Broadcasting System's butt, and my firing would be somebody else's cookie to crumble. (CBS's harshest critics employed the "Communist" label, which was about as stupid as it ever gets.) Nonetheless, in retrospect, It would have been an act of mercy to fire me and put me on the first plane back to Kentucky. As for CBS News being "communistic" and NBC being a "biscuit company," that was standard gallows humor.

Hell was rolling like hot lava in 1978 in Somoza's Nicaragua, and it was not from a volcano. CBS News desk assistants in New York were urging news crews to "be careful...we don't want you to get killed down there." Roughly translated, that meant: "Don't miss the story."

In Panama, I called New York and picked up that Bruce Hall and editor/producer Joe Carroll had descended by charter into Managua. Nobody knew how, but there they were. Their instructions were to call New York "soonest" and advise as to whether the same plane could continue to Panama, pick us up, and take us to Managua the same night. It didn't happen because the pilots balked. When a charter pilot tells you, "No," you'd better believe it.

My alarm went off at 4:30 a.m., Panama time, and fifteen minutes later I stumbled out of bed. I checked out, paying also for Roberto, who had not been a damned Yankee long enough to earn his plastic. We waited for Carl, who emerged about thirty minutes later than I had planned. It was a short ride to the airport, and there was the next surprise: Roberto, being a Venezolano, could not go to Nicaragua without a visa (the non-plastic kind). While he went off to the consulate, Carl and I boarded TACA 310. Roberto was temporarily left behind. Quixote would like to be permanently left behind in the "Switzerland of Central America." He could have taken up residence there and lived a simpler Peter's life.

Costa Rica, our first and only stop, was more lavish than pictures I had seen, and it looked *clean*, an answer to the prayer at St. Patrick's. I hoped closer inspection would not disillusion me. There were exceptionally green, contoured, cultivated hillsides, red tile roofs—signs of cultural pride—and there were cloud-covered mountains surrounded by a vast, rich green rain forest. We did not disembark because there was no time for it. I wished for even a slender chance to be living a different life, but Quixote had asked for *this* one and here it was. There'd be no running away.

HONDURAS

NICARAGUA

● Estelí
● Matagalpa

León ● *Lake Managua*
Managua ● *Lake Nicaragua*
Masaya

Peñas Blancas ● Liberia

COSTA RICA

● San José

Caribbean Sea

PANAMA

Panama City

Pacific Ocean

At 9:30 New York time we were on our way to Managua, leaving behind one of the most extraordinary countries I'd ever seen from the air. It made me pine for our own Plum Lick in Kentucky, as I wrote in my journal: *Big strawberries with thick cream...fatted pigs...cured hams the way Grandfather W.B. and Grandmother Lala would have liked it... springhouse full of cooling things to eat and drink...calves being born... lambing time...gathering black walnuts...then winter and stacking firewood for long winters' nights and love to keep us warm. Our first child."*

When we came in from the south over the Managua airport, a Venezuelan C130 was poised at the end of the runway. We crossed on our final approach and made a circle over Lake Managua, with the palace on the right. I strained to look, but it was too far to see anything. ABC and another crew had joined us in San José. Joe Carroll and a corporate jet pilot met us in customs. After we cleared, Joe helped Carl get ready to tape. ENG— Electronic News Gathering—was a new technological trick for an old pit bull, who had built his combat-centered career on film. Carl was giving it his best growl, but he realized, as well as anybody, that news on film was as dead as skeletons scattered on Nicaraguan street corners.

We took Joe's car rental to the East End of the airport and first took a wide shot of the planes. There was a Panamanian Electra as well as the C130. We climbed over barbed wire and tiptoed through hip-high grass to the planes. Buses were bringing freed political prisoners and the Sandinista gunmen to the planes. It was a certified, sure-fire media gangbang. I tried to interview a Catholic bishop.

"¿Qué pasa?" I asked, almost dreading an answer.

I didn't have to worry. The bishop looked through me as if I was Mr. Cellophane.

Carl found a guerrilla who could speak perfect English, and he told us (through a mask over his face) that the anti-Somoza uprising was for real. After we taped the takeoffs of the two planes, Carl and I took the CBS News jet back to Panama City. I was determined to try to obtain pictures of the arrival of the Sandinistas. Our stringer was superbly inept. I finally was able to send one minute of the arrival to the satellite, which was used as a "telop" on the update. (A "telop" is a picture usually positioned in the upper right-hand corner of the television screen above the anchorperson, who then reads the accompanying lines of the story). We received rave reviews from New York on our Managua footage. I fed a report to hourly radio, was debriefed, and sent up a *World News* Roundupper. I also fed new narration for *Morning News*. Before midnight, Carl's camera lost its color, making it impossible to do an on-camera standupper. My mother regularly wanted to know why I wasn't seen more on-camera. This was one of the reasons.

As Gordon Van Sauter used to say when he was president of CBS News, we had passed through a "shitstorm." Part of me loved it, but another part of me had never been more certain that I was ready to leave CBS at a moment's notice. It could have been arranged without a single look back over my shoulder. There might be many good and treasured memories, but no regrets. Well, not too many. I wanted to be a good gardener and animal husbandman. I wanted to stop playing electronic "journalism" games. I might have to teach and work at public television for a while, but basically I wanted an early retirement, which is to say when I was fifty-five years old. I wanted to be my own man. I was worn out with dangling on the end of a string, and I didn't want to be a puppet any more. I was cannon fodder, and it hurt my pride. It also scared me silly. Life was too short to dance with ugly network news executives. I wanted to do what I wanted to do while I was still able to do it, whatever "it" was. If anybody disagreed, they could take a royal, flying, full gainer with a twist into the shallow end of the pool.

It was Black Friday, August 25, 1978. Carl's camera was down—no blue in the picture. I called Feders and suggested that the crew and I pack up and leave on the first available flight, as if we had good sense, and head back to Caracas. He said, in his thundering, phone-slamming best, "Absolutely not." Sweet guy, that Feders. He said the *CBS Evening News* wanted a story from us on this day even if it was David Dick standing on a mountaintop. I knew better than that. They wouldn't have taken Moses on a mountaintop without first knowing what the words on the tablet were. I knew they wanted a story. I knew I wasn't Moses, even if that mattered, but since it didn't, Quixote figured he'd try anyway.

What the heck?

I peeled off $500 of CBS's shareholders' hard-earned money for a studio camera at Teleservicios, rolled it out onto the roof, and pulled off a one-minute and twelve-second situationer, which we looked at and admired. Although I may not have resembled Moses or Eric Sevareid, I didn't think I was any uglier than either one of them. We hurried back to Intercomsat. My friend from WTVJ in Miami, Mike Orloff, appeared during the night. He was handling the "feeding of the bird" (bouncing the camera footage off the satellite to CBS in New York).

All of a sudden I saw Bob Sirkin talking to his own birdbrains in New York, the ABC nitwits. I went to the water cooler and hung out there trying to overhear whatever it was he was saying. Finally, I sidled up and point-blank said to him: "I hope you're not going to tell me that you got into the garrison today."

He smiled.

It was a smile that was loathsome and painful for me, breathtakingly joyous for him.

"Yes, I did." He glowed.

"Did you talk to the Sandinistas?"

"Yes, I spoke with Céro."

"*¿Commandante Céro?*"

"Yes."

I pooped little green marbles on the tiled floor of the Intercomsat building. I called my co-conspirator crazies in New York and told them ABC had it but we didn't. All Hell did not erupt, but I had no earthly idea why. Sometimes it was as if I was the guy on the edge of the cliff and was trying to yell with a mouthful of buckshot. Everybody was whistling Dixie.

From Channel 4, I frantically cajoled some footage of the Catholic bishops at the airport. They were returning to Managua, and we fed that up to cover our asses with Moses' closing lines from the mountaintop.

Next upon the stage were two Third World reporters from a Spanish network I'd never heard of. They too had interviewed Céro. It was actually I who was fast approaching zero status. Sirkin offered to give me some of his pictures from the interior of the garrison, wallpaper stuff about as useful as the wrappings of a box with the frigging diamond taken out and put on a pretty señorita's finger. What I needed, of course, were faces speaking words no matter what language they were in. Spanish would do, even though I still was not much beyond the "¿Qué pasa?" point. The Third Worldies said I could have some of their interview, and Moses forthwith granted them full and final absolution for their sins.

I wrote new lines and fed them up to New York. I pranced back to the Continentál and called the Foreign Desk to find out how the piece had looked on the air. It really looked great. It wasn't seen at all—no Moses, no bishops, and no Sandinista rebels. The Spanish network had served papers on CBS News enjoining it from using the footage I'd sweet-talked out of the Third World guys. I ejected from my hotel room, jabbering like a mad cow drilled for the holler horn. I slobbered into the mirror of the tenth floor elevator of the Continentál Hotel. I considered getting laid.

"It isn't worth it. No, it is *not* worth it. It's for the birds. It is really for the birds. It is dementia. Demeaning. Fiendish." As we say on Plum Lick, "Sucked pond water." I went to dinner at Casa del Marisco with Carl, Mike, and Roberto. I scoffed ceviche. I didn't get drunk, and I didn't get laid. Three more mistakes.

About 3:30 on Saturday morning, John Smith turned up in Panama City. He was the CBS cameraman who specialized in driving bumper-to-bumper at super high speeds through the Ozarks, the Appalachians, and most reduced-speed areas in order to prove it could be done, while at the same time encouraging confrontations with an assortment of Barney Fifes. Through it all, Smith was collecting more books of Green Stamps for the pool table he wanted to install in his residence in Nashville. He called my room to say he had checked in at the hotel. Jubba, one of the original CBS Southern Bureau boys of summer, didn't come with him. Jubba was about to get his own staff job after all. Smith had come alone to take a cursory look at Sorensen's camera, and if John couldn't fix it we were to ship it back to New York for repairs. He couldn't, and we did.

Even the *Weekend News* had no interest in more of Commander Zero, but the Foreign Desk insisted that we try to get "our own" interview using Smith's camera. I checked with Fernando Eleta at Channel 4 and realized there was nothing he could do for us on this day. I was glad because I intended to slobber low. Besides, the cardinals were about to send up white smoke in Rome, and if Pironio was elected we'd have to move down to Argentina and follow that ecclesiastical storm. We'd have to be papal experts and look into all Pironio's closets to see what might be hanging around in there.

I bought a ten-band short-wave radio, and the first thing out of the box was the report that the new big guy in Rome was John Paul I, Patriarch of Venice. So much for the chances of a Western Hemisphere guy, much less a Third World soul to lead the Roman version of the universe. We returned to Casa del Marisco, all except Carl, who said he wanted to "turn off CBS entirely for a while." He accomplished that task by attending an erotic film, *Paradise in the Philippines*. What he did after that was anybody's guess.

At dinner, Smith began catching me up on the comings and goings in the Atlanta Bureau, the game of "what ever happened to...," which never failed to entertain on the cheap. With each tale of woe, each horror story, each expense account fandango, each spider web encounter, each breakup of a marriage or a love affair, my conviction was reconfirmed that as soon as possible I would be leaving CBS News—or maybe retreating would be the better word. I amused myself by building castles in the air on Plum Lick in Kentucky, where one day I'd watch the moon shine and might even drink some.

I lounged around the pool at the Continentál, glad-eyed the bikinis, took a nap like a good little boy, and went with Smith to pay a sick call on José Rangel, our regular driver. He was suffering from obesity and a broken foot, laid up for about six months. José had helped me pick out a mola to hang on our bedroom wall. The artistry interwoven in a mola was a pleasant relief from the pressures of storm centers. The reverse-appliqué stitching was an example of craftsmanship involving patience, a product of the Central American culture that symbolized a slower, simpler, more contemplative way of life.

Clemente Cohen (of the Venezuelan Office of Information and Tourism) surfaced in Panama City, and he went to dinner with us at Casa del Marisco. Almost every word and every thought added to what was becoming an all-consuming, blubbering obsession—I was ready to head for the barn and would begin talking to CBS at once about getting out of my contract. I was reading Robert Penn Warren's *A Place to Come To*, and I was making notes for my first book, *The View from Plum Lick*. I wanted it to say something about my experiences with CBS News, but more about conservation and survival with dignity, and about the beginning of our days in the house where my ancestors had lived and loved. A second book might be: *Follow the Storm: A Long Way Home*.

Oh, Lord, Eulalie, I am so ready to go fly back with you. Lalie's formal name was rarely heard, but it was the name I used when the occasion called for a sweeter sound. There was an Aunt Eulalie in *Gone With the Wind*, Edgar Allen Poe had a Eulalie, and the thought of writing a book with a Eulalie in it began to make its way through Quixote's fairy-tale mind.

The following morning, I called my old friend O. Leonard Press in Lexington, and he indicated to me that he was interested in having me work for Kentucky Educational Television in combination with a teaching position in the UK College of Communications. It wasn't the English Department, but beggars can't be picky. We set as our target date the fall of 1979. Len would speak with the director of the School of Journalism, Ron Farrar, and would write to me within two or three weeks. That would be an eternity, but there was no place to hide, nor did I want there to be one. As soon as I received Len's letter, maybe even before, I'd notify CBS in writing that I wanted to be released from my contract in order to begin teaching and writing.

There was a new feeling of elation, ease, and hope for the future. I saw myself climbing up out of a hole. Within one year I would be out of the red on the short term; my only debt would be the mortgage on the farm alongside Plum Lick Creek. In time, that indebtedness would be paid. I reminded myself that I did not want "to buy the farm" in Nicaragua. Getting killed was noble, maybe, but it was no way to acquire property.

Monday, August 28, 1978, I called New York from Panama and was told by Paul Byers (the Good Lord of News had seen fit to send Feders on vacation) that Nicaragua was expected to go "down the road," and we should make plans to be there. We booked on Pan Am 502 at 7:00 the following morning. A general strike was gaining ground in the latest assault to force President Somoza from office, and something approaching anarchy, or civil war, or both, was impending. I was anything but eager for it, but I was going because I considered myself a good follower of storms. I just hoped to live to talk about it. In the afternoon I received a "very urgent" call from Kate Skattebol on the Foreign Desk, asking me to check out the availability and cost of a charter to Managua, *immediately*.

New York found a corporate jet for us in Miami and sent it down to Panama to pick us up and bring us to Managua the same night. I headed for a telephone: "Does eight months in Venezuela sound better to you than three years?" Lalie said it did. I told her about the call to Len Press, and how I figured I'd give CBS at least six months' notice with a target date for leaving Venezuela on May 10, 1979. I would be in Atlanta in time to be best man in my son Sam's wedding and be there for my daughter Cathy's high school graduation. I would help Bill Gilvin set out the tobacco crop, begin getting the old house in shape during the summer of '79, begin gathering firewood for the winter of that glorious year.

Lalie said, "Gotcha covered."

Monday, August 28, 1978, I went to Tucomea Airport where, in a moderate rain, we took off in our Lear jet about 9:15 p.m. We came upon the lights of Managua about 11:00. After a delay at the airport (it had just shut down for the night), we finally arranged for rides into the city, where we checked in at Hotel Intercontinental. Managua was asleep. If Howard Hughes was there, I didn't know about it. He'd been known to come in and out of the country amid considerable mystery. Never mind the Hugheses or the Quixotes, the revolution had been conceived. Birth was a given. It would require less than nine months.

A few days later, in Kentucky, the first woman to go on trial for a self-inflicted abortion was found not guilty on a plea of insanity. In Nicaragua, where inhumanity if not insanity was the order of the day, the revolution would not be aborted, would not be halted by President

Somoza. It asked no quarter. It would roll on from the storming of the National Palace on August 22, 1978, to the execution of ABC News Correspondent Bill Stewart by a National Guardsman at a roadblock in Managua less than a year later—June 20, 1979.

At Bill's funeral in Ashland, Kentucky, on Sunday, June 24, 1979, anchorman Frank Reynolds said: "The West Virginia boy who grew up to be what he wanted to be, who saw the world and helped his countrymen understand it—a noble achievement—has come home." But I didn't want to die that way. I didn't want to come back in a body bag. And I wasn't ashamed to say it.

CHAPTER FIVE

We hooked up with Bruce Hall and the Nudelman crew, who had done a good job playing catch-up to NBC. It was decided in the coffee shop of the Intercontinentál, snug on a hill alongside President Somoza's bunker, that Hall, Nudelman, and George Natenson, the CBS News stringer from Mexico City, who was in Nicaragua without a crew, would cover President Somoza's 10:00 a.m. news conference. Smith, Roberto, and I would angle south to look for some good "bang-bang"—the sound and fury of a battle for the sake of noise and rage. Whether or not it signified anything was of less importance.

About thirty-six miles from Managua we found good bang-bang in Diriamba. The town was 99.9% shut down by the general strike, which seemed to be unquestionably effective only outside Managua. Concussion bombs were exploding short distances from us as we advanced through the outwardly deserted town. There was a burned-out bus. The arrival of the National Guard sent a small cluster of people scrambling. Soldiers leaped out of a jeep, and one pointed his gun directly at Roberto's chest.

"¿Nacionalidád?"

"Venezolano," responded Roberto, without flinching.

The soldier thought for an instant, then jumped back onto the jeep, which churned up dust as it sped down the street. Smith shot footage of a firefight as National Guardsmen opened up with their automatic weapons. John disagreed with me about the nearness of the bullets. To me, he seemed to be dancing out on the apron of the arena where the death wish capered, something I hated and resisted, even when it might seem cowardly.

I thought the bullets were much too close, and so did two civilians. We scrambled to a nearby stone wall and flattened ourselves on the ground behind it. The hair stood at attention on the back of my neck. I did a radio spot there but, after listening to it, decided not to offer it because I thought it was too breathlessly melodramatic and might have shown me for the chicken manure I actually was. We returned to Managua, where Hall and I fed separate pieces to Cronkite. Both were used. I also gave Douglas Edwards's *World Tonight* a companion piece to Hall's report on Somoza, who, contrary to everybody's wishful thinking, had not left the country and was still ruling it with an iron hand.

I went to dinner at the Lobster's Inn with Smith, Roberto, and Hall. The food was good. Influenced by Smith, I'd been eating a lot of fish, primarily ceviche. I was handling my fork gingerly when a fair-sized rat approached our table and passed directly alongside my feet. It seemed to be intent upon looking for anything resembling food that had dropped from the table. The waiter caught up to the rat and stomped it to death. Before it died, it ran in circles and sounded like a baby whimpering.

The Battle of Matagalpa was fought on Wednesday, August 30, 1978. Smith, Roberto, and I rented a car with a driver and went about eighty miles north through picturesque country where peasants were plowing the hillsides with oxen. Quixote wanted to stroll over and ask if he could help, or only sit and feel the breathing of the animals as they pulled the implement and turned the sod. He had a deep-felt desire to scoop up the dirt and squeeze it simply for the good feel of it. The campesinos, with their hardened hands upon the plow handles, and the campesinas who baked the bread and carried the water, were on the fringe of the war zone, where there were running battles between government troops and armed rebels. Civilians were caught in the middle. Whole families had been moving out to escape being trapped inside the no-man's land.

Noncombatants displayed white cloth in the thin hope it would protect them from rebel sniper fire and the retaliatory blasts from Somoza's soldiers. The Red Cross used utmost care. No one wanted to be a stupid victim of mistaken identity. I suggested to our crew that we carry white cloth. Smith refused. He reminded me that we were *periodistas*, journalists, as if that would be automatically recognized and respected by both sides. At the hotel swimming pool, most of us wore T-shirts with the words printed on the back "*Periodista—No dispare!*" Journalist—Don't Shoot! A white flag would probably not have saved Bill Stewart's life. He carried none–neither did we.

The National Guard troops knew they were moving targets for anyone opposing the government, and the soldiers took no chances at street corners. In the faces of the exceedingly young guardsmen could be seen the fear of surprise attack. Bullets flew in all directions. There were no guarantees, few second chances. There were bullets with names written on them, and when it was precisely the right moment the bullet would find its owner and would burrow in with the barb of unyielding pain.

There was no explanation for the death of a twelve-year-old boy who, Red Cross workers said, was killed inside his family's pitiful house. The child's mother, convulsing in shock, followed the small fiberboard coffin. All color was drained from her face. She climbed onto the back of the Red Cross jeep, where friends had placed the coffin. The mother raised the little door of the coffin above the child's face and looked inside. She slammed the door closed. Then she opened it again. She slammed it again. Later I heard that a stray bullet had killed the child. It bore the child's name.

A student and at least two other persons had been killed this day in Matagalpa, where only the very old still wandered in the open, only the infirm remained huddled on the sidewalks, not comprehending what had happened to a city that had become desolate. Except for the soldiers and the rebels, Matagalpa was largely deserted.

I fed via satellite to the Cronkite news the report on the dead and dying in Matagalpa. There was a briefing in the evening in "the Bunker" in Managua. Maj. Gen. Ormondo José Fernandez of President Somoza's National Guard fielded questions. He claimed that the national strike was a failure: Somoza had called for peace and dialogue, he said, and Communist agitators were upsetting peaceful stability. The general said people had been suffering because of subversive elements. He did not believe the rebels had widespread support. How wrong could one man be? Or how willfully was he distorting the truth?

On one occasion I had the opportunity to interview President Somoza one-on-one. Instead of looking at me, he looked directly into the camera. After a few seconds, I stopped the interview and said, "Mr. President, would you mind looking at me instead of the camera?" He replied: "You're right. I am the president." The interview resumed and Tacho continued speaking directly to the camera.

We returned to Matagalpa, where some of the injured were being brought into San Vicente Hospital on the perimeter of the city, but it was still so close that gunfire constantly sent Red Cross workers scurrying for cover. The injured had sustained a litany of wounds in faces, legs, midsections. Sister Martha Freche López of the Sisters of Charity made the rounds of the patients, whispering words of encouragement to each. Sister Martha said there'd been no time for sleep. "We have six days and nights," she breathed, "In the city there is no security."

As the wounded soldiers were carried out of the hospital and loaded onto a truck, other guardsmen took up defensive positions. One soldier who was brought out on a stretcher was not placed with the injured on the truck. His personal papers were taken from his pockets. He was shot between the eyes. The bullet with his name on it made a neat, bluish hole. It looked like a small grape stamped against his forehead.

One Red Cross official estimated that as many as fifty people had been killed in Matagalpa since Saturday. Back at Channel 6 in Managua the networks were making chicken salad out of chicken manure, and they were running low on mayonnaise and imagination. I longed for Plum Lick…

…tomatoes, potatoes, onions, corn, radishes, turnips, watermelon, cantaloupe, peas, lettuce, okra, strawberries, asparagus, rhubarb, peppers, pole beans, apples, pears, peaches, plums, walnuts, eggs, chickens, cured ham, sheep, goats, Irish setters, German shepherds, border collies, Australian shepherds, cats, cows, calves, horses, flowers,

a big front porch, firewood, children — and Lalie.

September 1, 1978, could have been a decisive day for Nicaragua and the government of Pres. Anastasio Somoza Debayle. There were two fronts, one in Matagalpa, the other in Managua. On the first front, National Guardsmen were expected to try once more to clean out a nest of rebel snipers. If the government troops were unsuccessful, as they had been for the past several days, it would be another victory for the Sandinistas, another major break in the linkage of Somoza's ironclad control of the nation. On the second front, which was economic, business leaders in Managua were saying that the general strike would truly commence on this day, shutting down virtually all commerce. But if the businessmen were unsuccessful, as they had been before, it would be another important triumph for Somoza.

The people were returning to Matagalpa. The war was over there, at least for now. The guns were stilled, at least for now. Most with whom we talked said it would only be a matter of time until it happened all over again — if not in this mountain town, then in some other part of Nicaragua. A woman who lived near the rebel bunker, then deserted, said there were maybe sixty young people holding off the National Guard. She said they were no more than thirteen years old. She said they had fled during the night into the hills or behind locked doors no more than a few blocks away. A seventy-year-old man said there would be battles such as this one until Tacho stepped down. And that, the old man lamented, "He's not going to do."

Sorensen came in to rejoin Roberto, and at the Lobster's Inn we had a little changing-of-the-guard dinner for Hall, Smith, Roberto, Joe, his wife Mary Ann, Carl, and Nudelman. The sound of concussion bombs echoed during the night in Managua. It had become commonplace, more symbolic and theatrical than menacing. A concussion bomb was usually lobbed into the middle of a street, and the effect was a loud act of defiance, a way for the anti-Somoza rebels to say, we're still here, we've not gone away, we will not go away, this is our country too. You think it is only your country, pero es nuestra pais, también. We are ready to die for our country. Are you ready to die for your country?

There was no way to foretell whether the weekend would be quiet. The indications were that the rebels seeking to force out President Somoza would like to have, and possibly felt they needed, a breathing spell after the cessation of the siege the day before in Matagalpa. It would be Monday before it could be determined whether a national strike would take hold in the capital city. Perhaps one indication that President Somoza felt the situation had stabilized was his public relations flack's strategic withdrawal to New York.

Fighting between Somoza's soldiers and the anti-government forces in Matagalpa seesawed to a cloudy conclusion. Both sides could claim victory, and did. Perhaps it amounted to a stalemate. The rebels, an estimated sixty in number, many of them teenagers, had managed to hold off the National Guard in Nicaragua's third largest city for five days. They escaped without a trace, and that could mean a psychological victory for the Sandinistas. But in the end, Somoza's military muscle prevailed. There were an estimated fifty dead and two hundred injured in Matagalpa. Most of the casualties were neither guardsmen nor rebels but civilians, including the twelve-year-old child cut down in the crossfire. At week's end a nationwide strike appeared to be sputtering, but strike leaders said it would be widespread the coming week. The long struggle between the Sandinistas and Somoza appeared no nearer to achieving a predictable victory for either side.

I called Atlanta about noon on Sunday, September 3, and talked to my son Sam, who seemed to be doing well as a young journalist at WSB-TV. Cathy was getting a 35-mm camera and was pursuing her interest in photography. Nell gave me a full report on Pat, our Irish setter; she had won the Golden Goodie Award at the last obedience session. Debbie was working in a shoe store. Rose may have been wondering if I would finally follow a storm so close it would wrap me in its arms and squeeze the life out of me. She did not want that. I did not want it.

"Please do not kill the messenger," I often prayed. "Be glad there are messengers, who will bring you the message so you'll know what to do about the problem, whatever the problem is."

On September 4, 1978, I wrote a rough draft of a letter to be sent to CBS News as soon as prudently possible:

Dear Bud [Benjamin]—

I am writing to notify CBS formally through you that I wish to be released from my current contract. It has been my expectation that one-day I would return to my alma mater, the University of Kentucky, to teach. It is my desire to give CBS six months' notice that I wish to be released from my current contract on or about May 10, 1979.

On this date I will have been on assignment one complete year in Caracas. During this time I will have reestablished the Latin America Bureau in a way that I hope will have fulfilled the expectations of CBS. Whether, as a practical matter, it is wise to continue to have this bureau located in Venezuela is, of course, a separate consideration, and if management wishes any input from me I will be happy to supply some thoughts. It seems to me, if the working premise is a 'presence' in South America, then the choice of bureau location is severely limited, and Caracas, with whatever native peculiarities it may have, becomes a logical place.

My desire is to be a credit to CBS, the network to which I've devoted myself exclusively and faithfully for the past twelve years. I would never feel comfortable working for the competition at any price. My teaching salary will be less than half as much as it is now with CBS. Money has never been an overriding consideration with me: the paramount factors have been and will be: dignity, professional excellence, self-worth. And to that greater end I desire now to move with full confidence that it is the best decision for CBS, the University of Kentucky, and myself. Please advise how I should now proceed to make the termination of my contract effective and satisfactory to both parties.

I'd like to take this opportunity to congratulate you, John Lane, and my other colleagues who recently received their promotions. I believe they greatly enhance the future of CBS News, the organization I admire so much and the one whose standards I will endeavor to uphold and to convey, if possible, to my students.

It was a letter never sent. Why? I'm not sure. Maybe it was as hollow as it sounded. Maybe I hated the thought of being a quitter. Possibly it was the old "go an extra mile" thing. Maybe there was just enough Quixote left in me to screw me up.

In Managua, "Tacho" Somoza tried again to tighten the leash on the insurgents. He took away the charter of the political opposition. Many may have thought he was a sonofabitch, but as F.D.R. said of Tacho's father, he was "*our* sonofabitch." During the father's dictatorship, on February 21, 1934, when Tacho was only nine years old, Sandino, patron saint of the 1978 rebel dogs, was ambushed following a dinner at the National Palace and was assassinated by the Somoza forces. Sandino's followers would never forget or forgive the treachery.

I attended a news conference called by INDE, the Institute for the Development of Nicaragua. We offered a piece, but the broadcast passed. No bang-bang. During the past two days the strike promoters had been saying that the showdown would become truly effective in the current week, but I had not gotten that impression. The reality seemed to me that Tacho had the guns and the money. He ran the country, and the businessmen could conduct a strike only so long, which meant until they ran out of will and cordobas. It was only a matter of time until the Sandinistas launched new attacks. The worst lay ahead.

As the week wound down, the National Guard took a deep breath, the Sandinistas licked their wounds, and the journalists began elbowing their way to the bar to feed on their own rumors. The most prevalent was the notion that there'd be a rebel attack on the Hotel Intercontinental, where the journalists were housed. Or National Guardsmen, disguised as Sandinistas, would attack. Or the rebels would attempt to take hostage a North American network television crew. In an effort to put some flesh on the bones of the predicament, a few of us requested and were granted a meeting with the U.S. ambassador. It was a "deep backgrounder," which meant that nothing that was said could be attributed to him. It lasted two and one-half hours, the ambassador outlining U.S. policy on Nicaragua down through the years. The theory was that the United States would like to see Somoza out but was reluctant to throw him out because there would then be a vacuum into which the Communists would move, creating another Cuba. The U.S. had supported Somoza, and now it was stuck with him. The ambassador assured us that there was no intelligence at the embassy indicating any real possibility of attack on journalists at the Intercontinental.

Later, reporters wearing their "¡*No dispare!*" T-shirts held a meeting at the hotel bar and decided if an attack did come they would stay off the elevators and descend calmly down the steps and gather outside at the swimming pool. All for one and one for all! If anybody was going to take hostages they'd have to take everyone, or spray us with machine gun bullets and leave our bodies floating in the pool. Big talk. Another whiskey on the rocks, *por favor*.

One early evening, several of us were sitting in the lobby when there was a loud explosion near the front entrance to the hotel. Nobody headed for the pool. We ran straight outside. It was only a percussion bomb. If it had been an attack we would have run directly into the jaws of it. We were that Doberman pinscher dedicated—and stupid. I called New York and discovered that it was beginning to look as if we might really be leaving Nicaragua.

Sweet Jesus!

As we came down to the end of the approximately two and a half weeks in Nicaragua, we drove back to Matagalpa in the north and did a "revisited." Everything was peaceful. I looked up Sister Martha Freche López. She was still smiling, fussing around an evacuation class for residents. I should have talked to her about saving my soul. Instead I interviewed a man who said the revolution was not only coming, it was here. We toured the town and then headed back to Managua. We also made two trips to Masaya in the south.

In Masaya I learned that the National Guard had shot its way into a Catholic school, dragged away at least one priest, and generally terrorized the faculty and students. We had an interview with a teacher who described in graphic detail how one student who recently had been arrested was tortured by having his testicles squeezed, an electric charge applied to them, and a rifle barrel rammed up his backside. The Cronkiters almost put it on the air, but it appeared they chickened out. Who knows? Maybe there wasn't room for it, which didn't keep from infuriating me that they had an opportunity to tell the United States public what was really happening in Nicaragua. My perception was that they couldn't bring themselves to put perfectly legitimate words, "testicles" and "anus" on the air. I wrote it down in my journal as a bad case of immaturity. I was partially vindicated. *Morning News* used the report next morning, testicles and all.

It was necessary for us to return to Masaya again, which later, along with León and Estelí, would be destroyed by the National Guard. There was a demonstration against the arrest and deportation of the Catholic priest in Masaya. Before we came upon the scene, the National Guard broke up the protest by dropping tear gas from helicopters. The mood of the people was anguish and determination to fight back. Open civil war was coming. There was no mistaking the signs.

It was a simple case of too much land and too much power in the hands of too few people, an elemental case of too little education, the old plantation mentality, and the old big-spread mind-set. The top guy was on top and would kill to stay on top. The worker ants had to be kept working in a variation of slave conditions. The people had to be suppressed because if they had power they would pull down the king from the mountain.

I wanted safe harbor. Crane's *Red Badge of Courage* preyed on my mind. I did not want it pinned to my chest. I wanted somebody else to wear it, anybody else. I knew, as everyone else knew, the struggle against Somoza and his children and his children's children would go on and on for decades after I was dead and buried in Kentucky. It would not matter whether or not I wore a red badge of courage.

Friday, September 8, we boarded our Pan Am flight to Panama. I was finally on my way to Caracas! As soon as I was home again I would sit down to the business of writing my letter of introduction to the dean of the College of Communications at the University of Kentucky. I would explain my purpose, my proposed timetable, and what I thought I would be qualified to teach: news writing for radio and television, voice development, reporting techniques, and broadcasting responsibilities. Maybe a little Expense Account 101.

The AeroMéxico flight that was supposed to leave Panama at 2:30 p.m. on September 8 was delayed until 11:00 p.m. Most of this time was spent at the airport. It had just recently been opened and it was handsome and efficient. We didn't know that all Hell was breaking loose back in Nicaragua. Even if we had, it would have taken a presidential order to turn me around and head me back in that direction. I was tired and in bad need of seeing my bride. I was in no mood to take any unnecessary chances, did not want to be a hero, did not want my butt shot off. We finally boarded our plane and soon were heading out over the rim of South America to Venezuela.

It was after two o'clock on Sunday morning when the wheels of our jet touched down at Maiquetía. When Paco came into sight he led Quixote to believe that Miz Scarlett had decided to stay at the apartment. My lower lip sagged. As we were standing there waiting to clear customs, I spotted her, all six-feet-two of her, on the other side of the glass window. She was flapping her arms like a seagull trying to take off from a swamp. She'd been trying to get my attention for I didn't know how long. I came through the door and we had ourselves a soul kiss, wet and warm.

A different reality appeared. Venezuelan marines were conducting their version of "crowd control." They tolerated no disagreements. "*¡Pase! ¡Pase!*" they snarled. Carl turned sour, which was standard operating procedure for most network cameramen, whose style was seldom to suffer fools kindly. We had under-tipped the porter and that had made the porter sour. It moved from there to the face-saving phase, which was on all occasions a no-win situation. After we loaded up Paco's station wagon we set out for Parque Central and by about four o'clock on that Sunday morning we had hauled in the last of our bags and boxes.

There was a message from New York on the telex. Michael George on the Foreign Desk wanted to know if we could go back to Nicaragua!

Sweet Baby Jesus!

I was ready to kill. The Saturday Night Sandinista special was roaring into Sunday. On the telephone, I reminded Mike that we couldn't leave Venezuela until we had reinstated our solvencias, and that anyway we were damned tired and wanted to go to bed. I tried to be gentle with Lalie, no matter how much I was like an animal breaking out all over.

Tenderness led to love.

The next morning, our first order of business was to apply for the reinstatement of our solvencias. But of course, just as I had predicted in a telex to Feders, Monday was one of the least productive weekdays for Venezuelans—the other one was Friday. I had another agonizing time of it in the Office of Information and Tourism and in Banco Mercantíl y Agrícola, where the manager disapproved of my reluctance to speak Spanish. She was right. I was the gringo. But she was wrong too because I was also the customer, and a damn good one at that.

I paid the bureau rent and mailed the letter to the University of Kentucky. As soon as we received what I hoped would be a favorable reply I would give my notice to CBS. It had been proven once again that the company should never have located the bureau in Caracas. Feders was certainly wrong-headed about a lot of things, but he had been absolutely right in his consistent opposition to Caracas. We had come to Venezuela with open minds and hearts and with enthusiasm, but we had been like cattle going to the stun gun. Hardly anything worked. The city and the people lived in filth and spread it as if it were their patriotic duty. The noise of the motorcycles was horrendous. Traffic jams were an affliction. Pollution was an abomination. *Goodnight, sweet Caracas. I do not like you. I know you don't like me. So we're even.*

As we tramped once more across the footbridge over the autopista we talked about how we might manage what then seemed to be a possible move to Panama. We discussed the prospect of putting our household effects into storage in the United States. I talked on the phone with CBS News Vice President John Lane and told him it was my recommendation that the bureau be moved from Caracas to Panama. I had been talking out of both sides of my mouth. I had written in my unmailed letter to Bud Benjamin that it would be best to stay in Caracas. John listened to me like the father confessor for which he had a well-deserved reputation, despite his frequent juvenile outbursts. I told him that Sorensen was in agreement. Later Carl would tell me that he and his wife Mirella had definitely decided to sell their apartment. We were floundering, and we knew it, but we finally received one-month solvencias, and Roberto was given his visa for Nicaragua.

CBS News Latin America bureau secured reservations on the AeroMéxico flight the following night to Panama, connecting with the TACA flight Thursday morning back to Managua. But we hoped to the Great Creator and all his angels in Heaven that we wouldn't have to go. Feders did not return my call in the afternoon to talk about his proposal that we postpone our vacations. Carl had canceled his trip to Europe because of the uncertainty of the future location of the bureau. Our gut feeling was that Nicaragua was going down, and it was going to continue to be a major story for years to come. Carl and Roberto came in and taped presidential campaign commercials off the air for our re-do of that story for Cronkite. I finished rewriting the script and we recorded it. That night, Lalie wept because she didn't want me to go back the next day to Nicaragua. I didn't want to go either. We went to sleep in each other's arms.

Because of the uncertainty of September 13, thinking it was highly probable that I would be leaving for Nicaragua, Lalie decided to stay home from Revlon. I was up about 7:00 and trudged across the footbridge to tell Maria Victoria that her friend was "sick" and would not be going to work until the next day at the earliest. I bought the *Daily Journal* (the local English language newspaper without which I'd be truly lost), and Nicaragua was still big on the front page. There was hand-to-hand fighting in Masaya.

Carl, Roberto, and Paco came in to prepare for the possibility of taking the trip that none of us wanted but for which all of us were willing to risk our loves, our lives, our only times on earth. It was time to update my will.

About two o'clock we finally received word from New York: We were not going to Nicaragua! *—we were all going on vacation!* Sonofabitch! It was like being on death row and receiving a stay of execution. Cupid took one long, deep breath. Carl was understandably annoyed, because even he could not be expected to turn his bravery off and on like a water spigot. He took two comp days prior to his vacation. Lalie and I decided to cook the last two of the world's toughest steaks from CADA, the supermarket built by the Rockefellers. It was a marvelous time to be together, laughing and loving.

We said we knew we had known we were in love before, but we never knew how much more we'd be after we were married. The next day would be the fifth-month anniversary of our wedding in St. Paul's Episcopal Church in Woodville, Mississippi.

I bought newspapers and once more read of the battle raging throughout Nicaragua. I called Atlanta: Debbie did not get a job with Braniff; Sam had not followed through on my recommendation that he borrow some money to help pay for the last of his college expenses. Nell thought Pat, the Irish setter, might have broken her leg, but no. Cathy was O.K. Rose was being what Rose was best at being, nurturing our children, worrying about their every move, feeding them well, nursing their wounds, tucking them into bed at night, reassuring them that, no, their father had not taken leave of his senses (whether or not she believed it).

Producer Rick Kaplan called from New York for more changes in the Venezuela presidential story. He said Feders's demise as CBS Foreign Editor was imminent. It was like that at the network—circular firing squads. Carl called and said a bulletin had just moved on Caracas TV that President Pérez was sending planes to Costa Rica. I called Clemente Cohen, secured the details, gave lines to the *CBS Evening News* while it was still on the air, did the same for radio, wrote, recorded, and fed a spot for the hourlies. New York called back and said we should cancel our vacations and catch the first available flight to Costa Rica. Hell was on rapid boil. It was spilling over into the fire in Nicaragua.

Feders was definitely "out" as foreign editor, to be replaced the next day by Brian Ellis, whom I'd known as the assistant CBS News bureau manager in Atlanta when I first went there eight years before. He was a "Brit," and that had both good and bad things attached to it—joviality mixed with tortured ambiguities. I made reservations, beeped Paco, could not beep Roberto, told Carl before he could say anything, "I don't want any more shit."

I tried my best to comfort Lalie. It was a tough time. Some women would have buckled under it. She mustered up the brazen Scarlett that was in her and probably would have gone off to kill Sandinistas or Somozas if somebody would only tell her which were which and where they were.

As the sun rose over Managua, it was clear to Anastasio Somoza Debayle what he was about to do in his bunker headquarters. The nation had been ruled by the iron hand of the Somoza family since the assassination of General Sandino in 1934 and the coup d'état against President Sacasa two years later. Managua, that "wonderful town" memorialized by the Andrews Sisters, was as much on the lip of destruction as it had been on December 23, 1972, when an earthquake registered 6.2 on the Richter scale in the center of the capital. Far more would die in the revolution sweeping Nicaragua in 1978 and 1979 than the thousands who had died on the day before Christmas Eve 1972, when untold hundreds of thousands of Nicaraguans had been displaced.

The decision for Somoza on September 15, 1978, was to order the mobilization of the National Guard, formalizing what it had already been doing from Matagalpa in the north to Masaya in the south—systematically grinding the opposition into submission. But the grinder was not working the way it was expected to. The Carter administration was losing stomach for what was happening in the nation that had once been a mock training ground for United States Marines prior to the assassination of Sandino. Somoza could not know that in less than a year the United States would sever its military ties with Nicaragua and he would be forced to resign and flee into exile. He could not know that he would not be welcomed in the United States, where he had been educated, where he had been admired and supported. Two years and two days after he mobilized his Guardia Nacionál, Anastasio Somoza

Debayle would be ambushed in Asunción, Paraguay. His assailants would riddle his car with bullets as if he was a poor man's Clyde Barrow. Then with bazookas they would blow the car to pieces. In Managua, the ruling Sandinista government spokesperson, disavowing any direct connection with the assassination, would say "an evil man" was dead. Somoza's family and others would say a courageous fighter against communism had paid the supreme sacrifice.

It was after midnight on the morning of September 15, 1978, when I took a cab to Roberto's apartment in the Far East end of Caracas. He had let the batteries of his beeper run down. I told him I wanted him at the office no later than 4:00 a.m. I returned to Lalie and tried again to be gentle. She was frightened. I had told myself that I had to be resolved for the two of us. I also had to be resolute for Rose, but she probably was being resilient. Her pure Sicilian blood was serving her well. The deep kindness of Mary and the raw power of Frank, her coal company parents, had melded in Rose's blood, and she was unselfish about sharing it. I slept for two hours, but not too well.

This day was not so much a day of hope as of fear. Quixote, however, wrote *"Happy Anniversary"* in his journal. *Thank you for five months of this sweet, powerful, and scary honeymoon.* Paco and Roberto showed up before 4:30 a.m. Carl didn't give an extra minute or inch, and we again had trouble moving our equipment past the Parque Centrál Mounties. I told them, in polished King's English, which they pretended not to understand, that it was *our* frigging property, and we were taking it someplace, and if they didn't like it they could call the police and have us arrested. They didn't, which was probably a good thing.

Lalie and I kissed and waved, as we had many times before, when she would stand at airport gatehouse windows and trace "I love you" on the glass before running to the top of the airport terminal parking lot. Up there, she'd wave her arms like a solitary seagull, still signaling as my plane lifted off the ground.

Carl, Roberto, and I took the 7:30 Viasa to Costa Rica via Panama. New York was then saying that the decision had been made to move the bureau to Panama as soon as the Nicaraguan situation was "under control." Gringo mentality at work again. We had no sooner checked in at Hotel Cariari near the San José airport, and New York had no more than told me they expected a piece from me for the *CBS Evening News*, than Roberto announced that the videocassette recorder had been left in Caracas.

I chewed hindquarters. Carl tried to get off the hook, but I wasn't going to hold still for that. We had our Costa Rica stringer, Rudolphe Carillo, shoot the Venezuelan and Panamanian Air Force planes and helicopters at the airport with a silent Bell & Howell camera. I scripted and narrated, and we paid a Costa Rican commercial pilot $25 to hand carry it to Miami the next morning.

Joe and Mary Ann Carroll came in by charter from Miami. They'd been in New Orleans for the Ali-Spinks World Heavyweight Championship fight. Ali had won back the title. The young man, whom I had deified as Cassius Clay when he was growing up in Louisville, Kentucky, was still floating like a butterfly and stinging like a bee. He was the World Heavyweight Champion for the third time, but a little more than two years later he would announce his retirement.

The videotape recorder arrived from Caracas, but confusion and frustration reigned. The national holiday of the day before splashed over into Saturday, and it would again on Sunday. There was no way to establish the San José end of the video-landline to Panama. The charter pilots were tired and in no condition to fly up to the Nicaraguan border. The weather was marginal at best. I decided to rely on the film and narration that had been hand carried to Miami. That was the straw that broke the day's back. The stringer gave the wrong flight number, which I had in turn given to New York. There were two early morning flights from San José to Miami. Our broker in Miami met the wrong one. The pilot who did have the film made the mistake of taking it to his motel and not calling anyone in New York to tell them. But by the time we finally realized what had happened, it was too late for the broadcast, which had definitely wanted it and had it in the lineup. I was too tired, hurt, and disgusted to say to hell with it.

We were a bunch of clumsy primitives born about twenty-five years too soon, predating miniaturization of electronic technology, high speed editing equipment, the digital satellite system, and the capability to communicate instantly almost anywhere in the world. .

Why didn't I quit on the spot? Maybe it was the paycheck stretching toward six figures. Might've been the expense account. Maybe it was pride. Old fashioned cowardice. Stupidity. Who knows?

I wanted Lalie to get her solvencia so we could travel together during our last days in Latin America. I wanted most of all to take her to Costa Rica and Argentina. She said she was ready to go. It would not be long, we thought, until she would give her notice that she was leaving Revlon.

I was up promptly at 4:30 a.m. and by 5:15 I was in front of the motel, enjoying the clean early morning air and listening to the birds singing. When we pulled up at the airport and were stepping out of our van, Carl put his camera on the ground. Roberto didn't see it and knocked it over. For half an hour I thought we were again out of commission, but fortunately Roberto tinkered it into working. I told Carl he was not to blame anybody else for accidentally knocking over a fifty-thousand dollar camera that he should never have put on the ground in the first place. We headed in our King Air charter up to the border area, where there were reports of battles between the Sandinistas and the Nicaraguan National Guard.

From the plane, Costa Rica was like bright colors melding into soft, delicate tapestry. Adrenaline was weaving too. We landed at the town of Liberia, hitched a ride into the municipality, and rented a jeep, which we drove the approximately sixty-eight kilometers to the Costa Rican-Nicaraguan border. We were stopped on the way by a roadblock because Nicaraguan fighter planes were in Costa Rican air space. They were bombing the border town of Peñas Blancas. Finally we were allowed to go through in a convoy of jeeps to a deserted customs house about two hundred meters from the border. Carl had good footage of the planes attacking the town and a fierce ground fight between the Nicaraguan National Guard and the Sandinista rebels.

The battle was intense. My natural reaction was to hug the earth and above all to keep my head down. Carl had come alive with the excitement. He stood up in plain view and took pictures as if he were in a drugstore, adrenaline shoulder deep and rising. He quickly whirled with his camera, pointed it down and put on record the cowardice of us brave correspondents as we hugged the ground as tightly as babes at mothers' breasts.

We drove back to Liberia and returned in our charter to San José. I scripted and narrated and gave the shipment to our charter pilot to take to Miami. I was doubtful it would make the late *Sunday News*, but it should have made the next *Morning News*.

Morning didn't use the piece, and it had come in too late for *Sunday Night News*. One more snowflake on a hot kitchen stove. One more blow struck for Mr. Somoza, one more reminder that risking my life was sucking more pond water. Our charter took us back up north to Liberia. We rented a car to supplement the jeep and again drove to the Costa Rican-Nicaraguan border. The battle was over, the planes had gone to their takeoff sites, and so had the Sandinistas, but we put together some excuse-me footage and headed back to San José, leaving the crew to cover when the OAS team appeared to make its inspection. The charter had me back as smooth as a breeze, only to be met by Joe Carroll, who told me the broadcast had passed, no matter what we had. He said it was due to the Israeli-Egyptian-Jimmy Carter-summit news coming out of Washington. The Camp David agreements had been signed, both the "Framework for Peace in the Middle East" and the "Framework for the Conclusion of a Peace Treaty Between Egypt and Israel." There was not room on the broadcast for a skirmish at Peñas Blancas on the Nicaraguan-Costa Rican border. If a CBS correspondent had been killed there, it probably would have been a respectful "tell" with a sad expression on the anchorman's face as the broadcast dissolved to a short, sanctimonious black screen before the next commercial.

I went to Key Largo in San José. I drank gin. I drank a lot of gin. There was a piano. I thought of Humphrey Bogart. He would have liked this place. It was *Casablanca*. Ingrid Bergman was there. I thought of Gary Cooper and *For Whom the Bell Tolls*. Ingrid was there too. My companions went to dinner at a nearby restaurant, but I returned to my motel room, missing Lalie terribly and thinking about nothing but starting our family. I didn't want to die before doing that. I resolved to do everything I possibly could to clear the decks for my retreat from CBS and my return to Kentucky. My morale was given a quick fix when

I determined from New York that our story that had not been considered worthy of *Morning News* had made *Cronkite* the following Monday night. I bought two miniature replicas of Costa Rican peasant carts. I loved holding them in the palms of my hands and against the side of my face.

The situation in Nicaragua had quieted down somewhat. I received word that Carl, Roberto, and I as soon as possible should book air passage to Managua to replace Ed Rabel and the Nudelman crew. CBS News was downsizing to the "cover your butt" stage. I was to join Smith, Jubba, Hall, and Natenson. Lalie didn't want me in Nicaragua. We had talked about adding a room at the old house on Plum Lick, and we talked about another fireplace. I was looking forward to growing our own meat: beef, lamb, chicken, duck, turkey, goose, my scrambled-egg mind racing ahead.

I didn't want to leave Costa Rica, the "Switzerland of Central America," but I was sure I would return one day. The crew and I were able to obtain seats on COPA's 11:45 flight to Managua. In less than an hour I was back in the thick of the civil war. The ride into town to the Intercontinentál was as depressing as Costa Rica had been encouraging, all the more so knowing how futile it was for President Somoza and the people who despised him. As we passed the pathetic shacks of flimsy wood and tarpaper, a little boy stood pissing, as if he might have been thinking, "Piss on it, á Dios, piss on it."

Somoza had won a bitter, bloody, and temporary victory.

I saw Jubba at the hotel for the first time in a long while. Smith gave us water, Gatorade, and cookies for the next day's trip. I went to the coffee shop and ate hard-boiled eggs and rolls. I decided not to try to call Caracas because I knew the phones were bugged. Some of us had been deluded into believing the revolution was winding down. It wasn't. It was catching its breath.

The nightly curfew in Managua ended at 5:00 a.m. Roosters announced the coming of another day in the capital city. We pulled away about 6:00 and headed north to Estelí. There were military checkpoints along the way, and near the town there was a series of trenches in the road that had to be gone around or over with utmost care. On the return we hit one and blew out a tire. While Roberto fixed it, Carl sulked and Quixote stared again at the farmers plowing the distant hillsides. They were in communion with the earth, some of the richest in the Western Hemisphere.

In Estelí, gunfire was intense at an intersection where the National Guard had positioned three tanks. From there, Somoza's tired, frustrated troops pulverized the streets of Estelí. A rocket-launching plane helped them from above.

I crouched low alongside a stone wall that enclosed a Catholic school and convent. I looked straight ahead and saw a young National Guardsman on the other corner. He was staring back at me. Everything seemed in slow motion. His rifle came up. The soldier sighted. The spot between my eyes was on the cross hairs at the end of the rifle barrel. The soldier's finger tightened on the cold metal of the trigger.

I had wondered if I might be shot on this day. I had wondered where on my body I most did *not* want to take a bullet. I had thought I did not want to take it in the groin. I was on my honeymoon. I hoped that God intended for it to continue. God did not want me to be shot in the groin. God was a good God. He created testosterone. But now that the tension in the soldier's trigger finger increased, I knew it was my brain I most wanted to be left untouched. The National Guardsman could have my groin but not my brain.

"Oh, dear God, please God, don't let him fire a bullet into my brain."

At the final nanosecond on the street corner in Estelí, I jerked down my head, and I heard the bullet grind into the stone wall a fraction above where my brain cells would have splattered. An officer approached the man-boy soldier, snatched away his rifle, and slapped him in the face.

I turned and crawled as fast as my hands and knees would carry me to the entrance of the school and convent. Sniper bullets whined across the weedy, scorched front yard. My brain was hot-wired to muscles and nerve endings in my arms and legs. Body and mind were cooperating with the one fundamental mission—survival.

At that moment nothing mattered, neither first wife nor second, nor thoughts of children born, nor babies yet to be conceived. The adrenal cortexes had secreted natural steroid hormones, and the euphoria lifted the usual onus of indecision. At that instant, I could not be sure whether I was dead or alive. I moved in a world of surrealism. I went inside and wandered among the dead and the dying. About 40,000 people had called Estelí *their* city. Most had fled days before. The School of Our Lady of the Rosary—the offices, the anterooms, and the courtyard—was filled with bleeding bodies. It had taken longer to convince the few who held on stubbornly, some perhaps too frightened to come out of their houses until now, when there was no other option. To do otherwise was to invite certain death.

I saw no priests, only nuns, and for a moment I remembered, fifteen years before, the sisters at St. Leonard Church in Louisville. They had believed in me, had let me teach English literature to the children in the seventh grade. The sisters had laughed with my reading of *The Adventures of Huckleberry Finn*—the rapscallions, the duke and the king, and Jim dressed up in a King Lear outfit on the Mississippi River. They had given me a St. Christopher cross for the dashboard of my car. They had inspired me to pray.

"St. Michael, the archangel defend us in battle, be our protection against the wickedness and snares of the Devil. Rebuke him, oh God, we humbly pray, and do thou, oh Prince of the heavenly host, by the power of God, cast into Hell Satan and the other evil spirits, who prowl about the world seeking the ruin of souls."

I relived the joy of reading the birth of Jesus lesson to the St. Leonard congregation at Midnight Mass. I remembered the sublimity of being an altar boy in the Navy chapel at Subic Bay in the Philippines, and I had wondered how Heaven would be—streets paved with gold, everybody fitted and flying with wings, no need for money, no government, no armies, no dragon seeds. I asked myself if I had died on September 21, 1978, the bullet from the National Guardsman's rifle making a bull's-eye, scattering my earthly brain.

At the School of the Holy Rosary in Estelí there was no check-in for judgment. There was no separating of goats from sheep. If it was not Heaven, then was it Limbo? Or was it Hell? Whatever it was, the nuns of Holy Rosary were doing one of the things they did so well. They were busy binding up wounds. After a while, when epinephrine had subsided in my body, I went outside where the destruction was almost total.

The town of Estelí lay in smoking ruins.

Yes, this was definitely Hell.

Vultures flew overhead. A Red Cross volunteer went down the street to see about his family. When he returned, he was crying. He was out of his mind. "My wife is dead. A dog is eating the body."

Carl, Roberto, and I inched our way down the empty street, past the point where the National Guardsman had shot at me. From time to time, a haunting face appeared in the opening of a door, an image would appear as seen through gauze in a second-story window.

None of the faces spoke.

The vultures continued to circle. Carl took pictures of them riding the low, hot, sticky currents.

We went to the house where the Red Cross worker's wife was dead. She was in a back room. The hungry dog heard us coming and ran past us out the front door. I looked at the woman. We covered her with a small, dirty rug.

The gunfire would ease off. There would be an almost unbearable, choking silence. The rebels, or their armed sympathizers—wherever they were they could not be seen—might be catching their breaths. Then Hell would come unhinged again. Bullets whistled over the School of Our Lady of the Rosary, where an estimated 4,000 people had sought a safer place to be, but there was not room for everybody. For some, the sound of war had become so commonplace that they accepted it as if it were what you were supposed to hear on a warm September afternoon. Others might never become used to it. I was one of those. We flinched even at the sight of a National Guardsman. There was no water for 4,000 people. No electricity. Virtually no food. Some supplies were on the way, but until they arrived no one could be sure of anything. The people of Estelí huddled at Our Lady of the Rosary, and the sisters tried to console those who did not know where their loved ones were. The National Guard continued the door-to-door search, determined to root out the last of the rebels and put to death anybody remotely connected with them.

Estelí was a graveyard with bodies scattered about the town. Some were already skeletons. The vultures had done their work. Red Cross volunteers used a long pole to move two bodies to the middle of the street. The bodies were doused with gasoline and set afire. A relative said they had been pulled from their house two days before and executed by the National Guard. Looting was widespread, mostly by women and children, but some men too were carrying off new sewing machines, mattresses, radios, television sets, refrigerators. Estelí was a destroyed piece of civilization.

At the Intercontinentál in Managua, I stared at myself in the mirror and said, "I do not want to die here. I do not want to be a hero. I do not want to be a fallen correspondent to be remembered on the *CBS Evening News with Walter Cronkite*." I had been to Hell and I had looked at it down the barrel of a National Guardsman's rifle, and I had hated what I had seen. Most of all I hated the dragon seed that had produced it.

In León, there would be no Mass at the Church of Virgen Pilar de Zaragoza on Sunday, September 24, 1978. The priest feared for his life. His flock was petrified with fright. The church was stripped bare. From the battered front door, past the pews strewn with fallen plaster, to the altar with every religious object removed, the church was an empty shell. Bullet holes marked the places where the religious statues used to be. And where were they now? They were in hiding in a nearby parsonage, where Jesus stood in a corner. There was a bullet hole in the heart of the statue of the Virgin. Her foot had been broken, and her fingers were blown away. The priest said these statues symbolized the martyrdom of the Catholic Church in Nicaragua. He said the National Guard used a rumor that Sandinista rebels were in the church as the pretext for destroying it. He said now was not the time for Mass at Virgen Pilar de Zaragoza. He said now was the time for quiet.

I negotiated with New York about the piece we were offering for the evening broadcast. I was given one minute and ten seconds for the Church of Virgen Pilar de Zaragoza. The previous evening in the NBC editing room, I had seen *The Last Picture Show*.

I called New York and was told that Carl, Roberto, and I could all pack up and go back to Venezuela. Natanson could go home to Mexico City. I felt like so much bailed and tied cannon fodder. We made reservations on the 6:20 p.m. TACA to Panama. I whiled away the time with some young Nicaraguan shoeshine hustlers at the airport, and I thought to myself, in about five years they'll be in National Guard uniforms and shooting at somebody, probably me, maybe my son, Sam. I didn't like the idea that once again it might be me crouching on the street corner alongside the stone wall. Quixote purchased a small marble peasant's foot to remind him of the part of the body that touches and tills the soil, the sacred earth blown out to sea after the dragon seed harvest.

The following day in Caracas there was a call from New York. After only thirty-four days as Pontiff, Pope John Paul I had died. I dropped to my knees, extended my arms outward and upward and spoke directly and harshly to God: "No more! That's it!"

I was more nervous than I could remember for a long time. My hands trembled. I needed rest. I wanted neither a Nicaraguan bullet nor a heart attack. I ached all over and was continuously sleepy. I persisted in having dreams about Nicaragua. I bolted upright. I couldn't avoid staring into the muzzle of the rifle barrel. I heard the bullet grinding into the stone wall, spewing pieces of rock above my head. I stepped again among the dead and dying in the School of the Holy Rosary. I heard a voice echoing, "My wife is dead....A dog is eating her body....my wife is...."

I was unable to sleep straight through, and my legs hurt to the bone. Sometimes lying on the couch, it seemed as if there was no feeling at all in my legs. Maybe I was not fully aware of all the pressure that had built up in me in Nicaragua. I told Lalie I thought we should spend Christmas in Mississippi. That delighted her. We thought maybe we could take some of our vacation at the end of the year after we had moved to Panama.

I played my own doctor in Caracas because I figured that if they couldn't run automatic elevators they might have trouble performing brain surgery. I decided I probably didn't have malaria or some other exotic disorder. It couldn't be dengue fever, for there was no mistaking that affliction when it came—the bones bruised so badly the victim began to contemplate death as a viable way out.

There were "civil disturbances" in Guatemala, but the death count did not bend the needle on the storm-o-meter. Besides, there was a brush fire on that "other" continent. I called the CBS Foreign Desk to discuss vacation for Carl and me. It was Brian Ellis's first day on the job as Sid Feder's replacement as foreign editor. John Lane was in Chicago and would not be back until the next day. I doped it out that Clemente Cohen had just happened to drop in on the CBS Broadcast Center on West 57th Street in New York and had given assurances that all our problems could and would be resolved, that I should come see him in his office the following day. I told them I had been receiving the same assurances for the previous five months.

Carl and I met with Cohen, but little good it did. After we'd hotly tap-danced the better part of an hour, I returned to the office, feeling low down and mean. The next communication on the telex was from John Lane, vice-president for News. He wanted to talk to me by telephone. It sounded ominous. He called a few minutes later and Brian Ellis listened in. Lane wanted to know how the meeting had gone with Cohen, and I replied, "Same old snowstorm." Then came the sledgehammer: Lane said the decision (if there had ever been one in the first place) to move the bureau out of Caracas to Panama had been reversed. We were staying in Caracas, and it was up to me to "make it work." He said we should "wheel and deal." At the Broadcast Center that usually meant, do whatever you have to do to get the job done, don't tell me about it, and if you get caught it's your patoot, not mine.

The following day, we made another hapless, fool's-errand trek to the solvencia office. Everything we had been assured we would obtain — a one-year solvencia — again came crashing down around our ears. The jefe, the hombre in charge, politely told us what he had told us three months before: in order for us to receive a one-year certificate he would have to have a letter from the Minister of Information and Tourism sent to the Minister of Finance requesting a special status. It was a letter that should have been written three months before, but all most officials did in the "Showcase for Democracy" was to promise, promise, promise and keep saying "Sí, sí, sí," when they really meant "No, no, no."

Hardly anybody was willing to admit the reality of the mañana problem, which was not only real but rampant. Yet for a North American correspondent to suggest it would incur the wrath singularly reserved for the worst of gringos who stereotyped their way through Latin America. Lalie, who had no urgent need to leave the country, presented her tax receipts and had no trouble obtaining a one-month certificado de solvencia. Maybe she batted her eyelashes. Carl and I, who didn't have the right kind of eyelashes and never knew when we might have an urgent need to leave the country—coup in Bolivia, earthquake in Chile, airliner crash in the Andes—received nothing except more promises from a functionary who promised that before the week was over he would speak to the vice-minister, who certainly, of course, would straighten everything out. I believed it as much as I believed the earth was flat. Paco taught me how to say "horse's ass" in Spanish, but he never told me how to write it.

Quixote asked Paco to report the following day and begin building a file on air charters in Caracas. If John Lane said "wheel and deal," that was what we intended to do, short of paying major or complicated bribes, which I refused to do. It became clear to me in future years of Monday-morning quarterbacking that a major bribe would probably have worked in the short run, but like blackmail it would have been another exercise in long-term, recoiling futility. Quixote was already in a free fall.

Paco helped us arrange an appointment with a charter company at La Carlota. The president of the company was a most attractive widow who managed one King Air and two Queen Airs. She spoke fluent English and seemed genuinely interested in helping us. I outlined our special requirements, and she said her company was ready to serve us. And then, like a strange lightning strike and a sudden clap of thunder, Carl and I received solvencias that would keep us covered for the remainder of October. Another contact assured us that he was a personal friend of the vice-minister and, indeed, by the time we had returned from our one-week vacations, we would have our one-year certificates. I told him if he pulled it off he would certainly have my vote for president of Venezuela.

Roberto took Lalie and me to the open market, where we laid in a supply of vegetables. I took along Edna Ferber's *So Big* and read in snatches between the sweet potatoes and the cucumbers. In the evening of the second Sunday in October I remembered Louis Bromfield's agrarian trilogy, *The Farm, Malibar Farm,* and *Pleasant Valley,* stories about the author's twentieth-century return to his Ohio home place.

On the first official day of our one-week vacation, we decided to forgo our planned four nights at a hotel by the sea to help save about $250. We said we'd use it for a down payment on a pickup truck at Plum Lick. We went to dinner at Gran Charolais in Caracas and enjoyed the best meat we had had since coming to Venezuela.

On October 10, *I woke up and began writing in my journal: I am Louis Bromfield, yet I am different and the task ahead for me is more difficult. The 1970s are more technologically advanced than the 1940s and '50s and the alterations of both man and matter are accelerating with geometric progression.*

After I plodded with Lalie over the footbridge, I returned to Apartamiento 4-M, cooked two pieces of bacon, heated up some leftover biscuits, reheated the coffee, and ate on the balcony with the chattering of our two lovebirds, the pericos, June and July. I held regular conversations with them, and they allowed me to stroke their rainbow backs. They cocked their heads and looked at me with gentle yet suspecting eyes. Quixote lunged forward to the chapter "On Being Teched" in Bromfield's *Pleasant Valley.*

Paco and Roberto knocked on our door by 8:00, and by about 9:00 we had loaded our picnic supplies into Paco's station wagon. Roberto had brought two loaves of French bread and a two-gallon rattan-covered jug of red wine. We headed out of the city in the direction of Colonia Tovar. Instead of going through the tunnels as we did on our runs to Maiquetía, we went east into the mountains, through Carayaca, winding over Río Tuy, each mile carrying us into cleaner air and greener countryside. Along the way we stopped and helped a lady and her family, who had had a flat tire. Traffic was heavy going out of the city as it was when there was a holiday. The Columbus Day exodus was another institutionalized reason to leave Caracas as far behind as possible.

A few kilometers before the village of Colonia Tovar with its blond, blue-eyed, Germanic pioneer stock, Paco veered off on a road to the right. We wound through the mountains until we found a spot we liked, southeast of El Limón. We were famished and thirsty and it was about noon, so we fixed our plates and poured our glasses. Leprechauns feasted deep in damp moss and ferns dripping with cool moisture. Paco and Roberto fell asleep and had a snoring contest. Scarlett and Quixote began exploring for hidden treasures arising from their readings of Ferber and Bromfield.

We strolled up the road to a higher place where we could look down into the valley. Clouds had floated in and around us, wrapping us as in a veil of vapor. The saturated air left us feeling cool, and the dampness refreshed our spirits. Then, as if on cue, the clouds magically cleared. One by one, the forms of people appeared in the valley. They were hoeing, planting, and cultivating as if Ferber's *So Big* were playing on stage. Bromfield's "My Ninety Acres" came alive. I wanted to join them, as I had wanted to join the plowers of the fields in Nicaragua. I wanted to plant seeds to grow good things to eat. I did not want to broadcast suffering.

On the way back to the picnic glen, we gathered ferns, wildflowers, dirt, and burro manure. We tickled Roberto and Paco with pieces of grass along the backs of their necks. Then we explored above their eyebrows and finally along the entrances to their noses. They sat up and rubbed their eyes and laughed.

We were truly happy.

About three o'clock we headed back to Caracas in gridlock traffic. As the crow flew, the distance was only about thirty-one miles—five hours later we stepped into the elevator at Parque Centrál. We said goodbye to Paco and Roberto, and we fell into bed, too exhausted to do anything else.

Lalie bought four more flowerpots, and I filled them with dirt and put into them some of the wild flowers from the mountains. I re-potted some plants that were in bad need of it. I regretted that the South American experience had become such a colossal dead duck. It was, we were convinced, the fault of Caracas, CBS News—the duck pond—and ourselves. I wished I could have made things different, but I couldn't. We were stuck with it. We could have said it was not the fault of Caracas at all. We were arrogant and refused to acknowledge it. We were ugly

Americans, lacking the intelligence to be sensitive about a culture other than our own.

The normal arrogance of a journalist in her or his own country is only topped by the arrogance of a reporter in a nation not her or his own. We acted as if there were never any problems in the United States. New York had no slums, no crime, and no street people. We expected Latin America to be something it wasn't, something that none of us was. Venezuelans were proud of their nation, and Caraqueños were just as proud of their city. Why couldn't we visitors act with more respect? I don't know. All I know is, we didn't.

We now had Pope John Paul II. I read aloud from *Edge of Sadness* and broke down and cried twice. With only seventy-five more days in 1978, surely nothing big would happen to disturb Thanksgiving, Christmas, and the New Year.

CHAPTER SIX

"Heal me, Lord, for God's sake, somebody's sake, make me feel better." I was in and out of bed throughout the day and up and down from the couch. I was sick. In body, in mind, in spirit. I'd been taking a liquid antacid, and it seemed to be helping a little. I confronted Carl with my firm conclusion that the last footage he had shot was "blue," out of color sync, and he finally accepted it without further argument. I played footsie with the story of a kidnapped official of the upcoming chess tournament in Buenos Aires. I was a coonass juggler and my banquette was South America, with Central America thrown in around the corner.

Out on the balcony, I wrestled with the plants and whistled back at the pericos. I had a big fern in my lap and was trimming out dead growth. "Foreign Desk, you're out...New York news producers, out...ill-tempered cameramen, out you go." I separated two African violets and tried my first root division. I'd resown tomato seeds, along with some parsley. How green was our balcony!

I was the grateful recipient of a face massage and chest rub. We finished reading *Edge of Sadness*, and I again choked up on the last line. I was continuing to read *The Yearling*. My favorite nurse fixed me a light meal of chicken soup and cheese toast. She came and sat with me as I tried to send a telex to New York. She fixed me hot tea, and I fell asleep by her side in bed.

I prepared a telex to New York proposing stories in Venezuela, Paraguay, and the Caribbean. I'd show *them*. In early evening there was a telex from Ellis on the Foreign Desk, asking me to do a quickie report on freedom of the press to be shipped ASAP for *Cronkite*. What a joke.

There was another message to call Ellis in New York. I knew what had happened. John Lane got on the phone with the two of us, and I was told Sorensen had called, complaining that "we had problems down here," namely, I didn't speak Spanish, I was living in the bureau with my wife, and I wasn't treating Sorensen right. I explained my position forcefully and well, I believed, and we agreed that Carl and I would "start anew," but I had the good sense to know that that motorcycle tire was flat.

I hoofed it with Lalie over the footbridge and then returned to the office/apartment to "start over again" with Sorensen. There was one thing about which I had made up my mind—I was not going to apologize, and I expected no apology, because I had deduced from my Latin American experience that machismos did not take kindly to expressions of weakness. I was going to do no more than absolutely necessary. I felt betrayed. Castrated. I was counting the days until I could climb out of this abyss, go back to the United States without one glance back over my shoulder.

Sheik Yamani slipped into town to have a pre-OPEC conference talk with President Pérez, and we were not there with our camera when the meeting broke up—no great loss, because he didn't say anything about oil price increases. But just as I expected, a message came in during the night on the telex from New York, asking if we could find Sheik Yamani for a statement. I said we'd try. Paco drove us through smoking, honking, doorlatch-to-doorlatch traffic to a military installation, but Yamani was said not to be there, and we returned to the office. I tap-danced with Roberto on a script for the Freedom of the Press piece, which would go up to New York the next morning on the Pan Am flight. We recorded the narration, and Paco delivered it to the airport.

I was continuing to read *The Yearling*, and it was a positive source of pleasure. Literature was helping, as the University of Kentucky English professors had long ago promised it would. Books became our peace at the center. Out on our balcony, the flowers and plants were sustaining us too. So was the warm feeling growing in our Valentine hearts. I arose early and gave my honeymooner a special treat. I sneaked out of bed and stopped the clock on the wall so it wouldn't strike the hours. It was the antique clock we had bought in Jackson, Louisiana, at a time when all we had was faith that we would one day marry—the same clock that now hangs on the kitchen wall on Plum Lick. Lalie slept until almost noon. She asked me to read from *The Yearling*. We grieved when we came to the death of Fodder-wing.

I was up again early and again stopped the wall clock. Roberto came at mid-morning. Lalie heated biscuits and turned them upside down in syrup and butter in a plate. She was tearful as she packed into a trunk the unneeded, stylish winter clothes that had meant so much to her when she was working for Revlon U.S.A. We had decided to send the trunk to New Orleans. I knew I was responsible for what was happening, but she said she'd follow me wherever I went.

It was to be another day of abject frustration for the Caracas Bureau. Our October certificates of solvency had run out, even though I had warned Clemente Cohen the past Thursday please not to let it happen. He was still talking about a one year solvencia, but either the minister didn't show up or the vice-minister didn't want to sign a letter of authorization. In any event, it was again and again, mañana, mañana. I advised New York of the situation. The Dominica story was off. All that was about to happen there was independence—it had become a British colony in 1805. Correspondent David would not go there on November 3, 1978 (but hurricane David would on August 30, 1979). The honeymooners had a long talk, which left them both in down-and-dirty blue funks. After supper I read aloud from *The Yearling*, and then we went to sleep.

I commemorated November 1 by putting on my jogging suit and footslogged, too out of shape to run. I trudged along a disgracefully, inexcusably dirty street, returned to the office/apartment, heated a piece of cornbread, and had it with a cup of coffee. I washed a few things in the pint-size machine. For the third day in a row Clemente Cohen failed to provide us with a one-year solvencia, a six-month solvencia, even a three-day solvencia. We could not leave the country if there was a storm to follow. I decided not to be upset about it.

The shah appeared to be falling in Iran, where there was a nationwide oil strike. Oil fields were shut down. Within a week, after days of rioting, the shah would call out the military, and in Paris the Ayatollah Khomeini was summoning revolution. I fixed a little supper for Lalie and me. She told me about the dockside importation problems Revlon was having in Caracas. She needed to talk, and I needed to be a good listener. I brought her Scotch on the rocks and fixed a plate of caviar on crackers with chopped onion and a shredded hard-boiled egg. Roberto had given us a full quart of caviar, which had been given to him by Russian sailors who couldn't speak Spanish or English. Roberto could not speak Russian. Somehow, they had found a common ground in a mini-mountain of caviar and enough vodka to fill a wading pool. Why or where or when or how Roberto had fallen in with Russian sailors was never revealed, and we didn't ask. Vintage wheeling and dealing! After we almost OD'd on caviar and vodka, Lalie took a hot shower, and we fell into each other's arms. We finished reading *The Yearling*, and I began reading *Lamb in His Bosom*. We were gloriously, wonkily, dead drunk.

After four days of badgering the Venezuelan bureaucracy, Clemente Cohen finally obtained for Carl and me a six-month solvencia. It was good until May 2, more than adequate for our purposes. Now all we had to do was rescue from the clutches of customs at the airport a shipment of cassettes sent to us by CBS News. We were in the final month of the presidential election in Venezuela, as if anybody cared at CBS News.

We took the AP bureau manager, Henry "Hank" Ackerman, and his wife, Mell, to dinner at Castellano. Hank was a native of Louisville. In July, he and his wife had moved from Lima to Caracas. The main conversation was, how screwed-up could Venezuela become? I did my usual fire dance, predicting Armageddon in Caracas "during my lifetime." I gave Hank the information needed for the staff and me to become members of the Foreign Correspondents Association. Hank was fluent in Spanish, and it embarrassed me to have to admit that I wasn't. I didn't know how much longer I could expect to be paid for doing so little reporting. Long enough, I hoped, until blessed word came down from the University of Kentucky that I had a teaching job.

I said I needed "peace at the center," and by that I didn't mean the eye of the hurricane. It was a Quaker expression meaning calm and confident living, caring about small things, having nothing in common with being on the leading edge of storms. I watered all the plants and made another division of our African violets. The parsley seeds I'd planted had come up and had promptly died. I sent a telex to New York, reminding the Foreign Desk that there were independence dates for three Caribbean mini-states, but I knew there would be no interest. Some at CBS would say I wouldn't know a "story" if it bit me on the end of the nose. Touché.

I talked to Lalie on the way to her ride, about how I felt about leaving CBS News, the institution I had said was my motherland and fatherland, my nation, my religion, my be-all-to-end-all. I made it clear that I didn't need to attend another Southern Governors' Conference, knowing it probably wouldn't get on the air, but if it did, then chartering back to Atlanta in a small plane through a storm to feed. I didn't need to climb aboard another helicopter and fly out over the Gulf of Mexico to circle a burning oil rig and return to New Orleans and speed to WWL-TV to learn that the *Evening News* had passed on a piece but would take fifteen seconds of footage for a "telop."

New York telexed a query about a Human Rights Conference in Santiago, Chile, during Thanksgiving weekend, and we began making inquiries. A seminar on democracy would open in Caracas. Arthur Schlesinger, John Kenneth Galbraith, Mr. and Mrs. Richard Goodwin, former Venezuelan presidents Betancourt and Caldera, British and French writers, and other intellectuals would attend. Any rational human being would have thought CBS News would want me to be there. I told New York about it early in the morning, but it was not until afternoon, and too late, that they said, "Cover it for radio." I told the assignment editors that I'd make the effort the next day. We were jacking around with the Office of Information and Tourism about a trip on the coming Saturday with the president of Venezuela to open a new steel mill. It was doubtful we would go. If there had been an explosion, hostage taking, or coup d'état that would have been *news* and we would have covered it like Dixie dew.

I enjoyed going alone to the seminar on democracy at the Institute for Higher Studies. I spoke briefly with Galbraith, Schlesinger, and Goodwin. I would have liked to be able to say that I'd read their books and could challenge their theories. That, of course, was anything but the case. I marched back to Parque Central, did a quickie radio spot, and fed it to New York. Before sleeping, I read aloud from *Lamb in His Bosom.*

Efforts to set up an oil exploration story involving a trip to the interior, the Orinoco region of Venezuela, came crashing down with a thud. Basic to the problem was that I could not reach Brian Ellis on the Foreign Desk in New York for a decision, and on such a speculative adventure, including an extremely costly charter and other expenses, and particularly because there was no great loss of life, there was only one thing to do—forget it. If it had been a natural disaster, and if the coverage would be competitive, we would have covered it as if it were the great humanitarian, philosophical thing to do. In truth, we saw ourselves as some kind of God's servants spreading the word of storms and human suffering on the grandest of scales.

I was now reading Frederick Jackson Turner's *The Frontier in American History.* Lalie was worn out. The wind was all gone out of our honeymoon sails. The bride was tired and homesick and her face and eyes showed it. In seven months the beauty that had glowed in all her facial features on our wedding day, April 15, had drawn tight with tensions spiraling out of the madness of Caracas and CBS. Despite best intentions, the honeymooners snapped. Words backfired. Boomeranged. We took pot shots at each other. We didn't know what had taken hold of us and would not turn us loose. It was like a boil whose festering would not ease until it had been lanced. By nightfall, exhausted with the internal combustion of our emotions, we were like babies in each other's arms, our confidence in ourselves bruised and barely restored.

I made the final arrangements for a therapeutic weekend mini-honeymoon. I set the alarm for 4:30, because I wanted us to get an early start to Maiquetía to take the 8:00 a.m. Aeropostal vuelo 110 to Margarita Island. I was sleep-whipped, but by 6:00 I had found my glasses, shoes, comb, and keys. My soul mate was all prettied up in her white slacks and red, white, and blue striped jacket, and we were soon on our way by taxi to the airport. Shortly after 8:00 we were airborne. It was our first flight together since arriving in Caracas.

At first there were no cars available at the Margarita airport, but Scarlett charmed one out of an agent, and we were on our way east from the airport into Porlamar and a little farther to the Concorde Hotel. We were given room 1720. Scarlett and Rhett went to the beach and sunbathed for forty-five minutes, ate club sandwiches, and drank the local version of margaritas, returned to the room, and fell asleep in each other's arms. We were in another world, entirely.

We woke up shortly after four o'clock in the afternoon. We showered, and drove into Porlamar, thinking we would find a string of Margarita's "famous" pearls. We found nothing that even came close. They were all imported from the Orient. Margarita Island was surprisingly arid and the Venezuelans were well into their don't-give-a-rat's-ass selves. And we were supposed to be the "ugly Americans"? Give us a break.

We browsed around and bought at half price two bottles of Tanqueray gin, one bottle of Old Forester and a liqueur. We visited a Catholic church. We lit candles and prayed for our families. I prayed for Rose and the children. We prayed that all human beings could be as happy as we were. We drove around. I was running off at the mouth about how dirty mankind was on Margarita Island. But it was, and that was all there was to it. Margarita is such a beauteous sounding name, but that was about all the beauty there was to the island. There were more yahoos per square inch on Margarita Island than in downtown Miami Beach. Jimmy Buffett's *Margaritaville* was surely someplace else.

We managed to have an adequate dinner at Restaurante Chipi's and then returned to the Concorde to sit for a while on the balcony. We sipped the liqueur and looked out upon the Caribbean.

We had not set the alarm, but we woke up about 7:30 the next morning. We told each other about our dreams. I had dreamed that my honeymooner was sitting in the same chair with an old boyfriend and that she was not wearing her wedding band. I dreamed I asked him if he loved her and he said yes, so I said, "Take her!" I also dreamed this mini-honeymoon was part of a presidential trip and that I had missed the candidate's plane.

Scarlett had dreamed that she was in a confrontation about how to divide up Rhett's estate.

We decided to check out of the hotel and spend as much time as possible driving to the northern part of the island. We went through the little towns of La Asuncia and Santa Ana to Juan Griego, from there to Altagracia and finally Pedro Gonzalez, where we eventually concluded there was little if anything pretty, certainly nothing green, to see on Margarita Island. We passed up an imitation safari, which was nothing but a flea-bitten, poor man's Lion County Safari. We returned to Juan Griego, where we took pictures atop a fortification that also overlooked La Galera. We sunbathed at Juan Griego and then lunched at the nearby Hotel El Fortín. We ate mouthwatering fish: Rueda de Sierro for Lalie, Parquito Entera Frito for me and six Zulia beers for the two of us. We drove south back to the airport and checked in for Aeropostal flight 129.

Back in Caracas, I said I was concerned that we were drinking too much. There was a thin line between drinking socially with "the best of them" and drinking to relax with the shades pulled down and a darkening margin for error. I was all the more sensitive about it because my father had died of alcoholism when he was thirty-six years old. Other members of my family had become addicted in varying degrees. I knew that I had it in my genes to become an alcoholic. It was ironic that both alcohol and tobacco, such lethal drugs in their own ways, were legal, and Kentucky led the nation in the production of both.

I read aloud from Eudora Welty's *The Optimist's Daughter.*

CHAPTER SEVEN

It was another day across the footbridge, the foul, dirty, stinking, creaking, steel footbridge, where the yahoos and two gringos *came and went, cheerless.* What was there to cheer? Maybe somebody knew something we didn't know. It was not the bullfight season. Hemingway would not have liked this footbridge! Most people could not afford tickets to the opening night of the Ice Follies. I watched Lalie seat herself inside Marie Victoria's car, stood, and saw them pull into the autopista to be swallowed whole in the swirling traffic, the little orange car like a bright pill going down a giant gullet.

I had my overdue close-up look at a barrio in Caracas. It upended my thinking. What it said to me was that the end of the world is within reach. This was how it would be when all rural people finished flooding into the urban areas: New York, Chicago, Los Angeles, Houston, Mexico City, Port au Prince, Paris, São Paulo, Seoul, Bombay, Calcutta, Moscow, Cairo, Jakarta, Tokyo, London, Singapore, Hong Kong, Manila, Buenos Aires, Río de Janeiro, and Caracas. The density of population per square mile was stacked as high as 247,000 souls in Hong Kong. The great urban centers of 1978 were more vulnerable than Pompeii in A.D. 79. Mount Vesuvius erupted again in the seventeenth century, but in the twentieth century the causative would be lack of water quantity as well as quality, soil erosion, acid rain, and pollution of every kind. I knew there was little we could do to reverse the trend. The die was cast, indifference was bred, and the inspiration to improve was dying like a plant without water. We only thought we knew what Hell would be.

As it turned out, Hell was waiting for us next door.

James Warren "Jim" Jones was a Disciples of Christ minister, born May 13, 1931 near Lynn in east central Indiana. He moved to Indianapolis where, in the 1950s and 60s, he built his charismatic ministry. Jones had a powerful hypnotic effect on his congregations and was known to have mesmerized his followers into believing he could cure cancer of the throat. The faithful would fall upon their knees in order for Jones to slap them on the neck while at the same time making a sudden upward jerk of his hand to reveal a bloody chicken gizzard hidden up his sleeve. He waved the object in the air as if the cancer had been miraculously removed.

In 1965, Jim Jones took his ministry to Ukiah in northern California and from there, in 1971, he moved to the San Francisco Bay area. He established the People's Temple, safe house for drug addicts, prostitutes, and those who no longer believed in the capitalist society of the United States. In 1977, Rev. Jones led nearly one-thousand of his faithful to Guyana in South America, where he effectively imprisoned them at "Jonestown"—in exchange for promised tickets to Heaven, Jim Jones confiscated his followers' passports, siphoned millions of their dollars from the sale of homes, and threatened with death anyone who disputed his claim to power. Reports of these transgressions reached family members left behind in California and they brought the situation to the attention of their congressman, Leo J. Ryan, who took up their cause after he'd become convinced that something sinister was happening.

The Guyanese jungle was a nearly perfect place for Jim Jones to be God. Neither the U.S. State Department nor the Venezuelan government apparently knew exactly what he was doing, or if they did, they didn't try to stop him. Jones was in the middle of nowhere with a license to play the most vengeful of deities. The working theory was that an arrangement had been made between Jones and the Guyanese government. Jim Jones was committed to socialism and often spoke of his dedication to communism as well. It would be difficult to fault the Guyanese government for welcoming opportunities to develop remote, relatively inaccessible areas of the jungle, the deal made all the sweeter when the pioneers were Socialists and Communists who felt alienated by a capitalistic society in the United States.

On Monday, November 13, 1978, the passengers on the redeye from San Francisco to New York included members of an organization called "Concerned Relatives." Representatives of the two major San Francisco newspapers, the *Examiner* and the *Chronicle*, an NBC television news team, the *Washington Post*, and a reporter for *National Enquirer* were on that fateful journey to Guyana. The *Examiner* had sent reporter Tim Reiterman and photographer Greg Robinson. The *Chronicle* had sent Ron Javers. On the flight east were correspondent Don Harris, cameraman Bob Brown, technician Steve Sung, and producer Bob Flick, all of NBC News. Charles Krause, Buenos Aires correspondent for the *Washington Post*, boarded in New York, along with Congressman Ryan and two members of his staff.

On the same day, I was taking down pictures from the walls of Apartamiento 4-M in Caracas, including the clown with soiled white gloves looking with great hopelessness at the front page of the *Wall Street Journal*, a print I'd purchased during a George Wallace campaign stop in Boston. I likewise solemnly removed the antique clock from over the telex. We were disassembling a honeymoon that had managed to last seven months. We knew the party was over.

The San Francisco to New York flight continued to Guyana on the eastern border of Venezuela. The jet came in for a night landing on Tuesday, November 14.

The next morning, November 15, Lalie and I celebrated the seven-month anniversary of our marriage. I put on my jogging clothes and stalked with my weary wife over the footbridge. After she left for work,

I paced about one mile. We discovered that the president of OPEC would be meeting with President Pérez at Miraflores Palace at 6:00. We were there in time to catch him as he came out at 7:00. I managed to ask three questions; the answers were not headlines but were faintly newsworthy. Paco fought the traffic back to Parque Centrál, a painful reminder that Caracas was a no-hoper. It must have been what the final inferno would be like, I had told myself so many times. Major reasons were the appalling attitudes and actions of most of the Caraqueños with whom we came in contact. We seldom moved in the sphere of the elite, those who paid others to stand in long lines where line-jumping was an art form. The view from our balcony at Parque Centrál was a doomsday still life. The hills to the south were covered with people who lived like ants, a culture entrenched.

"What are we going to do to reverse it?" Lalie asked. "The destruction of our planet, I mean. "We agreed there was probably nothing we could do about it. "They're crawling over it like tumblebugs rolling a ball of dung to lay their eggs," wailed Quixote.

On Thursday, November 16, in Georgetown, Guyana, the American embassy was showing slides to Concerned Relatives that depicted Jonestown as a model community in the jungle. California congressman Leo Ryan knew a scam when he saw one, and this was one he was determined to pry open.

One of the most definitive accounts of the life of the Reverend Jim Jones, Jonestown, the People's Temple, and the events that would occur there two days after this slide show is Tim Reiterman's extraordinary book, *Raven*. My involvement, more peripheral than his, was also a personal one, mine drawn largely from what I saw with my own eyes as a CBS News correspondent, following what at first I believed was just another storm.

According to Reiterman, there was confusion in Georgetown concerning who, if anybody, would get into Jonestown. Congressman Ryan told reporters there was a plane to take him, journalists, and only a few relatives to the People's Temple. It was a twenty-passenger plane arranged through the U.S. Embassy. Ryan decided there was room for all nine newsmen, two attorneys (Charles Garry and Mark Lane), and four relatives—Jim Cobb, Beverly Oliver, Anthony Katsaris, and Carol Houston Boyd.

Thursday, November 16, Quixote wrote in his journal: *There may be a democracy here in Venezuela, but the elite in European gray suits still run things for the poor campesinos in the desperately impoverished barrios. In the early afternoon, Paco drove the crew and me to the West End of Caracas for the start of a symbolic promenade through the city by the Social Democratic candidate Herrera and his followers. It was bedlam, a pedestrian's grave misfortune.*

San Francisco *Examiner* reporter Reiterman was probably peering out the window of the twin-engine Otter as the plane crossed the wall-to-wall jungle of northwestern Guyana, which Venezuela claimed but did virtually nothing to administer. Reiterman was seeing what I would see two days later—the mammoth jungle—but what he was about to experience I would miss only by the grace of God.

That Friday morning, I was waking up and looking again at the most beautiful woman in the world. The Latin America Bureau had collapsed and the only thing I had to hold onto was Lalie. She was the center of my universe, and we had come to understand that what we wanted most of all was peace at the center.

The CBS Foreign Desk wanted a report telexed every Monday morning as to the condition of what was working and what wasn't, as if it mattered. Whether our minds were working, whether our morale was up or down didn't seem to be a consideration. Marty Housman of UPI called to say he and his wife could not be our guests for dinner on Saturday night. Neither of us could know that none of us would be dining out the evening of November 18.

I washed clothes and read more from *The Store*. I awaited Lalie's return from work at Revlon, then fixed a hot dog supper. I had been cracking some of the black walnuts we had brought with us from Plum Lick. They tasted good on top of ice cream and syrup.

I sent Lalie off to bed while I put the dishes to soak. When I came to bed we did not know that the tenderness we shared would be our last for three weeks.

I had brought my honeymooner a nightcap of fine Nicaraguan brandy. In the middle of the night, she bolted upright in bed. "Ooh, ooh," she shrieked. A huge cockroach had started up her left leg, crossed her midsection, darted between her breasts, scurried over her right shoulder, and exited through the screenless open window above our heads.

According to Reiterman's account, the pilot of Congressman Leo Ryan's plane at first had agreed with air control in Georgetown that the Port Kaituma landing strip was not serviceable. The alternative was to land at Matthews Ridge, a mining town about thirty miles away. After banking over the People's Temple, the pilot decided to have another look at the Port Kaituma airstrip. He said he thought it would be O.K. to land. The airstrip, which was less than a half-mile long, could accommodate the twin-engine Otter.

The landing was successfully executed and People's Temple guards relayed word of the arrival to Jones. At first, only Congressman Ryan and Richard Dwyer from the U.S. Embassy in Georgetown and Ryan's aides were allowed into the People's Temple. It was about 6:00 p.m. when Jim Jones and Congressman Ryan agreed that everybody could come to Jonestown the next day except Gordon Lindsay, who had written a negative story about the People's Temple. At 6:20 the Otter lifted off with Lindsay on board to return to Georgetown. He could not know how fortunate he was.

While Ryan and his aides stayed inside Jonestown the reporters were forced to spend the night in a shack at Port Kaituma, with a muddy, forty-five minute truck ride the next day to the People's Temple. Jones didn't want them in Jonestown overnight.

It was Saturday, November 18. "Eternal Spring" in Caracas was as balmy and boring as it was every day. I sneaked out of bed at 5:30 and fulfilled the promise I'd made to myself to write a "here-I-am-still-ready-to-teach" letter to Dr. Rush at the University of Kentucky. I started a pot of coffee.

I later wrote in my journal: *It was probably one of the loveliest days I had ever spent with you, until late afternoon. Our lives changed in a split second after that. I had planned to take you to dinner, but we decided to stay in our own digs. I worked on records of the bureau. It was good being comfortable with my best friend. I grilled a steak on the balcony, and you fixed biscuits to go with the honey I had picked up, and okra and tomatoes.*

I was sleeping on the couch, when the telex clicked on.

Mendelson for David Dick Urgent

This D Dick

This bulletin just in from state dept who say U.S. congressman Leo Ryan of California has been shot and is thought dead after an attack on his fact finding mission at the airport in Port Kaituma Guyana.

Ryan was reportedly leading a delegation investigating a controversial religious settlement at Jonestown in the South American country. Mainly Americans populate the settlement.

Can you find out logistics for coverage. Any stringer or local TV coverage Etc If you can relay plans soonest Ellis will give Okay or No-go.

Will outcheck.

I began calling charters. Nothing. I kept an eye on the telex. The story came in bits and pieces. It was believed Ryan had been killed along with two unidentified NBC television newsmen. I wondered if they had been Ellen McKeith and Fred Francis. I had drunk Nicaraguan brandy late into the night with Ellen in Panama, and I had worked with Fred to cover the crash of the Eastern L-1011 in the Everglades when he was a reporter for WTVJ-TV in Miami. They were my friends.

New York, with stupidity rivaling my own, queried as to whether I had considered driving from Caracas to Jonestown.

Have we ruled out driving overland to this place?

Long way through jungle.

Just so that eye have firm answer your saying we should not even consider it query.

Right. Eye don't have mileage's exact but it seems totally out of question.

Okay fine that last we talk about it.

Quixote beeped Roberto and called Carl, and they came in. I alerted Sancho Panza. Soon it was midnight and a sorrowful moon frowned down; it was clear that the CBS Latin America Bureau based in Caracas was about to go down in flames, burning into meaningless ashes.

There had been a delay in the return of the doomed news personnel from Port Kaituma to Jonestown on Saturday, November 18. It wasn't until late morning that a promised tour of the People's Temple started. While at first there appeared to be no defectors willing to step forward and say they wanted to leave Jonestown with Congressman Ryan, by approximately midday, according to Tim Reiterman's book, a good many were making it known that they did want to leave. First there were about eight, then more than a dozen.

By Reiterman's count, sixteen boarded the truck that headed toward the Port Kaituma airstrip. They included Edith Parks, her son Gerald, and his wife Patricia, their son Dale, teenager Brenda, and her boyfriend, Chris O'Neill, and the wistful little pre-teen, blond-headed Tracy. There were suddenly too many defectors for the space available on the Guyana Airways Otter, so a six-seat Cessna was ordered in from Georgetown. Even the additional space might not be sufficient.

Shortly before the party left the People's Temple compound, a man tried to cut Congressman Ryan's throat. The violence was thwarted. Larry Layton, one of Jim Jones's lieutenants, positioned himself among the defectors headed for the airstrip. The Cessna came in, followed by the Otter. They were still several seats short of the number needed. The defectors would go first.

The temple dump truck and a tractor with a trailer pulled up about 100 to 150 yards down the airstrip. Almost a dozen men emerged and stood in and around the two vehicles. They raised their guns.

It was almost 5:00 in the afternoon, and the CBS Latin America Bureau's correspondent was asleep, dreaming of life on a farm in Kentucky.

The shooting began.

Cameraman Bob Brown recorded his own death.

The video image and Brown's brains went to black.

Correspondent Don Harris was dead.

Congressman Ryan was dead.

Photographer Robinson was dead.

Patricia Parks was dead.

Their bodies marked the space around the Otter like the broken hands of a clock where time had stopped. The left wheel of the Otter was flattened. One engine was shot out. The Cessna took off and returned to Georgetown. Guyancsc police from a Port Kaituma substation took Larry Layton away.

Two days before the Jonestown massacre, a remorseful Quixote had scribbled in his journal: *The solution, the fundamental solution is in the Colonia Tovars, not in the Parque Centráls. It is in our quiet, meditative, pastoral places, not in the concrete dungeons and towers of a race gone mad. It's like a climax with a stranger in the night: you've got to look at each other in the morning or sneak away in the night, only you know you won't run away because you've got no place to run. So you'll have to look at her, look deeply at her, even if you don't say one word to her, God knows love her, because you know you can't love her because she's only the mechanical, fat, laughing lady in the chicken-wire cage at the entrance to the crazy house. She's that way when you go in, and she's that way when you come out. And each and every time she'll be that way, until somebody decides the whole thing is a bad idea.*

CBS should have fired me for not being able to launch like a cruise missile to Guyana, and all-knowing management probably would have except there were too many other things to do first. The Foreign Desk located Bernard Goldberg on vacation in Miami, put him on a corporate jet, and pointed him in the direction of Guyana. It was the same Bernard Goldberg who would, after twenty-eight years of following storms, hang it up in the twenty-first century and write the best-selling book *Bias*, the story of his own personal travail at CBS News. He never stopped considering himself to be the messenger, and then, as now, it's open season on messengers. Goldberg, not I, did the first CBS News report on the Jonestown massacre. Later, Lalie, not I, helped Bernie in his futile effort to feed the story from Caracas.

The crew and I were up all night fielding telephone calls and telexes from New York. My windmilling efforts to "wheel and deal" with charter companies and pilots had crashed and burned.

Roberto went out knocking on doors, yelling up at windows, finally locating one J.J. Bichier, bush pilot. Arrangements were made to meet J.J. at 7:00 the next morning at Aerodromo Francisco de Miranda, the small airstrip within the city. Paco had picked up Carl at his apartment.

I gave Scarlett O'Hara a quick kiss and headed out of the door at Apartamiento 4-M. She stood outside the iron security door, seeing me leave to follow the biggest storm of my life. There was good reason to believe that I might not come back.

"Put your bags down so you can kiss me right."

There was a soulful meeting of lips.

When I stepped away, I left behind the bag containing socks, underwear, change of outer clothes, and my shaving kit.

On the way from Parque Central along the Autopista del Este, the mood in Sancho Panza's station wagon was stony silence. Months of waiting for a storm to cover had been like standing on the sidelines for an entire season, hoping to see action and not getting into the game until the final seconds. We did not then know that Venezuelan bureaucracy had doubtless saved our lives. If we had been at Jonestown on

November 18, we would have been dead.

As we passed the Monumento a María Lionza, with its grotesquely out-of-proportion forward-thrusting breasts on an Amazonian riding a phallic-nosed tapir, Quixote wondered if after all that had gone wrong in the ill-conceived, ill-located Caracas Bureau of CBS News, we might finally do something for which some would be proud. But we were already a day late.

As the original Sancho Panza admonished the original Don Quixote: *"Well then, Señor, I say that for some days past I have been considering how little is got or gained by going in search of these adventures that your worship seeks in these wilds and crossroads."*

CHAPTER EIGHT

At 7:45 a.m. on Sunday, November 19, we were taxiing out in J.J. Bichier's Yankee Victor 515 Charlie Papa Aerocommander 560. Quixote was in the co-pilot's seat. Carl and Roberto squeezed in behind us. As the little twin-engine plane's wheels cleared the runway and headed east over Río Caurimare, I said a short prayer that such a small plane would take us where we had directed it to go—Guyana and as close as possible to the Port Kaituma airstrip and the People's Temple. We should land there if possible.

J.J. held the Aerocommander on an eastward heading alongside the more than mile-high mountain range towering between Caracas and Mar Caribe. He cleared the last of the elevations south of Chuspa and crossed over the crooked little finger of the peninsula at Carenaro, where we were finally above the blue waters of the Caribbean but still not free of Venezuelan air control. We headed for Isla Margarita, the same forlorn island where Lalie and I had spent our mini-honeymoon. Isla La Tortuga lay off to our port side, and I penciled it in on the map I was constructing in my journal. As soon as we landed at Aeropuerto Internaciónal del Caribe on Margarita Island we blustered into battle with one more Venezuelan immigration and customs officer. J.J., Carl, and Roberto, all fluent in Spanish, could not speed up the functionary, who wanted nine copies of a piece of paper J.J. didn't have. It took an hour and a half to wear down the official, while I paced back and forth, watching the tail end of my career fizzling out like a small sliver of a shiny, spent meteor. Didn't he know a United States congressman had been killed in Guyana? Didn't he care? Didn't he know that we were reporters, messengers whose only desire was to go and report a story? Did he want to be held responsible for the loss of our jobs? Did he know how richly he would be rewarded in Heaven if he cooperated?

We finally prevailed.

We took off again, and at last we were free of Venezuelan immigration and customs red tape, provided we didn't crash-land along the northeastern coastline. Briefly, we were back over the Caribbean where the weather was blue and sunny, but the water was muddy from the flushing of the Orinoco River. There was little left untouched by human greed and stupidity. J.J. steered Yankee Victor 515 Charlie Papa over Peninsula de Paria, Golfo de Paria, and the southern tip of Trinidad and Tobago. He held to a southeasterly heading, which again put us over Venezuela's barely inhabited Territorio Federal Delta Amacuro, where the Orinoco River fans outward into hundreds of water systems. The only two roads came to dead ends at the villages of Los Guires and Boco de Macareo. From there we flew over the Amacuro River, which formed the boundary of the northwest passageway to the Zona en Reclamación, the habitation of remote Indian tribes.

Zona en Reclamación, or Guayana Essequiba, was approximately 150,000 square kilometers, larger than the state of Arkansas, an expanse of almost impenetrable jungle and serpentine waterways. Venezuela and the former British Guiana had disputed the territory for more than 150 years.

There was nothing to suggest Venezuelan interest in Guyana other than its ongoing hunger for more natural resources, chiefly gold and diamonds. What Venezuela wanted were exploration and development rights in the western sector of the former British Guiana, which in 1966, my first year with CBS News, became the independent Cooperative Republic of Guyana, a socialist state.

The Dutch had settled Guyana in the seventeenth century. The British had colonized it and remained in control from 1814 until 1966, when it gained independence and its name was changed from British Guiana to Guyana.

At the time we crossed the disputed zone, we believed the center of the storm, Port Kaituma and Jonestown, was located in the southeastern part of Guyana. The information, given to us by some other lost soul at CBS News in New York who had done poorly in high school geography, was exactly the opposite of the real location, which was in the northwestern sector, only five miles from the internationally accepted Venezuelan border. The misinformation was compounded by the fact that J.J. was a Venezuelan bush pilot using a Venezuelan map, which differed from Guyanese maps.

J.J. was taking his Aerocommander directly over the area where more than nine hundred bodies were beginning to rot in the sun at Jonestown, but that was something else we didn't know. If we had, we probably would have tried to land and might never have been heard from again. As many as eighty World War II planes had been reported missing over the Guyanese jungle; about sixty of them had never been found. The jungle in the northwestern sector was densely matted and tangled. There were no roads connecting it with Georgetown. One way to travel from the capital city to Jonestown was to fly directly in a small plane to the Port Kaituma airstrip and then trek the last jungle miles to the People's Temple. Another way was to fly in a somewhat larger plane to Matthews Ridge and continue on a small train the twenty miles to Port Kaituma. Helicopter was another possibility. One more option was to go by trawler from the port of Georgetown, up the coast to the mouth of the Waini River to the Moro Passage, up the Barima River to Morawhanna.

And then there was this guy in New York who'd asked, "Have we ruled out driving overland to this place?"

We didn't ask J.J. if he knew what would be our chances if we had to make an emergency landing, and he didn't share with us any concern he might have about boa constrictors, bushmaster snakes, the black-rosetted jaguar, and the night-prowling ocelot. There were poisonous pit vipers and rabies-infected vampire bats. We had no jungle training, and although I assumed later that we had first-aid supplies—a knife, matches, surely—we wasted no time on drills. The way you played the game was to pinpoint the location and fly into it with little regard for survival. If we had gone down, we would have been dead meat falling from the sky.

We were about to cross over the easternmost rim of what Venezuelans called the "Lost World." Venezuela encompassed more than 352,000 square miles, about as large as Texas and Oklahoma. Lost World included most of Bolivar State and the Territorio Federal Amazonas, but it spilled over into Guyana. The higher elevations of the Guayana Highlands, one of the oldest regions of South America, formed millions of years before and designated the Guayana Shield, lay off to the southwest of our flight path. With islands of flora and rain forests, Lost World with Angel Falls in Bolivar State, the highest falls on earth, might as well have been on another planet. The water cascaded down 2,916 feet, more than seventeen times higher than Niagara Falls. The blessing at that time was that civilization had not caught up with and desecrated Lost World; Amerindian tribes respected it, and it stood as living proof that earth without modern man is often times magnificent.

J.J. brought us in over the wide Essequibo and then crossed the Demerara River to Timehri Airport, which served Georgetown, Guyana. CBS News correspondent Goldberg was at the terminal with cameraman Bernie Nudelman and his Miami-based crew. After talking for a few minutes, we were saying what journalists should never say—that the story was probably over. Goldberg had interviews with two survivors of the shootings at the Port Kaituma airstrip, including NBC producer Bob Flick, physically a large, burly man. During the interview he seemed beaten and stunned the way a huge bear is brought to its knees. He had been standing at the plane, which would have returned the congressman, the messengers, and those clamoring to leave Jonestown. When the shooting began, Flick would escape the bullets by hitting the ground at just the right moment. Other survivors, including reporter Tim Reiterman, ran for the nearby tall grass and hid until the gunmen returned to the People's Temple. A detailed description of the five murders at the airstrip is included, with pictures, in Reiterman's book *Raven*.

The San Francisco *Examiner* had been working the People's Temple story two years before it became "the Jonestown Massacre" in Guyana. The newspaper, above all reporter Reiterman, deserved credit for being on the story long before others took up the challenge, predominantly television journalists such as myself. Our specialty was paramilitary: hit the ground running, find the storm, go to the eye of it, and serve it for dinner between "Andy Griffith" and "I Love Lucy." As Bruce Morton of CBS News once said of network television news: "We have a vested interest in chaos." As Bernard Goldberg said in his 2001 book, *Bias*: "In an 'entertainment culture,' even the news is entertainment."

I faulted myself as much as CBS News for not caring about Guyana until there was a monumental disaster. We'd come swooping down in our corporate jets or our pathetic little Yankee Papas, giving the appearance of serious journalism, when in truth we were like vultures circling for carrion. Television news had its moments, sometimes its glorious moments, but too often it was a contrivance sliding on the slippery slope of losing its way. At Jonestown, television valiantly tried to climb back toward excellence.

NBC cameraman Bob Brown stood his ground and demonstrated raw, rare courage when he recorded his own death. NBC correspondent Don Harris asked tough questions in the last interview with Jim Jones, who was surely a madman, on the last day of his life.

I watched Goldberg thunder away in his charter jet to Caracas to make what he believed would be the first televised report for CBS News. The New York Foreign Desk personnel had instructed Bernie to go to Caracas, which would have made sense if Caracas had made any sense. I told him I thought it was a mistake to go there, and I recommended anywhere but there—back to Miami, for example. The contorted oversimplification was that CBS had a news bureau in Caracas, this was a South American story, and everybody should be getting their money's worth. Maybe that was a reasonable assumption.

Another kind of night of horrors awaited Goldberg in Caracas. In my absence, Lalie tried to smooth the way, but the Lord himself would have been forced to use miracles. There was no feed out of Caracas because the transmitter was down and had been, we discovered later, for two weeks. Reason: bad fuse. Lalie had been assured that there was "no problema" in providing the service CBS News had requested. Goldberg limped out of Caracas the next day, probably thankful to be able to continue his vacation and doubly grateful that he'd not been sent to Venezuela to establish the CBS News Latin America Bureau.

The Nudelman and Sorensen crews and I took taxis into Georgetown. Quixote and his buddies found rooms at the Park Hotel, which resembled a minimum-security detention center. The Pegasus Hotel, the pride and joy of the Guyanese elite and the relatively few tourists who ever bothered to travel to Georgetown, was filled. Tourists would be out of their minds to spend good money on a trip to this formerly British but now darkly brooding land. On my first night in Guyana it reminded me of a miniature Port au Prince, Haiti. The people were practically all black, either African black or West Indian black. The two cultures were constantly at each other's throats, and about all a white person could do was to like it or leave it. I was sentenced to Guyana until CBS News decided to grant me parole.

The quickest food on the first night was fried chicken brought in from a nearby kitchen. The Guyanese government imposed rigid regulations on foodstuffs: garlic was forbidden. Even garlic seed could get you into a lot of trouble. It was a way for one culture to punish another culture. Back in Kentucky, I knew about bootleg whiskey, but bootleg garlic seemed a little farcical. We ate in a small, dank room called The Bar. I drank fruit juice without the gin, fed radio from up on my abstinence wagon, and went to bed. It was smotheringly hot in Guyana. Room 210 was more like a minimum-security cell than a hotel room. The telephone was at the end of a stumble down a dark hallway to a desk downstairs. For the second night in a row there would be terribly little sleep.

As I drifted in and out of consciousness, I still did not know that more than nine hundred people were already dead at Jonestown. I still had no earthly idea exactly *where* Jonestown was or *what* it was. I did not associate the name with the People's Temple. Nor did I know that a short distance from my room in Georgetown, in the People's Temple headquarters known as Lamaha Gardens, one of the Temple leaders, Sharon Amos, had butchered her three children and slit her own throat.

About 3:00 a.m., Guyana time, there was a knock on my door. The voice said I had another phone call. I lurched out of bed, jammed my legs into my only pair of trousers, already becoming stiff with sweat and dirt, and followed the desk clerk to the telephone downstairs. The CBS News Foreign Desk assistant read me wire copy: "The State Department has announced that an estimated four hundred people are dead at the People's Temple settlement."

My brain did not seem to know how to process such bizarre information. It was 3:00 in the morning. I had no idea where anything was in the capital city of Guyana. I felt overwhelmed with the enormity of the report. I considered for a moment the possibility of running away from what was developing into the worst storm I'd ever experienced, but I knew there was nowhere to run and nowhere to hide. I was trapped in a country that the day before I didn't know existed. Anybody who might have asked me yesterday where Guyana was would have heard me say, "Isn't that somewhere in Africa?" On top of everything else, my umbilical cord was still attached to Sorensen, the cameraman with a reputation for refusing to accept the possibility of fear.

I told CBS in New York that I would call back with a radio spot for the 6:00 a.m. broadcast, another for the *World News Roundup*, and a separate voicer for the television program then called *Morning News*. Jennifer Siebens came on the phone, and the sound of her voice was reassuring. I had worked with her on a Southern Baptist Convention story during the Atlanta Bureau days. She was a natural producer, the kind correspondents appreciated. Too many news producers were correspondent wannabes. Jennifer was calm, creative, and relentless in her belief that all stories deserved to be "fleshed out." I was writing copy in a vacuum. She provided me with more facts, and I included them.

We believed that people at Jonestown had committed mass suicide by drinking poison. They did it because Jim Jones told them to do it—he said they would all go to Heaven together. Jim Jones's henchmen would shoot those who didn't drink the cyanide potion. Mothers would squirt the substance into the mouths of their babies. Jones would take a revolver and blow out his own brains.

I was at the point of nausea, but I told myself to behave, be calm, and do the job I was paid to do. At 9:00 a.m. on Monday, November 20, I went to a news conference held by the Minister of Information and Culture, Shirley Field-Ridley. She announced that there would be only "pool coverage" of the scene at the People's Temple, and she proclaimed that since NBC had lost its crew at the Port Kaituma airstrip, then in honor of them, or out of respect for them, NBC would be the pool team. Bernard Shaw, who was working for ABC after leaving CBS, spoke in a loud, no-nonsense voice from the side of the crowded room. He said it should be up to the networks to make the decision themselves. He, of course, was exactly correct. But no amount of arguing would change the ruling. Minister Field-Ridley wouldn't budge. NBC was the pool.

After thirty minutes I broke away from the news conference and fed a status report to radio, a copy of which was designated as an update for *Morning News*. Radio failed to provide it. It may have been poetic justice, because television loved to give the shaft to radio whenever there was the slightest opportunity. "F--- radio" had been the watchword among CBS television news producers and many correspondents. I hated it because I knew how intimate, immediate, and powerful radio was—if there was ever a tradition at CBS News to be respected and revered, it was the Edward R. Murrow "rooftop" reports he did for radio during the bombardment of London in World War II.

I thought we had scored a major triumph by obtaining permission to use J.J., our bush pilot, to fly to Jonestown. I invited my friend, Pulitzer prize-winning reporter Gene Miller of the *Miami Herald*, to join us, along with a still photographer. Six years before, Gene had been one of the reporters standing watch outside Holy Cross Hospital when Gov. George Wallace was brought there after Arthur Bremer almost killed him in the Laurel, Maryland, shopping center. I liked Gene, and I thought I owed him one. Also I felt more secure having along for company a really intelligent reporter.

We were in the Aerocommander with the engines running, but when we advised the tower that we were ready for takeoff, the air controllers wanted to know if we had permission from the Director of Aviation. J.J. stalled as long as he could, but it was to no avail. It was sweltering hot inside Yankee Papa. Several times we climbed on and off the plane, like pouring in and out of a tin of sardines. We made phone calls until we were blue in the face. My pant legs were becoming stiff as cardboard, dirty, smelly, stomach-turning cardboard. Madame Minister had gone back on her word, or, more fairly, she had overstepped her authority. It was probably just as well. We would have screwed up the pool coverage and the competition would have screamed "foul." I'd been raised on the Plum Lick philosophy that things generally work out for the best.

I was wheels up in our Lear jet to San Juan, Puerto Rico, on November 20, with the first material for the Monday night Cronkite broadcast. Joe Carroll edited. Correspondent John Sheahan had come in to help out, and so had my old cab driver buddy, Frank Smith, from Atlanta. In the early '70s, when CBS News made us stop renting cars at company expense at our place of residence, I found Frank, good old Frank, and he found a gold mine. Frank was my Atlanta Sancho Panza. When he met Quixote at his house on Seaton Drive to head out to the airport, Frank brought coffee and the morning paper. All of this was much better than renting cars.

We managed to make air on the second broadcast at 7:00 p.m., New York time, but not on the first broadcast, which went live at 6:30 Eastern Standard Time. After a cold Kentucky Fried Chicken dinner beneath the wing of the corporate jet, we decided it would be off the rocker if not impossible to make it back to Georgetown the same night. We checked in at the Holiday Inn at the San Juan airport, where with a grateful thud I crashed into bed. I went to sleep thinking what a staggering day it had been in the life of one menial messenger.

We were up at first light and on our way back to Guyana. There was an increasing flap over the pool arrangement for coverage of the grisly scene at Jonestown. Several of us thought that NBC was being a little too sanctimonious about the deaths of its correspondent and cameraman. We wondered if the pool producers were holding back at least some better footage for themselves, reluctantly doling out what was left to the other networks. Joe Carroll returned with us to Georgetown to log cassettes and have a better feeling for what was happening.

In addition to the pool footage of Jonestown, Carroll had rounded up enlarged still photographs taken on the first "news pool" visit to the

People's Temple, and I studied them before taking off in our Lear, Tuesday, November 21. Joe was doing what Jennifer Siebens had insisted we should—"put more flesh on the bones of the story." I focused on the pictures and let their images burn into my brain. Nothing else mattered. Self-seeking thoughts were short-circuited and routed to remote corners of my mind. There was one picture of what we believed was the body of Jim Jones, who either had committed suicide or was killed by someone else who delivered a bullet to his demented brain. One thing was certain—he was dead.

On our way out of Guyana everybody in our crew had the same idea. We would fly over Jonestown. Why the hell not? We'd been denied permission to do so, but it was an unenforceable command. Although we knew we would have trouble slowing the small jet down for Sorensen to take usable pictures, we would do it anyway for the best reason of all, so the CBS News correspondent could take pictures with the mythical camera in his human mind.

The sky was overcast and it required two or three passes before Quixote could see the carnage. It lay three hundred feet beneath him in unspeakable awfulness. The bodies looked like fire ants doused with deadly chemicals. The victims hugged the ground with their arms draped over the shoulders of family and friends. Bloating had begun. I imagined that I could smell it. I talked quietly with myself: "Don't throw up...you are the one who is seeing this...this is your job...it is your responsibility to get it right...keep it simple...keep it clear...remember Hemingway... remember Dreiser...remember Crane...remember Steinbeck...remember Warren...start writing NOW."

The pilot of the Lear, Bill O'Neal, looked back at me. I gave him thumbs-up and began to write. There was nothing left to do but to resume normal speed and altitude and streak northward across the Caribbean to Puerto Rico. Sorensen seemed subdued, chastened. He knew his electronic camera had produced nothing that could be salvaged. Possibly he also knew, as did I, that we'd been overtaken by events. It wasn't World Cup and it wasn't Estelí, Nicaragua. It was Jonestown.

What I had seen had surpassed comprehension. The bodies of most of the people were face-down. I remembered from the still photographs that Jim Jones was face up. Sickening. It was as if they'd fallen asleep in the palm of Gulliver's hand. My mind was stormy, and I fought to keep my thoughts and my writing under control. I thought of an obscene decay of mind and spirit. Maybe that was what it was. I wasn't sure. I was not prepared to accept mothers filling syringes with cyanide and Kool Aid and squirting it down the throats of their babies. What madness! What a sin against all that was good and decent. These were the words in my journal that could not be included in a straight news report. We were expected to count bodies and sometimes describe how bodies looked, but as street reporters it was not our business to make overwrought judgments. That was the work of commentators, editorial writers, and other godly people. We were messengers, only messengers, and we must not forget it.

By the time we flew into San Juan, I had my script written. We raced to WAPA-TV, where producer Bill Willson was waiting. He finished editing the piece with only seconds to spare. It was the lead story on the *CBS Evening News* and throughout the world. By now it was the biggest storm I'd ever covered or probably would ever have the misfortune to report. I didn't want to see another one like it.

Fifteen years later, after I had returned to Kentucky, I was relieved that I did not have to sit for fifty-one days outside the Branch Davidian cult's compound near Waco, Texas. I did not have to be the messenger who described the inferno that burned it to the ground. I did not have to account for the initially estimated eighty-six people, including seventeen children, consumed in the flames, and did not have to chase after the eight known survivors of another mass suicide/murder. I would remember the printed words that had hung from the pavilion beams at Jonestown:

Those Who Do Not Remember the Past Are Condemned to Repeat It.

We checked in at the San Juan Hilton. The preceding three days had seemed like three years. I joined a pleasant dinner with Willson, Carroll, the jet crew, and Frank Smith, the best damn cab driver in the state of Georgia. I went to my room and fell asleep and was too tired to have any dreams.

We gathered at 5:30 a.m. on Wednesday, November 22, for the ride to the San Juan airport and the flight back to Guyana. It was to be John Sheahan's turn to feed Cronkite. John was not a "Big Foot." If we'd been big-footed by one of the network's superstars there would have been no question about whose face would have been on television. Cronkite, Kalb, Kuralt, Mudd, Rather, Schieffer—they *were* the Big Feet, and that was that. From time to time they fueled their careers by cruising in at precisely the right moments to authenticate what the Quixotes had already begun to report. Sheahan and I and later Steve Young, three lesser players in the star system—we scrambled and shared the crumbs falling from the table. While Sheahan, who had replaced me in the Atlanta Bureau after I moved to South America, went with the Nudelman crew for a more carefully planned aerial inspection of Jonestown, I patiently waited at Timehri Airport for a "photo opportunity" of the arrival of the first bodies. Teams of U.S. and Guyanese personnel filled the bags and loaded them onto the choppers at the People's Temple and television crews recorded the offloading at the far end of the Georgetown airport

We worked for hours in the sweltering heat. We made a trip to the side of the airport opposite the terminal for a briefing with an Air Force lieutenant colonel. In an interview he said the priorities were 1) to identify the bodies, 2) to transport them to Georgetown, and 3) to look for possible survivors. Quixote asked the obvious question: "Sir, don't you have your priorities reversed? Shouldn't you be looking for survivors *first*?"

The lieutenant colonel seemed to be confirming the growing suspicion that there were no more survivors. But it didn't make sense because eight hundred and three passports had been found in a trunk at the settlement. We rushed our cassette to Willson and Sheahan in San Juan by putting it on NBC's Lear jet. The squadron of Lear jets representing U.S. television news networks occupied a large portion of one of the Timehri Airport aprons, more air power than the entire nation of Guyana would ever hope to have.

Steve Young had come in with cameraman Clarence Gibbons and his technician, Louis Ledford. Clarence had worked his way up from electrician under Laurens Pierce to the prized stature of cameraman without whom Big Feet and Little Feet would have no place to stand. I returned to the Park Hotel and went to dinner with Nudelman and Dan Céfalo, the soft-spoken, generous, and gentle soundman who would later die when the helicopter in which he was riding disappeared in a storm in the Bermuda Triangle. This Dan was one of the many unsung heroes without whom television superstars would have little reason for being.

The Park Hotel reminded me of a poor man's Sydney Greenstreet movie set. There were traces of British influence: bland and tiresome breakfasts, tea at midafternoon, and accents that caused West Indians and Guyanese blacks to sound generally better educated than they typically were. There was no hot water in the rooms. I squatted for my bath like a broken-down streetwalker.

On Thanksgiving Day in 1978, it was my turn to be on the *CBS Evening News with Walter Cronkite*. We had temporarily moved the feed point from Puerto Rico to Barbados until the networks could negotiate a satellite uplink with the government in Trinidad and Tobago. I wrote a five-minute piece for radio's *World of Religion*. Sorensen, Moreno, and I again were escorted with the rest of the media to the other side of the airport, where we obtained footage of the unloading of helicopters, the transfer of the body bags, and the placing of them into shiny aluminum caskets. One was numbered 13B. With a black marker, the name "The Rev. Jimmie Jones" had been written on it.

Tape editor Al Balisky and I ran and jumped on our Lear because we felt we didn't have time to call New York and we didn't know where the rest of the CBSers were at the time. We were on our way to Trinidad and Tobago and hadn't gone far when we received a message from Willson at Timehri Airport in Guyana. The message was a simple, "Return." After taking a deep breath, we turned back because we were good soldiers. So were Jim Jones's followers. When we opened the door of the plane back in Guyana, Willson told me that he and Sheahan had "better material." I was pulled off the Lear, they boarded and were quickly airborne for Port-of-Spain, Trinidad and Tobago. I'd been shot down many times, and this one was rougher than most—but Quixote was alive, and that's what came first. When messengers are killed, other messengers appear—even one dead messenger can produce one hundred new messengers. I was one of those, and I did interviews with survivors and sent several spot reports to radio in New York.

The day after Thanksgiving, November 24, I was among the media who interviewed an eyewitness to the Jonestown murders and suicides. O'Dell Rhodes described himself as a former drug addict from Detroit. He had seen one of the mothers inject the poison into her baby's mouth. "She went over and sat down and gave herself the poison. I didn't know how a mother could do that," he said with a soft, quavering voice.

Rhodes had escaped the compound and gone to police at Port Kaituma. "Get somebody to Jonestown," Rhodes said he told them. The quavering turned to sobs.

Back in Louisville, Kentucky, when I was working for the CBS affiliate, WHAS Radio and Television, I used to wonder, "Who lives on the third floor?" There were buildings along Jefferson and Main Streets, and I frequently looked up to the third floor windows, because they appeared particularly lonely and deserted. "Who lives on the third floor?" became a personal watch-phrase, a mantra meaning to check one more source, go an extra mile, and make one more telephone call. I decided to check out the third floor of the Park Hotel.

When I reached the top of the stairs, a young Guyanese soldier glared at me, his automatic weapon at the ready. He was barring entrance. I took a chance. I told him in my best no nonsense tone of voice that I had every right to be there and brushed past him. I never looked back. The bluff worked. On the third floor of the Park Hotel was where I found Mrs. Claire Janaro of Redwood Valley, California. She had recently come in from the United States, and she believed her two children were probably dead at Jonestown. I summoned Sorensen and Moreno, and I interviewed the grieving woman.

"Is this on television? Please somebody do something. Call the State Department, call President Carter, please, do something to help the people of Jonestown," said Mrs. Janaro, her body convulsing with hysteria. "Nobody does shit...somebody HELP us down here," she wailed.

I went to the telephone and called CBS in New York and said I thought there was ample material for a special, "The Final Horror." I interviewed a spokesman for the U.S. Embassy in Georgetown, who said an effort was being made to look for survivors. About 375 people were still unaccounted for. I went to the airport and was doing a "standupper close," when new numbers hit like a thunderclap: another 370 bodies had been found at Jonestown.

My brain lost feeling. It processed the information as if it were a commodity report. I redid the standupper, and Willson and I boarded Nan One Two Hotel Jouliette and headed for Port-of-Spain. We led the Cronkite News with another wrenching account of the story unfolding at the People's Temple. We followed that with another report for "The Final Horror," which was aired on CBS the evening of November 24. Sheahan came in and put together a second piece using the interview I had done with the Gerald Parks family of Ukiah, California.

Members of the Parks family—sixty-four-year-old Edith, her son Gerald, and his daughter, twelve-year-old Tracy—said they had spent three days in the jungle. They had survived the Saturday afternoon ambush of Congressman Ryan and his party. They had seen Patricia Parks's head blown to bits, and memories of it would remain with them for the rest of their lives.

My God, I thought, what a hideous hour in the history of mankind. Wars are horrible. So are plane crashes. But how could seven hundred and eighty people commit suicide at the same time by swallowing cyanide? How could so many innocent babies be murdered? How could one man become so powerful as to dominate the minds and the wills of all those people?

We were in the lobby at 7:30 a.m. on November 26 for the ride to the airport and the flight back to Georgetown. I had bought four bottles of Scotch for the customs and immigration officers at Timehri Airport. It was no different from the way People's Temple members had smoothed their way past Guyanese authorities. We weren't smuggling guns or cyanide, but it was bribery all the same.

127

I remained at the airport while Willson and Sheahan went into Georgetown. I lay down and grabbed thirty minutes of sleep in the VIP lounge. About 2:00 p.m., Sorensen, Moreno, and I were taken with a few other reporters across the runway to the place where bodies were being transferred in bags from helicopters to the caskets. It was there we were told that the final body count had reached nine hundred and ten.

"Jonestown: a place, an event that again today, Saturday, November 25, 1978, demonstrated that there are no limits here to the grotesque. As if 409 bodies were not enough, then there were 780, and if 780 were not enough, now there are 910 and there is no certainty that the body count won't go higher." That was the beginning of my script for the *Saturday News*. The 910 figure did not include Sharon Amos and her three children, which made the total at least 914.

I fed radio.

Sheahan came to the airport with more interviews with survivors. Willson and I hurried back to Trinidad and Tobago. My old friend from Washington, Bill Crawford, a fine CBS News producer, put in his appearance. We went to the station, and I fed the bird. We went to the Hilton where I bought shaving equipment for myself and cigarettes and chocolate bars for our Guyanese "friends" at the airport. I took a hot bath, but the dirt did not seem to want to come off.

On Sunday, November 26, one week after my arrival in Guyana, I was up early in order to leave for the airport to return to Georgetown with Willson and Crawford. I took more booze and cigarettes to Timehri airport personnel, and I wondered what would happen if there were no need for the alcohol and tobacco industries. Other "sins" would have to be invented, while Kentucky would go through bankruptcy.

Willson returned to Port-of-Spain with Sheahan and Young to do early and late *Sunday News* and *Morning News*, and Crawford filled me in on many CBS changes. Threldkeld and Stahl were out as *Morning News* anchors. Schieffer was now *Morning* maestro. Stahl replaced Schieffer at the White House. Mudd would anchor Cronkite in the summer of '79, exclusively from Washington, an indication that he was probably Cronkite's eventual replacement. Somebody forgot to tell Dan Rather.

My CBS Roundupper for the next morning was drawn from my journal: *The government of Guyana is taking to Jonestown today a planeload of reporters and cameramen from the United States. It will be the first opportunity for newsmen en masse to have a look at what's left of The People's Temple settlement. The last body was brought out yesterday to be placed in a metal casket at the Georgetown airport to await the flight to the United States.*

I saw Jonestown on Monday, November 27, 1978. The media met at the Ministry of Information and were bussed to Timehri airport, where we boarded a Guyana Airways turbo prop. At 2:53 p.m. we touched down at Matthews Ridge, an outpost in the northwest Guyana jungle. The view along the way was an almost unbroken canopy of trees, vines, palms, and growth in every hue of green. I was to see this even more clearly and to absorb it more deeply on the helicopter ride from Matthews Ridge to the People's Temple, a flight covering about twenty miles.

I imagined the feeling of supreme isolation that must have captivated, deluded, and destroyed whatever mind there was left to Jim Jones and set the backdrop for his imprisonment of the minds of more than nine hundred of his followers, his prisoners. There was an aura of omnipotence, of the last rung on a ladder to Heaven.

It had rained. Jonestown was a quagmire of mud and the stains left from more than nine hundred decaying bodies. The bodies had all been removed, but the sickly sweet smell of death hovered over the settlement, moved like an enveloping, virulent fog. It penetrated living nostrils and produced a natural aversion to its being inside healthy lungs.

Willson, Sorensen, Moreno, and I went to Jim Jones's cabin and made our way inside. Drug paraphernalia was scattered around. It looked as if an evil wind had swirled through. There was no time to waste. As I was coming out through the front door and turned right to proceed across the long porch, I spotted boxes filled with letters. Sorensen was rolling, and I knelt and read on-camera pathetically stated "Dear Dad" letters. Jones expected everybody to call him "Dad," encouraged them to write self-analysis letters to him. At the preschool nursery I did another piece for *Morning News*, and another sequence at Jones's mother's grave for the Cronkite news. I did on-the-scene adlibbing for radio, and we hurried back to Matthews Ridge and on to Georgetown, where Willson, Sheahan, and I bummed a ride on NBC's Lear to Port-of-Spain. We fed the preschool nursery footage to *Morning News* and the audiotape to radio. Producer Paula Sturtevant was on the other end of the line in New York.

She cried.

There were tears in San Francisco, too. Mayor George Moscone had been shot to death in his city hall office. Minutes later, Supervisor Harvey Milk, the city's first official to acknowledge that he was gay, was shot and killed in the same building. A short time later, thirty-two-year-old Dan White turned himself in to police. White had resigned as Supervisor but had been trying to reverse the resignation. He described himself as an opponent of homosexuals, a defender of "family values," and a foe of users of marijuana. The coinciding of the San Francisco murders with the Jonestown massacre fed fires of dismay and disbelief. In May of the following year, Dan White was found guilty of murdering Mayor Moscone and Harvey Milk. Two days later, at least 140 people were injured in violence following the conviction.

I checked in at the Hilton in Port-of-Spain, and I called Lalie in Caracas. She told me there had been a telex from Brian Ellis complimenting my work and saying I'd be back in Caracas in "a couple of days." It turned out to be a premature message. Storms hardly ever conform to births or deaths or honeymoons or trains leaving stations on time. Storms are imprecise, with a mind of their own. They roar. They quiet down. They disperse. They gather again. After the storm comes the quiet with an illusion that there won't be any more storms. Then they strike again with little or sometimes no warning—and so it will be so long as there is devilry. The Branch Davidian calamity would go up in flames in Texas in 1993, and the inevitable comparisons would be made with 1978's Jonestown in Guyana. The terrorist attacks on the World Trade Center in 2001 were a part of an unbroken linkage, more sowing and reaping of dragon seeds.

On the day following the San Francisco murders, twenty-one bodies were found buried at the domicile of John Gacy in Illinois. The connection between the violence of 1978 and that of 2001 suggests a common thread of behavior born of egomania leading to megalomania and finally, as in the case of the Rev. Jim Jones, omniscience. David Koresh, too, proclaimed that he was Jesus Christ. Osama bin Laudin said he acted in the name of Allah.

I went to TTTV, Trinidad and Tobago Television, to begin working on the evening's Cronkite piece. I thought it was one of the finest I'd ever done, one in which I would not be ashamed to be the ugly duckling becoming the swan singing as it died. I believe the Jonestown suicides and murders, or whatever name they would take into history, would be the high point in my career in broadcast news, which had been based almost entirely on following storms. The one thing I wanted more than any other was the magic moment when I could head home to Kentucky.

Near the end of 1978, twelve years with the Tiffany Network and its vested interest in chaos, Quixote had decided it was time to write, to teach, to farm, to garden, and to raise a second family with Lalie. There was no doubt that the word would be going back that the Caracas Bureau should be shut down and moved to Miami. That's where the other networks were located because that was how most storms could be most conveniently covered. It was more cost-effective to charter corporate jets and dispatch them at a moment's notice to the latest mudslide or drug bust in Colombia, the latest plane crash in the Andes, particularly if the survivors started eating each other.

I did not divulge my plans to leave CBS and return to the University of Kentucky. I looked into the faces of my fellow storm followers and I thought to myself, there has to be more than this. There has to be more to mass communication than the chronicling, however faithfully, of disasters, which leads inevitably to cynicism, itself as poisonous as cyanide.

On November 29, word came from Guyana that the first survivors, a small group of older people, would be leaving Georgetown on the afternoon Pan Am flight. Correspondent Steve Young hooked up with them and continued with them to New York. It would have been nice if I had been the one to go to New York to be debriefed on *Morning News*. But I was well contented with what I had, grateful for what I'd been able to achieve. If the Jim Jones test by cyanide had taught me anything at all, it had taught me humility, and it had given me a sense of when enough was enough.

I returned to Georgetown on the NBC Lear, taking with me Cutty Sark and Marlboros to put smiles on the faces of the customs and immigration officers, police, survivors, anybody. The ride from Timehri to Georgetown was more depressing than I'd felt it before. I supposed it was because I was becoming burned out on the story that was quickly losing its sex appeal among the mass communicators, who were on guard for other storms, somewhere, anywhere.

It had been nearly two weeks since I'd left Lalie in Caracas. She'd have been encouraged to know that along the way I'd managed to pick up some Fruit of the Loom. At the Park Hotel, members of the Parks family were still there, waiting for word on when they might return to the United States. So were O'Dell Rhodes and the others. I talked with Brian Ellis on the telephone, and he said he and I would talk the following day about pulling out the crew and me. We were the last CBS personnel left in Guyana. We were often the last to leave. I went to my room early and treated myself to a huge chocolate bar filled with whole almonds.

After I was pleasantly asleep, I was awakened for another telephone call from New York. I received unusual praise from the CBS Foreign Desk muckamucks for the work I had done on the Jonestown story, first of all the piece in which I read the "Dear Dad" letters. It would have been good to hear personally from Cronkite himself, even his executive producer, but I don't remember a peep out of either of them.

By November 29, all the bodies from the People's Temple had been returned to the United States, and it was our expectation that we'd be flying out of Guyana on the following day. We'd go for brief R and R, then prepare for Sunday's Venezuelan presidential election. There had been an earthquake in Mexico registering 8 on the Richter scale, but there were no known deaths—the body count remained the chief yardstick for judging the importance of news coverage.

I discussed with the U.S. consular office the situation with survivors and was told that none would be going anywhere on this day. I tried to interview a judge on the case of "John John," one of Jim Jones's sons, who died with him, but the judge refused. I did an interview with an attorney on the case for a piece coming out of Los Angeles, and requested and received a one-on-one backgrounder with U.S. Ambassador John Burke. Then late in the day I found out we would not be leaving Guyana after all. New York, in the person of CBS vice-president John Lane, wanted us to stay "protectively" for several more days. I advised that the Venezuelan election was low priority, and privately I was relieved I wasn't going to have to worry about that gangbang. I talked to Lalie on the phone and asked her to telex our shipping situation to New York and to request more money. I believed it would be only a short while until the Caracas Bureau would be mercifully shut down, most probably to be relocated in Miami. Quixote doubted he'd be living in Coconut Grove with a secluded swimming pool where he could swim nude at full moon.

On Friday, December 1, I wrote in my journal: *I'm going to do all within my power to return to Plum Lick.* Even to myself I was sounding like a broken record.

It was a slow day. At 5:00 New York time, Quixote's "Venezuelan Image Makers" was an "either-or" with a Mike Lee piece from Northern Ireland, an either-or on the Cronkite broadcast. Being "either-or" was like being jerked around in a dating game.

Carl was mugged in the early evening just after I had left him. The attack occurred in front of the U.S. Embassy. The muggers made off with his watch and his passport and a hunk of his pride. Maybe they loved him and didn't want him to leave the country. They ripped the watch off his wrist, but otherwise he wasn't hurt.

I wrote in my journal: *I want to hang new wallpaper inside my mind, set new tables, invite in new people, talk in new rounds of conversation, at times engage myself alone in quiet meditation. I won't allow myself to be jabbered to death by Elmer Fudds with screwed-up minds. I want no Jim Joneses to guarantee me passage to Heaven. I feel uncommonly*

133

young as I approach my forty-ninth birthday. As I near the half-century mark of my life I feel and know I am hugely optimistic.

I woke up the following morning so "bad off" even a cold shower didn't have much effect. The crew was not ready to shoot at 8:00 a.m. on Saturday, December 2, and as a result we missed sixty-four-year-old Edith Parks hugging and kissing the rest of her family goodbye as she grimly left the hotel on her way to the United States. So I proceeded by foot with her and the Julius Evans family up to the U.S. Consulate—I, the lone reporter and no cameras, which may have been poetic justice. Sorensen and Moreno came running up too late. I scolded them, but little good that did. We made it to Timehri Airport in advance of the little party of six, and I did some fast Q and A, then played cops and robbers with the embassy people and the airport authorities. We managed to obtain most of the pictures we wanted and needed. I took the ABC pool Lear jet to Port-of-Spain. Al Balisky and I put together a decent two-minute piece for *Saturday News*, and over the telephone I fed a spot to radio. It had been raining in Trinidad and Tobago for two days. There was "trouble with the voltage on the carrier" in and around the ground station, and for a while it appeared we would lose the bird. Somehow the God of satellites was with us, and we fed New York's greedy gullet.

By 6:00 a.m. the next day we were battening down the hatch of Nan 17 Jouliette Foxtrot for the flight back to Georgetown. Quixote had so far missed much of the Venezuelan presidential election and with a little luck he would miss all of it. I took a cab to the U.S. Consulate in Georgetown, where Carl and Roberto were staked out. I feared we'd dropped the ball by not going to the People's Temple house in Lamaha Gardens when a bus went there to pick up about twenty-four of the surviving followers of Jim Jones. As it turned out, it didn't matter. We had a great deal of footage, including a few remarks from one of Jones's adopted sons, Tim. But he would say nothing of substance—as if substance was something we were looking for.

We raced to Timehri, beating the bus there. Then the story changed—the pilot would not take off because he said FBI agents were not on board.

I jumped on the Lear and took off to Port-of-Spain before Pan Am flight 228 cleared the runway. It was time to take our footage and report the unfolding story, bit by bit. It was the third day of rain in Trinidad and Tobago. Balisky and I barely made the feed for the *Early Sunday News*.

I grabbed a sandwich and a piece of cake, ate them on the way to the airport, then rode the Lear to Georgetown. When I was back in room 210 of the Park Hotel, I fed radio a spot for the next morning's *World News Roundup*. There was a temporary power failure, but I had the Saturday and Sunday *New York Times* and was catching up on news. Sparky Anderson had been fired as the manager of the Cincinnati Reds. What old Sparky needed were Lombardi, Blackwell, the McCormicks, Frey, Walker, Joust, Post, and all the ever-loving Good Old Boys of Crosley Field days.

On Monday, December 4, we went to the Georgetown courthouse to await the arrival of Charles Beikman, the ex-U.S. Marine allegedly associated with the murders and suicide of Sharon Amos and her three children on the same day as the mass suicides and murders at Jonestown. I never knew to what extent he was actually involved. I interviewed Beikman's son, talked to the defense attorney, and had our piece essentially finished by 10 a.m. The Danish consulate gave Carl a new passport. I fed radio a spot live into the telephone and advised the Foreign Desk as to what we could offer for *Evening News*. I rode the Lear jet back to Port-of-Spain, where Balisky and I put together an adequate two-minute piece, and we fed the bird.

Quixote went to dinner at a fairly good Indian restaurant where he died and went to Heaven on curried goat. I returned to the Holiday Inn and placed a call to Lalie in Caracas. First reports indicated Luis Herrero was the new president of Venezuela, defeating Piñerua handsomely and swamping Diego Arria. She said Caracas was a madhouse.

David Charles or Ravy Bradford, I wrote in my journal of our unborn child, *please know how much your mother and father love you before your creation. You are already living genes inside our bodies wanting to be unified in the personality, character, and intelligence of your individual self.*

Tuesday, December 5. I was in the lobby of the Holiday Inn in Port-of-Spain well before 6:00 a.m. to meet the charter crew for the ride to the airport and the return to Georgetown. I was now using the last notch of my size 34 belt. My next belt would be a 32. I smiled to myself. I'd never felt better. I'd quit drinking and was looking forward to running again. I had reacquired my taste for fruit juices, a taste destroyed by alcohol, caffeine, and carbonated drinks. The new pages in my passport were filling up, making it look like a long foldout postcard. There was nothing to bring back to Trinidad and Tobago on this day. Three more Jonestown survivors flew out, but there was no coverage of it. I was informed that last night's piece was passed by the Cronkiters but was used on *Morning News*.

Sam, the driver, went shopping with me. I wanted to see what I could find for Lalie for Christmas. I found an oil painting titled "Old House and Sunset." I thought it powerfully stated what I felt Guyana fundamentally was: raw nature, primitive living, oppression, desperation; dark, moody, mysterious conditions; an unfamiliar, forbidding culture. Sam and I visited the Starbroek Market with the huge clock on top reminiscent of Dutch colonial days. I bought a preciously thin thirteen-carat Guyanese gold nugget. I thought it would look lovely resting between my lover's breasts.

The market was a crowded place, but cleaner than anything I'd seen in Caracas. I ate a pretty good steak with the current NBC crew at the Tower Restaurant, then went to bed early. I remembered the congressman, the other NBC crew, the San Francisco photographer, and Patricia Parks—the messengers who had been killed for wanting to seek the truth and for wanting to tell it. That is all, too, that Bill Stewart wanted to do in Nicaragua in 1979. They were all messengers. I hoped God had saved a quiet and safe place for them, a corner of Heaven.

On Wednesday, December 6, I arose and then said private prayers on my knees, something I had begun doing morning and night since coming to Guyana. The Jonestown catastrophe had brought me to my knees.

I checked out of the Park Hotel after feeding a Roundupper to radio. We staked out the Tower Hotel and picked up footage of seventeen members of the People's Temple when they boarded a bus for the airport. There was one sequence in which Stephen Jones, the natural son of Jim Jones, embraced Tim Jones, one of the adopted sons. I did a short interview with Stephen, who was forced to stay behind while Tim and the others left for the United States. We watched as Pan Am 228 gracefully rose from the main runway at Timehri, then I boarded my Lear jet to Port-of-Spain, bringing Carl and Roberto with me. I fed a piece to the *Evening News*, placed a call to Caracas, took a hot bath, and went to bed. I woke up several times during the night and tried to reach Lalie on the telephone, but the overseas circuits, at least the ones to Caracas, were down.

On December 7, 1978, I woke up and included in my prayers a "Happy Birthday" to my sixteen-year-old daughter, Nell, in Atlanta. It had been a long night because I kept waking up and trying to get through to the overseas operator. "I'm Dreaming of a White Christmas" was playing in the restaurant. I took another good hot bath and tried another time to call Caracas but could not get through. Finally, in a rage, I gave up at 7:05. I sat on the balcony of the seventh floor and scowled at the harbor activity. I made up my mind that I was going to return to Caracas on the afternoon Aeropostal flight or know the reason why.

The news director at WTTV interviewed me, and I tried to give my impressions of Jonestown and what I thought made Jim Jones do what he did. There were no easy answers. I was not a cult expert. I felt more comfortable describing things I'd seen and heard than making judgments about them. Later, after I left CBS News and began giving talks on Jonestown for the Kentucky Humanities Council, I constructed five causes for what had happened: authoritarianism/egomania/megalomania; isolation; charismatic leadership; sex and drugs; and ultimate truth. I challenged audiences to construct their own causes, and I asserted my belief that it shouldn't take more than nine hundred to make a story— one sacrificial lamb would be too many.

CHAPTER NINE

I confirmed with New York that Sorensen and I would return to Caracas in the afternoon of December 7. Roberto would stay back and baby-sit our equipment. At Port-of-Spain airport I bought a bottle of the finest brandy for Christmas and a couple of Trinidad and Tobago record albums.

Aeropostal was forty-five minutes late. When we disembarked at Maiquetía, our red-tape troubles began. Immigration refused to pass Carl through because his new passport did not have a transeunte visa stamp in it. They told him he must either surrender his passport or they would deport him. Carl argued for about two hours to no avail. They confiscated the passport. Paco drove us to Parque Centrál, and everything I loathed about Caracas seemed ten times worse.

I rang the buzzer to the office, and there she was, all five feet-fourteen inches of her, standing in the doorway, the first time in nearly three weeks I'd laid eyes on the most beautiful woman in the world. We kissed hungrily. Later, she began preparing supper, for I was hungry for good food too.

The following day, Friday, December 8, I began receiving telexes and telephone calls about a tape that had been found at Jonestown — babies and other children could be heard screaming and the voice of Jim Jones could be heard exhorting his followers to drink the poison. I gave

Brian Ellis a couple of names the Foreign Desk assistants might call in Georgetown, where the tape reportedly was. I washed the dishes while Lalie prepared for work, and then we padded again together across the footbridge over the autopista to meet her ride. I wore my jogging outfit. Stripped, I weighed one hundred and fifty-nine pounds.

I had not been back in the office long when I was told to find a charter and return to Guyana. The humane society should have been onto this—three weeks of cold-bloodedness in Guyana, out for one day, then back again to the outrage. Pilot William Marquez and co-pilot Luis Narcano took me in a King Air, Yankee Victor 152 Charlie Papa. We didn't take off from Carlota until 1:00 p.m. Three hours later I was in Georgetown, where there was a delay in clearing customs. The agent was eating supper. Then he had to tend his dog's hurt leg. It sounded perfectly logical to Quixote. I located a driver and finally signed in at the Pegasus Hotel, where I located "Jack," the Guyanese government spokesman. "Jack" was refusing all requests even to hear his copy of the tape.

I was too numb to be angry. The whole thing was beyond stupidity. The only possible redemption of this lunacy was when I did a debriefing with radio and received permission from Ellis to return on the same charter to Caracas the same night. It was as if I'd taken a taxi across town.

A partial text of the tape was published the following spring in an Associated Press story in the Caracas *Daily Journal* after the audio had aired on NBC. Jim Jones was heard saying it would be an act of kindness to administer poison to the children. He said it was not suicide, it was the same as others had done in ancient Greece. He called it a revolutionary act.

A woman in the People's Temple pavilion argued that as long as there was life, there was hope.

The Reverend Jones was in no mood for disagreement. He said, "Someday everybody dies."

The crowd shouted its approval. "...We're all ready to go. If you tell us we have to give our lives now, we're ready," another woman wailed.

A nurse was heard giving instructions about how to administer the poisoned solution to the children. She said the taste was bitter, but that there was nothing to worry about.

"Please, for God's sake, let's get on with it," said Jones.

There were sounds of confusion and applause.

"Die with respect," said Jones. "Die with a degree of dignity. Stop this hysterics. This is not the way for people who are socialistic Communists to die....Children, it's just something to put you to rest. O, God!"

There was crying in the background.

Lalie and Paco met me about midnight after the futile trip to bring back the tape. We ate a quiet, late dinner by the seashore. The next morning, Paco showed up about 10:00 to take Lalie and me to buy our first Christmas tree. We went looking even though the spirit of Christmas had been raped. We found a nice tree without much trouble, brought it to Apartamiento 4-M, and Paco helped Lalie set it up and begin the decorating.

I placed a call to Bill and Lena Gilvin on the farm in Kentucky. They said it was snowing on Plum Lick. Bernice, the Jersey cow, was heavy with her Simmental calf. Bill said he felt for me having to cover "that mess down there."

It was the beginning of our seventh month in Venezuela. My feeble attempt to learn to speak Spanish fluently was fluttering in bits and pieces, but I didn't care, because I thought I knew where I was going and how I was going to spend the rest of my life. The trouble was, I didn't know there'd be many more turns in the road before that happened.

It was raining when we galumphed forlornly together over the footbridge. There was little to say, and I was lost in thought. I told Lalie I knew I had to continue with CBS until there was confirmation of a position at the University of Kentucky and Kentucky Educational Television. It might take several years and who knows how many miles?

"I'll go anywhere with you," she said.

I'd been thinking about the fundamental shift in our lives. On the one hand, maybe I was robbing Lalie of a huge opportunity with Revlon in New York. And did I really want to stop short in my own career? Did I really not want the Big Apple? Did I not want one day to succeed Douglas Edwards as the anchor for radio's *World Tonight*? Didn't I want to be the smooth and calm voice for the nation?

I believed I could predict how "New York" would turn out. Neither of us would be happy. We would meet at Harry's Bar in early evening and each have three drinks—one for you and one for me and one for the angels that we used to be. Maybe Scotch on the rocks tonight, maybe perfect rob roys tomorrow night, as if there was a drop of truth in the bottom of the glass. I'd waltz through Robert Service's "Shooting of Dan McGrew" and we'd go in a velvet fog to our East 52nd Street apartment. We'd look out the window at the Chrysler Building, and after a few years we would know how old and empty that could become. Too doddering to go see revivals of *Grease* and *The Best Little Whorehouse in Texas*, too feeble to watch reruns of *Jonestown* and *Beirut*, we'd play gin rummy and bitch at each other. New York would not sustain us in our final hour of need.

Thank God, our hearts, minds, and better senses reached toward sunsets on the other side of the Hudson. Over there stretched the long road home to Kentucky. One day we'd make it there if we were patient and if God thought it was a good idea.

I received a panic call from Brian Ellis in New York that we were "going back to Georgetown" right away. I told him I thought it was truly unnecessary and for once I prevailed. Later, it was confirmed I was right. I made a stew and grilled cheese sandwiches.

Days moved by on silver strands. I worked all afternoon on a candlelight dinner for the two of us. I put together some good sauce for the pasta, made a nice olive and egg salad, fixed a loaf of bread with garlic and butter, and opened a bottle of Medoc wine. It was the first alcohol for me in a long, long time.

We lay in bed and talked about the meaning of Stribling's *The Store*, which both of us now had finished. We agreed it was a terrible indictment of the South we both loved, especially as it was emerging from the devastation of the Civil War. I began reading Bernard Malamud's *The Fixer*—if the slaves in the Old South thought they had

had it bad, what was to be said for the Zhids in the Russia of Nicholas II? I decided I needed a good Laurel and Hardy fix.

Lalie was in high spirits about a phone call she'd received from her first boss, going back to what she called her hell-raising days in Baton Rouge. She said everybody had to learn about life for her or himself, usually the hard way. Instead of eating out, we heated up biscuits and jambalaya and stayed bedded down. We began reading aloud from Edith Wharton's *Age of Innocence*.

About midnight, Paco hauled Quixote to Avenida los Procerel for the traditional roller-skating and noise making in celebration of Christmas. I recorded the sounds on my tape recorder. Paco shipped it to New York. I climbed into bed after one o'clock the next morning.

We received a Christmas card, which included the rumor in the CBS Southwest Bureau that we were being transferred to Dallas. I had two Scotch on the rocks, the first for me in months. I had to be up at 3:45 the next morning to make a church recording for *World of Religion*. Soon we would have been in Venezuela eight months. It seemed like eight years.

The alarm went off at 3:45. Paco was supposed to show up at 4:00, but he didn't because my Spanish had thrown him off. He thought I meant 4:00 in the afternoon. I caught a cab at 4:30 and went like a blind man to find a Catholic Church in Chico. I had been told that La Misa de Gallo started at five o'clock at La Iglesia de San José, but it was buttoned down tight as a confessional. A nearby market was open and Ferber's *So Big* people were setting up their vegetable stands. I ambled along Avenida de Francisco de Miranda all the way to Chacrito, thinking maybe I had the wrong church, but I couldn't find another one.

The Lord spoke. He said, "Listen, little amigo, Quixote, if you don't get back to San José de Chacao I'm going to have to let somebody mug you, and in case you wondered, you're going to miss the *six* o'clock mass."

I took a cab, and the instant I stepped inside the church, the Mass began, just as God had said it would. A group of young people and a few adults sang and played guitars. I wrote, recorded, and transmitted to New York my *World of Religion* offering. I called Atlanta and told my daughter Cathy that the funds were in hand for her first year of college.

On the Friday before Christmas, Lalie received a raise and a letter of praise from her boss at Revlon. I was absolutely proud of her. She had worked hard and deserved it. I fixed us a little breakfast and fell asleep reading *Age of Innocence*. I shuffled up the street and bought a bottle of Scotch for Roberto and a bottle of gin for Paco. Lalie wrapped them prettily, making a bow out of a CADA bag. By late afternoon, we were in tears over Wharton's Neland and May Archer and the countess Olenska. Roberto and Paco came to the apartment and invited us to go to dinner, a taking of the boss and his wife, el jefe y su esposa, out to eat. I did some Christmas drinking, which did not entirely please me and hardly satisfied me. We went to a little restaurant that was uncrowded and quiet. We invited Paco and Roberto, two of the best friends we would ever have, to come up to the apartment for nightcaps, and we gave them their Christmas presents.

The next morning, I finished reading *The Age of Innocence* to Lalie. We lay silent for a time, and then we talked quietly about Edith Wharton's masterpiece. I fixed a little breakfast for us and began reading H.L. Davis's *Honey in the Horn*. We made a batch of beaten biscuits that turned out too thin, but we ate them anyway. We took a long nap in the afternoon, both of us saying we needed some time in warm sunshine.

The year 1978 was almost history, and I was anxiously looking forward to hearing from Len Press at Kentucky Educational Television. We decided not to attempt midnight Mass, and I rejoiced over that decision. Why? Perhaps distrust, a stern foreboding of ultimate truth. Being a day late and surviving at Jonestown had left its mark between the eyes of reason. Holy incense, shadowy confessionals, charismatic preaching, faith healing, and gifts of tongues left us suspicious of any pie in the sky theology. Quixote grilled two little pieces of lomito steak and three sausages that were left over from Friday night.

After supper, Lalie read aloud and sobbed her way through Irwin Russell's *Christmas Night in the Quarters*, a story tenderly close to her New Orleans heart. With fireworks popping all along Avenida Lecuna and across the way in the barrios, we went to bed early. Lalie was reading Malamud and I was reading H.L. Davis, and the two of us were reading each other.

On Christmas Day, I woke up my Lalie with several "Merry Christmases." There were smiles of love on her face. She prepared all day for our Christmas dinner. I called Atlanta and talked to Rose and the children, wishing each a merry Christmas. Rose said she had heard that CBS News correspondent Ed Rabel had gone to New York and had asked that the Latin America Bureau be moved to Miami. I said nothing would please me more than to see Big Ed cover the South Shetland Islands, or the South Sandwich Islands, or the Falkland Islands—from Miami.

We talked with the extended families in Mississippi. On our first married Christmas, we opened our presents beneath the tree. Dinner was superb. Lalie cooked Revlon's Christmas gift of ham, and she made the traditional Cumbo/Harvey stuffed mirlitons grown in the side yard of the shotgun house on Navarre Street in New Orleans, where Uncle Jimmy and Aunt Fritz had lived. There were potatoes and shrimp remoulade, apple strudel and ice cream, champagne, and brandy—a feast fit for royalty, our first and last Christmas in Caracas. Scarlett said as long as she lived she'd wear the gold nugget necklace the kindhearted Quixote had brought from Guyana.

The Caracas Bureau was about to be history—shortly after the New Year the administrative function of the bureau would cease, and CBS News would relocate its correspondent to the United States. The cameraman and technician would be left in Venezuela at least for an interim period. CBS probably didn't want to bear the expense of moving Sorensen again if it could be helped. Moving some gnarled veterans of CBS News could be as complicated and expensive as landing on the moon.

I began rereading *Dragon's Teeth*, Upton Sinclair's masterful description of Earth in the years leading to World War II: "*He had traveled here and there over its surface, and everywhere had seen men diligently plowing the soil and sowing Dragon's Teeth—from which, as in the old legend, armed men would someday spring.*"

On Friday, December 29, after my alarm went off at 4:00 a.m., I lay there thinking what my New Year's resolution ought to be. I decided: to have peace at the center and to let my intellect roam free. As the morning wore on there was less and less peace at the center and more and more need of it. Little things seemed to throw me off balance. I stumbled over things. I dropped things. I cursed things. I told myself how stupid that was, because the fault lay with me and no other.

I looked to the future. From this day forth, I was ready to get on with our lives as they were, not as we might wish them to be. I felt a new surge of energy. I felt dignified, proud of myself, courageous, not needing to be shy or defensive.

Fireworks were going off in Caracas as if there were a coup. We went in the evening to Mel and Henry Ackerman's for dinner at their residence overlooking the city. From high up in the hills we watched the fireworks exploding over the length of the valley that is metropolitan Caracas.

Scarlett had begun keeping her own journal. This was her entry for New Year's Eve, December 31, 1978: *I begin here because I feel the events of this particular night bear recording—an absolutely unforgettable occasion in an otherwise despised city. This evening we had been invited to share New Year's Eve with Hank and Mel Ackerman and two other couples.*

By cab, we wound our way up through the higher elevations to Edificio El Cerra at the top of the mountain above Las Mercedes. As 1978 drew to a close, we all went (stumbling, mostly, after so much food and wine) out to welcome 1979 from the quite large patio.

The view of Caracas, spread out far below us as far as we could see both east and west in a myriad of lights, was breathtaking.

This city, which we have damned and cursed for lo these eight months, exploded from all corners with the most fantastic, unbelievable, children's-storybook, mind-bending fireworks display on earth. Caracas has no ban on fireworks and for once we were grateful: rockets, Roman candles, sparklers, firecrackers; three million Venezolanos, and every one of them shooting off something. But all of these rockets and sparklers were nothing compared to those inside me when David kissed me and wished me Happy New Year!

The most unusual, lovely-scary sight was the fragile globos that some enterprising Caraqueños had made—translucent globes made from rice paper and bamboo with a candle in the bottom. When set free, they floated up, up, and up, high over the mountains, the city—and we two, taking our hopes and our hearts with them far away from Caracas to a longed-for little farm on Plum Lick in Kentucky.

I love you, David. Happy 1979—Homeward bound!

We had a quiet lunch together and talked more about our lives beyond CBS. We cooked southern ham, cabbage, and black-eyed peas for New Year's Day dinner, which would become a tradition in years to come.

On the first day back at work in the New Year, I made reservations to Georgetown, Guyana, for one week later—more Jonestown-related legal proceedings. I also made plane reservations for Lalie and me from Caracas to New Orleans for June 2. I had Roberto pick up $3,000 in advance money for the Guyana trip the following Tuesday. When the sun went down, I read aloud passages from *Dragon's Teeth*, and Lalie read some to me.

The next morning Lalie said she had slept like a rock, and I had too, both of us with our share of troubling dreams. *Dragon's Teeth*—its six books, especially "Blood Hath Been Shed"—must have triggered it, and events raced ahead. At the beginning of the New Year, 1979, there was a summit meeting in Guadeloupe attended by President Carter, Britain's prime minister James Callahan, West Germany's chancellor Helmut Schmidt, and France's president Valéry Giscard d'Estaing. Near the end of the month, Pope John Paul II visited Mexico. In Puebla he attended the opening of a meeting of the bishops of South America. The Pope said he believed the future of the Catholic Church lay in Latin America, but the papal belief left CBS News unconvinced that its future was there. The Latin America Bureau was not called upon to help cover the Guadeloupe summit conference or the Pope's visit to Mexico.

The current storm that most fascinated the network television news producers was the return of the Ayatollah Khomeini to Iran. He was another kind of Jim Jones, and some of the rhetoric sounded as extreme:

"I beg God to cut off the hands of all evil foreigners and all their helpers." On February 14, 1979, an armed band of Iranians attacked the United States Embassy in Tehran, and a new storm was forming that would cause most Americans to forget there had ever been a Jonestown.

In the mail was a letter from Dean Ramona Rush at the University of Kentucky. It sounded as if I would be offered a faculty position in what she described as the News and Public Affairs "preference" of a new Department of Telecommunications in the College of Communications. We guessed the starting date would be August 15, 1979. We were wrong. There was a storm subset on which we had not counted—the academic storm. We had no way of knowing that I was still six years from joining the faculty of the University of Kentucky, and we knew nothing about faculty unrest and disagreements that would result in Dean Rush's resignation.

What to do?

We went to a disco so dark John Travolta would have fallen on his face. Lalie was smashingly sensuous to dance with—she was mondo sexy, and as all good coonasses say down in southern Louisiana, we "passa good time." I had my first Scotch of 1979.

I talked on the phone with Latchman Kissoon, my attorney acquaintance in Georgetown, Guyana. He told me the Larry Layton trial would not begin for at least two weeks. He had become a symbol for partial redress of a grievous wrong. After I advised New York of the delay, it became a question of whether we would go to Nicaragua the following day for the first anniversary of the murder of the editor of *La Prensa*, Pedro Joaquín Chamorro Cardenál. Correspondent Ed Rabel and producer Phil O'Connor had been scheduled to go. At the last minute, Roberto realized his visa for Nicaragua had expired. He hurried to the Nicaraguan Embassy to have it updated and then proceeded to lose his passport altogether. In the meantime, New York decided that Rabel and O'Connor would go on as planned. We would become the backup crew, the embarrassing new role of the now "so-called" Latin America Bureau.

Scarlett and Quixote took down the Christmas tree, carefully removing each icicle and ornament however small, and then she broke the tree into manageable pieces, not helping her psyche in the process.

We began to feel low down and mean because new thunderheads were forming over Nicaragua and I might have to leave the following morning. All our little words and little actions went off like little firecrackers in our little faces.

The next morning there was no loving. There were few words between us until Lalie left in a taxi. We said we'd get better. I called Sorensen and suggested that he come in packed and ready to travel if necessary, and he gave me some nonsense about "having a big problem packing" and that he needed to know for sure whether we were going. I told him *I'd* be ready to leave on a moment's notice. "Goodbye." He came in without his bags.

I called Atlanta. Rose had selected Peachtree World of Tennis for the rehearsal dinner for our son Sam's wedding. I suggested to him that he check with the priest and find out for sure whether it was all right for me to be the best man. I had not played by the rules: marriage was one of the seven Sacraments; divorce was forbidden: "let no man put asunder." And so I told my son not to worry about it if the priest objected. After all, a sinner was a sinner.

The trip to Nicaragua was called off. There were riots against higher gasoline prices in Jamaica, and it looked as if we, or somebody, might have to go there. The top labor leader was murdered in Managua, but as yet there was no word on our going there. One of the reasons I wanted to leave CBS News was because so much of what we did was to sit around waiting for another storm to roll out of the sky somewhere. We moved from one violent visual to another.

I was the proud but weary father of two-dozen bouncing baby tomato plants on the balcony overlooking Avenida Lacuna. When Paco came in to pick up the shipping bag, Quixote sadly told him he'd give the tomato plants to him when he left. He didn't say when he was leaving.

After Lalie and I had gone to sleep, the telephone rang. It was Lalie's sister, Cornelia, with the message that Aunt Fritz Harvey was back in the hospital in New Orleans, that she was on a life-support system, in a coma, and not expected to live much longer. Cornelia was in Woodville. Fighting back tears, Lalie sang a belated "Happy Birthday" to her sister, and then she came to bed and let her grief flow. She remembered her last telephone call with Aunt Fritz in which she'd said she was looking forward to summer so she could see her niece and "touch your sweet face."

Next morning, hand in hand, I walked with Lalie to her ride. Then, in my jogging outfit I made a grand circle back to Parque Centrál. I picked up two powdered milk cans and one oil can along the way and used them as new hostels for three more of my babies. I wrote a letter of consolation to Uncle Jimmy in New Orleans. I also wrote a letter to "Little Jimmy," Aunt Fritz's and Uncle Jimmy's only son.

Lalie came home later than usual because she had been involved in a non-injury automobile crash on the autopista. Thank God she wasn't hurt. I made her relax on the couch. I called Woodville to see if there was any new word on Aunt Fritz. When there was no answer I sensed what in all probability had happened. I called the Harvey residence in New Orleans, and Little Jimmy's father-in-law told me Aunt Fritz had died at one o'clock that morning. I tried to comfort Lalie, who said, amid all the tears: "She would have been so pleased, so happy if she could have known I was pregnant."

I looked at her. She returned a look that said: "No, I'm not—not yet."

The funeral would be the following day. Cornelia and Lalie's mother had driven down from Woodville, Uncle Audio and Aunt Louie came down from Jackson, and Uncle C.B. from Key West. The wake was to be until midnight at the mortuary—Shoen's on Canal Street. I went to bed. Lalie came in later. We kissed goodnight.

The next morning, we held each other. Lalie, I knew, felt helpless because she could not be in New Orleans for the funeral. When we called and talked to Uncle Jimmy, I told him I was sorry, that I wished we could be there, and for him to take care of himself. Lalie talked with Cornelia, and her mother came on the phone and said it was just like a Harvey reunion.

I said I had no choice but to book passage to Guyana on Tuesday for the Larry Layton trial, although I hoped I wouldn't have to leave that soon. I had begun reading *CBS: Reflections in a Bloodshot Eye*, the beginning of my personal library of books critical of the "Tiffany Network." The same year that was published, 1975, saw the publication of Sally Quinn's *We're Going to Make You a Star*. Barbara Matusow's *The Evening Stars: the Making of the Network News Anchor* appeared in 1983. Peter McCabe's *Bad News at Black Rock: The Sell-Out of CBS News*, was published in 1987. The following year came Peter J. Boyer's *Who Killed CBS: The Undoing of America's Number One News Network*. Ken Auletta's *Three Blind Mice: How the TV Networks Lost Their Way*, appeared in 1991. The most recent of the genre, Bernard Goldberg's *Bias*, in 2002, almost immediately soared to number 1 on the New York Times Best Seller List.

I called Delia at Candes and requested reservations on the next day's flight to Georgetown. I heard from my contact in Guyana that the Layton trial had been temporarily set for February 14, and the Stephen Jones/Charles Beikman trial would begin in two days. I called New York, and Larry Doyle, who was still sitting in for Brian Ellis, called back and said we were definitely to go.

Lalie and I handled ourselves pretty well on the morning of my leave-taking for Guyana. There were no tears when we kissed goodbye. I had said last night that I wished she could go with me, and she had said she wished she could do so too. I gave the tomato plants a last watering, said goodbye to the pericos, and shuffled off with Paco and the crew to the airport. Wheels were up at 6:50 p.m. for Trinidad and Tobago.

CHAPTER TEN

In the Port-of-Spain in-transit room, Quixote watched a man and his two young adult sons and wondered what our David Charles would look like, be like. How tall would he be? Would he become a doctor or a carpenter? Or would she be a daughter whose name would be Ravy Bradford, named for my great-aunt Ravy Jane? And would Ravy Bradford be tall like her mother? Would she become a doctor or sing in Broadway musicals? Ravy Jane's granddaughter, Maurine Dallas Watkins, had written the original play *Chicago*.

I wished the whole world could be with me to hear the melodies of one man in our transient midst. He had eased over to another traveler who'd been aimlessly picking on a guitar, the stranger in the night quietly asking if he might use it, holding it close, then playing and singing at the top of his voice. He ate out my heart and soul with the words of a father and his son, "When Are You Coming Home, Dad? I Don't Know When, Son."

I thought of my Sam, who was twenty-two at the time and had finished his journalism degree at the University of Georgia. Later I would see a picture of NBC correspondent Don Harris's son, Jeffrey, as he carried the urn containing the ashes of his father following memorial services at First Baptist Church in Videlia, Georgia. I did not want that to happen to me, selfishly I didn't, and I didn't want it to become a fate for any member of my family.

The minstrel had a group of people sitting on the floor around him in the airport terminal. It was an unbidden concert without ticket or program. The songs rolled over us: "There's an Old Crow Sitting on the Cold Stone Fence," "I Do Not Have a Mansion," "Kiss You and Give You Seven Daffodils," "She May be Pepper to You M'Boys, She's Sweet as Sugar to Me," "You're a Living Walking Dream," "He's a Pore Damn Fool, He Never Knew How Much He Had," "All My Life's a Circle, Sunrise and Sundown."

The tall, curly-haired man stopped singing and returned the guitar to the somber man from whom he'd borrowed it. I went up to the stranger who'd sung with such feeling.

"What's your name?" I asked.

"Harry Chapin," he replied.

The troubadour soared away to Antigua and New York, and I, better for having my spirits lifted, took my leave for Georgetown, Guyana. Years later, I read the account of Harry Chapin's fatal car wreck on July 16, 1981. He was only thirty-nine years old when he died; his birthday was celebrated on the same date as my daughter Nell's. I had attended only one of his concerts, the impromptu one he performed in the in-transit room of the airport at Port-of-Spain, Trinidad and Tobago, on January 16, 1979. And he had only two more years to sing.

Today, when I hear Mary Chapin Carpenter, I think of her father and the role he played in convincing me that there are only so many storms to be followed and only so much courage in one human heart. And whenever November 18 comes around, I remember the congressman, the three journalists, and the woman murdered on the Port Kaituma landing strip. Later I would add to my memories ABC correspondent Bill Stewart, executed by a Nicaraguan National Guardsman, and I would think how brave these people were. To me, their deaths represented the insanity of "killing the messenger," and I took renewed faith from the truth that after messengers are killed, more will appear, and truth-seeking and truth-telling will be as Milton said it should be: "...who ever knew Truth put to the worse, in a free and open encounter."

Because of a mechanical problem with our Pan Am 707, we did not leave Port-of-Spain until after 1:00 a.m. on January 17, 1978. The remarkable CBS News artist Howard Brodie was on the flight from New York. We didn't arrive at Timehri Airport until past 3:00 a.m. After the long, jolting ride into Georgetown, it was almost 5:00 before we were checking in at the Park Hotel. I dropped my shoulder bag and suitcase in room 44, slept a short while, and was trudging back out of the room at 7:45 a.m. We got to the courthouse in time for the arrival of Steven Jones and Charles Beikman for what was supposed to be the first day of the preliminary inquiry into the murder charges brought against them. But Rex McKay, chief defense counsel, was absent, and his staff asked for and received a delay.

I had a truly close call at lunch at the airport. I swallowed a chicken bone, and it wedged in my throat—wouldn't go up, wouldn't go down. I thought I would choke to death. Brodie, who made a practice of distributing Heimlich maneuver pamphlets wherever he went, was at the table, but there was no way I could tell him I was dying. Was God talking to me? I was too afraid to move. It was a repeat of the slow motion I had felt in the split second when I was in the cross hairs of the National Guardsman's gun on the street corner in Estelí, Nicaragua.

My life flashed again across my consciousness: there were Eulalie and the courting days on the edge of Lake Mary in Mississippi; and there were Rose and the young married days in Iowa. A burst of frolicsome good old girls and one-night standers soared like shooting stars through a full moon sky. There was my mother running off to be married to my father, who was running from his father's Bible preaching—days of mint juleps, medical school, and early death by laboratory gin. My children appeared with smiling faces, broken arms, and the night the baby rabbits escaped. High school graduations and birthdays returned, and college days reappeared. There was the U.S. Navy, the light cruiser *Manchester*; the Philippine Islands, my first communion as a Roman Catholic, and the young man who violated me as I slept naked in the Long Beach YMCA. There were shreds of WHAS Radio and Television in Louisville, CBS News in Washington, D.C., Atlanta, Caracas, and Georgetown, Guyana.

Something told me to stand up slowly and sneak carefully to the men's room. I looked at myself in the mirror, saw the blanched face, saw the eyes looking back at me. There wasn't time for ten Hail Marys and ten Our Fathers, not a moment to spare for "Bless me father, for I have sinned." My prayer was without words. I turned loose of myself. Let myself go. Almost stopped breathing. I was as ready as I ever would be for divine intervention. And then—it came.

The chicken bone dislodged.

One more time a miracle had happened. After Nicaragua and the Laurel, Maryland, shopping center, it was one of my closest calls. Quixote would not be remembered in the annals of journalism and the Jonestown massacre as the reporter who choked to death on a chicken bone.

Did I fall on my knees and thank God? I did not. Not then. I had work to do. Maybe God would understand.

Howard was still jousting with the bureaucracy as to whether there would be art in the courtroom. I talked briefly with Brian Ellis on the telephone. He said discussions would begin next week on a number of things, including the status of the Caracas Bureau. In the evening, all of us except Roberto went to Latchman Kissoon's house, where there was conversation, rum, ice cream, dressed eggs, and pastry. Little wonder I was sick so often.

We received official word that, after all, Carl and Roberto were to travel with Pope John Paul II in Mexico, so we were leaving for Caracas and they were to go on to Mexico City on Monday. On the flight to Port-of-Spain I talked with my professional colleagues about divorces and rumors of divorces at CBS News. The "world's greatest communicators" were constantly having trouble talking to their wives. After a three and a half hour layover in Port-of-Spain, I was back in Caracas. Scarlett, Quixote, and Sancho Panza went to dinner at Hostel de Castellano and became magnificently smashed.

It was an A1, bountiful Sunday in "Eternal Spring." Never had I found Eulalie lovelier, a good friend with whom to live out my years. I went to the newsstand but was unable to find Saturday's *Miami Herald*—it was ridiculous to have to settle for Friday's paper on Sunday. CBS News in New York could not have functioned for one second if it had had to wait until Sunday to read Friday's *New York Times*.

Roberto came late in the day to prepare for his and Carl's trip to Mexico the following morning. Lalie made spoon bread as I remembered it when I was a boy in Kentucky, perfect steaks stuffed with clams, green beans, and raisin pie with coffee and brandy. We took the television set into the bedroom to watch the Super Bowl, but it was a delayed broadcast and I wished I hadn't heard on the radio that the Steelers had already defeated the Cowboys.

Carl and Roberto headed out for Mexico, and I naturally had some why-ain't-I-going feelings. I knew why I wasn't going. I wasn't a heavy hitter, much less a Big Foot or a superstar. I wasn't quite on the "A" team. I was a flake and a fluke in a place called Caracas, a word that in some parts of Latin America meant "chocolate." As far as I was concerned it might as well have meant old fruitcake. I got even by going out and running a mile in the park of the mahogany trees and felt great, but Lord, what a litter-ridden place Caracas was in 1979. With a clear sense of purpose, I fed and watered the pericos. Lalie brought in a huge pizza, and she suggested that I pick up a six-pack of Zulia beer. We feasted and reminisced.

A year ago, I had told Lalie of the phone call from Bill Small saying that I'd probably be transferred to Venezuela. Today, when I talked to Brian Ellis on the phone, there was nothing more specific about moving the bureau out of Caracas. He said I might be needed any day now "somewhere in the world." I supposed Antarctica was as good a guess as any. I talked to Zeke Segal in the Atlanta Bureau, and he suggested I would be the fall guy for mistakes made in the impossible situation in Caracas. As a child, one of my best-liked stories was the little boy who stuck his finger into the dike to prevent the great flood. Another favorite was the foot soldier who gathered into his chest as many enemy swords as possible in order to create an opening for victory.

After we hiked to Lalie's ride, I did my running in Parque de los Caobas, and I returned to the office feeling refreshed and at peace, although the headline in the *Daily Journal* said "World War III Feared over Mideast." In the space of one month, the shah of Iran had been forced into exile, and a million people demonstrated in the streets of

Tehran for the triumphal return from exile of the Ayatollah Khomeini. Israelis killed forty Palestinians in a raid on Lebanon; and Abu Hassan, the one believed to have planned the 1972 raid on the Israeli compound at the Olympic Games in Munich, was killed by a bomb in Beirut.

Subsets of storms, spin-offs of woe "prowled about the world, seeking the ruin of souls," and the networks deployed their reporting teams like moving chess players on a board emblematic of Earth. I was feeling more like a pawn than a knight, as if I might be my own Sancho Panza.

Even Plum Lick in Kentucky was not safe. If they could come down there and pick young men to fight in Vietnam, they could come anywhere, anytime, take any people and turn them into armed men. With a vengeance I transplanted ten tomato plants—I had thirty-six growing. Then it was time to feed the pericos. The call of the day was to Len Press at Kentucky Educational Television. He told me he'd be talking to Dean Rush that day, that he believed everything was settled at the university, that I would have the position. But wait—the special session of the legislature was still up for grabs and there could be budget cuts resulting in layoffs at KET.

There was good music on the FM radio station in the afternoon, including "Ole Man River." I had almost finished reading *CBS: Reflections in a Bloodshot Eye*, and I told Lalie I was going to be in good company leaving CBS: Edward R. Murrow and Fred Friendly had become leaders of the rats deserting the USS *CBS*. In time, some by retirement, others by dissent, they would be followed by George Herman, Daniel Schorr, Marvin Kalb, Bruce Morton, Bill Moyers, Roger Mudd, Robert Pierpoint, Bert Quint, Ray Brady, John Sheahan, David Schoumacher, Howard K. Smith, Bernard Shaw, Bernard Goldberg, Connie Chung—even Walter Cronkite. Alexander Kendrick, in his 1969 *Prime Time: The Life of Edward R. Murrow*, had summed it up: "Ed Murrow was dead. The Beverly Hillbillies lived on."

I ran twice, each time a little further than the preceding laps, and each time I ran well. I did not run for time but rather for distance. I began running at the foot of the stairs on the mezzanine at Edificio Catuche, and continued to the park, where the next day there would be a carnival for the new president. I ran to the end of the park, turned around, and jogged to the entrance. In the evening I stretched it out to the portable police station, where a Barney Fife "pssssssted" me. I ignored him. He was trying to make me put my jacket back on, so my little pink nipples wouldn't disgrace Caracas. I put the top back on, not wanting to have to explain it in some weekend pokey. With all the littering and spitting on floors in restaurants, all the noise and pollution in the Hell that passed for a city, all the skintight jeans and see-through blouses and every conceivable form of suggestive hot pants on women, with all the skateboards and motorcycles running amuck, I was "pssssssted" for baring my top. Quixote's nipples weren't all that great, and there was no hair on his chest. Give him a break.

In the afternoon, Lalie and I took a stroll in the park. It was a solid mass of people drinking beer and making noise. Scarlett told me two men had pinched her on the buns. So much for a Norman Rockwell ramble in the park on a Sunday afternoon in Caracas. Two months before, Rockwell had died in Stockbridge, Massachusetts. I went out for my second run of the day, again through the park, which by late afternoon was fouler than it had been in the morning. Kids were wading in the pools where beer cans bobbed. Lads and lassies were throwing the cans out into an area that had been gone over once lightly with brooms. The whole park smelled. Venezolanos were simply defiling Earth, and the Copeiano party, which had elected Luis Herrera president, had the cheek to call itself the party of "The Green."

In the morning, after we crossed over the footbridge, I went to the park, the only area for miles around where running made any practical sense, and I ran well, but the park's stench was worse. There was still a little half-hearted raking going on, but no picking up or hauling away of the tons of celebration residue.

January 31, 1979: I was jogging in the park and had an impulse to call Rose and the children. When I returned to the office I placed the call shortly after 7:00 a.m. Atlanta time. Cathy had a new job keeping records and running the office for a cabinetmaker. I reminded her she'd be eighteen soon, and I would be forty-nine. Nell related that her riding instructor had said her legs were getting stronger. On her last report card she had made all A's except a B in biology. Pat, our dog, was fine and was remembering what she'd been taught in obedience school. Debbie had changed jobs. She was going to become a telephone reservationist for Days Inn. I reminded her to keep her résumé up to date. I asked her if she was happy.

"Yes, are you?" she said.

"Yes," I said. I told her I loved her.

Sam told me Laurens Pierce and his wife, Patricia, were going to be the photographers at Sam's wedding. He was doing O.K. as a substitute at WSB-TV. If the priesthood had a problem with me being best man, nothing was said.

Rose and I talked about Sam and Val's wedding present. He wanted a roll-top desk. I agreed with Rose that his suggestion was too expensive and, in any event, too heavy. Rose seemed fine, calm, and confident. She wasn't asking for advice, and I was not attempting to give any. The important thing was that we were talking, reaching out to each other with no strings attached. It was time to get on with our lives.

I jogged with my greatest ease so far. As a bonus I found a big can for one of our tomato plants. I transplanted one of the more promising plants into my newfound treasure. I needed more dirt and more cans. I hadn't heard a peep out of the Foreign Desk in New York. They probably had forgotten I was anywhere in the world. They might have thought I had turned into a penguin and wandered off the ice at Tierra del Fuego.

The Foreign Desk editors were preoccupied with the return of the Ayatollah to Tehran. Millions of his worshipful countrymen greeted him upon his arrival, and Iran had come unglued. Demonstrators did what demonstrators historically do—look for the television camera and crank up their fist shaking and their American flag burning. The Chinese vice premier was touring the United States, the Pope was on his way back to the Vatican after his trip to Mexico, there was a bad winter in the United States, and Nelson Rockefeller had died. Everything that was happening appeared to be happening outside Latin America, where we were having our regular little mudslides, soccer matches, and trifling coups du jour.

Thursday, February 8, 1979. My early morning jog was faster and further and more enjoyable than ever before, for it was nice and cool in the park. I was refreshed when I sat down at the telex and sent a message to the Foreign Desk reminding Brian Ellis that the Larry Layton trial was supposed to begin one week from Monday. By nightfall, I'd had no reply, only notice of a "rate of currency exchange" for all overseas bureaus and a note about scheduling vacations. My reply was to tear up one of my old shirts and tie six tomato plants to the concrete slabs outside our kitchen window. I might as well have been a prisoner with privileges. I made a protective reservation for myself for Tuesday to Guyana just in case New York wanted me to go early to do an advancer, but it was hard to believe that I'd come through Friday without any word of an assignment from the Foreign Desk. By the end of the day there had not even been a reply to my telex concerning Guyana. Probably a case of benign neglect.

On Saturday, at 7:00 a.m., I ran my longest run so far—from the overpass between the Anauco and Caracas Hiltons to the museums, into the park, to the end of it, then a new way over sod, back to the overpass, again to the museums, back into the park, and to the end of it again. It was about two miles.

I lay in bed early Sunday morning, letting thoughts find their own way. I called Len Press in Lexington. He said that in one week we should know whether the legislature had approved budget cuts for KET. My teaching position (two three-hour courses) at UK was firm. If there were budget cuts at KET there would be no opening for me, but maybe later in the year. The teaching position would pay $15,000 a year, but without benefits. We talked over the situation. The crux of the matter was one of simple dollars and cents--$15,000 a year wouldn't pay alimony and child support. Since I was neither Socialist nor Communist, I didn't expect anybody to turn mountains into level playing fields. I was capitalistic, and I understood a little something about taking personal responsibility for myself. After I'd gone to bed and pulled the covers over my head, I woke up resolved to accept whatever was inevitable, to face up calmly to reality, to give my tea leaves a good, hard study.

I began to consider dispassionately the possibility of staying with CBS News—if CBS News would still have me.

Lalie gave me bread to feed the pigeons, the kind with feathers, reddish legs, darting eyes. At the end of the run, I threw out some crumbs, but not even the usually famished pigeons were attracted. They probably distrusted gringo also-rans. I went to Centro Plaza to Candes Travel Agency and picked up my ticket for Guyana the next day. I tried to find a nursery for soil but couldn't do it on foot. I found three more big milk cans for our tomatoes, and sent a query via telex to New York concerning travel to Guyana. Shortly thereafter we received the long awaited official word:

CBS was transferring me to Dallas! It was February 5, 1979, eight months and twenty-six days after arriving in Caracas. There had been the rumors, so it was not a total surprise. John Lane said the Caracas Bureau would be closed and moved to Miami. I asked why I was not going with the bureau, and he said because I was not a "self-starter" and that I had not done "a very good job down there." A cold, wet penguin said there was partial truth in his pronouncement but that it had not been quite that simple.

"Being in Caracas is like being put on a rock with both hands tied behind your back," I frigidly said. "Your best 'self-starter' at CBS would have been in trouble here. The only way I could have done a good job would have been to scream to you people months ago that a Caracas Bureau was goofy. I think you people should give me credit for trying to make it work and suffering with it as long as I did...." Blah...blah...blah.

After I'd spilled my guts, I was told I was "a good correspondent," which sounded a lot like a "good little boy," that it was not my fault Caracas had failed. Whether or not it was my fault was beside the point. It happened on my watch. I had sufficient strength left in me to gather in the swords and take the blame. There was at least one shivering penguin who knew when it was on thinning ice, there were breaking sounds rippling beneath his feet, and he was ready to head for shore.

Guyana was a "go" the next day. I'd be working with Bill Willson again. Lalie called from her office and I told her about John Lane's telephone call. We agreed that going back to Dallas wasn't half bad. Of course, we still hadn't heard the final-final word from Len Press, but it looked as if Camelot on Plum Lick might have to wait a couple of years, maybe longer. Sometimes events can't be controlled exactly the way you'd like to have them. First thing I said to Lalie when I met her at the street corner was: "Pleeeeeze don' throw me inta thet brar paadch."

I was booked on the next day's flight to Guyana. In the morning we lay in each other's arms, telling of dreams of the night just past, talking about Dallas, about things not working out in Venezuela. At the same time, we were grateful that I had been one day late at Jonestown.

After talking to New York I canceled my reservations for Guyana for the day and requested the travel agency to book me for the Saturday flight. Then came a call from New York asking me if I could travel to Georgetown sooner because now somebody wanted an advancer. Damn it to Hell and gone. It was as if I had never sent all those inquiries about going to Guyana for this precise purpose, and now it was back to the travel agency to change the flight plans again. I was also told that correspondent John Sheahan was coming down with Bill Willson and the crew. I had mixed feelings about that. I could detect the sounds of bigger feet. The whole thing upset me so much I wanted to break dishes. Somehow we managed to get through supper, and Lalie noted the possible flights on Friday to Georgetown via Port-of-Spain. We went to bed and I broke my no-drinking rule by having a Ponche Crema and a Crème de Cacao.

Early next morning, I ran even better and farther than before in Parque Las Caobas. I idled my mind and permitted no bad thoughts to come in—I floated. I made it all the way back to the overpass at Avenida Bolivar, and I finished powerfully. As soon as it was nine o'clock I called Delia at Candes and asked her to work on new reservations for me for the next day to Georgetown.

In the morning I gave Paco seven more really nice tomato plants, left notes for Lalie on the refrigerator door, on her pillow, and on the wall across from the john at eye level. I made myself two sandwiches, which I called my $35.00 per diem meal, and Paco drove me to the airport at 11:00 a.m. for the 1:00 p.m. flight to Port-of-Spain.

I spent the afternoon and early evening in the in-transit lounge in the Port-of-Spain airport while awaiting the arrival of Pan Am 227 from

New York. Harry Chapin wasn't there, but I could still hear his song: "When Are You Coming Home, Dad? I Don't Know, Son." I ate the $35.00 lunch I had brought with me from Caracas, and I waited from about 2:00 in the afternoon until 10:00 in the evening, never knowing that a message had been left for me by CBS (at the Pan Am check-in counter, CBS later said) with instructions to keep me off the plane. When I boarded the Pan Am flight to Georgetown, much to my surprise and disappointment, nobody from CBS was on board. I felt downcast and blue. And alone. Very alone.

I had no idea what had gone wrong. But there was nothing to do but remain aboard and ride off into a darkening night. Author Graham Greene was on the plane, but I was too dismayed to try to talk with him about *The Power and the Glory*. I assumed his Catholicism had given up on me a long time ago as one of the true lost causes. We stepped into the terminal at Timehri Airport about midnight, and by that time I had regained most of my sanity.

Any hopes I may have had that the CBSers were already in Guyana were quickly dashed. Thank the Lord, Emerson the driver had come out to the airport for the third night in a row to see if any of us had come in. He said NBC was in town, but that was all. The whole episode was still a mystery. Emerson drove me to the Pegasus, where I thought everybody had reservations. There was none, and no message for me. I checked into room 407, called New York, and the mystery was finally solved. The Larry Layton trial had been postponed one week, and everybody else had been contacted and given the message. I was floored. It was about 2:00 a.m. when I released Emerson, requesting he return at 7:30 a.m. to pick up a mighty lame Quixote and return him to the airport. I would try to confirm booking on the KLM flight at 9:15 to Port-of-Spain, connecting with Viasa to Caracas. I asked Kate Skattebol in New York to send Lalie a message to have Paco meet me at Maiquetía. I tried to go to sleep, but it was a fitful business. I woke up about 6:45 a.m., showered, and checked out. Emerson was on time. Sam, the older driver, was up and around, and I gave him a chocolate bar, and I gave the other two bars to Emerson. I made the flight O.K. and fortunately was able to get a seat on the Viasa flight out of Port-of-Spain to Caracas. Good old

Sancho Panza was waiting for me, all bright-eyed (with dollar signs) and finger-popping. He was a damned good man, and I was lucky to have him on my side.

"Ah! Don't die, Master, but take my advice and live many years, for the foolishest thing a man can do in this life is to let himself die without rhyme or reasons, without anybody killing him, or any hands but melancholy's making an end of him." So Miguel de Cervantes's Sancho advised Quixote.

Saturday, February 10. After placing a number of calls I finally got through to Len Press. The special session of the Kentucky Legislature had ended without hurting the KET budget, but Len said he could not at this time make any public declarations concerning my hiring because of "some changes" that were being made. I told him that CBS was reassigning me to Dallas, and that I had no choice but to go through with it. There was no way I could be without income for an indefinite time, no matter how short it might be.

Lalie and I exchanged Valentine cards. It was my day of days for jogging—I ran an estimated three miles in the morning and four miles in the afternoon. I began dismantling the collage I had stuck up over my desk—the airline baggage tags, the cocktail napkins, the matchbook covers, the motel keys. Sorensen and Moreno had sent a message that they were returning from Mexico City on Saturday.

I spoke with New York and was told the time had come to contact May Wong at CBS concerning the details of our move. Robert McCarthy called from Business Affairs and instructed me to see the attorneys before leaving for Guyana (to sign the bureau's termination-of-lease papers). We were actually closing down Apartamiento 4-M, Edificio Catuche, Parque Centrál, Caracas 101, Venezuela S.A.

My alarm went off at 5:00 a.m. Paco came to the door about 7:30, and we rode with him to Revlon. Then I was on my way with Paco to the lawyers' office in Central Plaza, where I signed the bureau lease-termination papers. I also turned over the telex and beeper agreements. Traffic was heavy going back to the office. I gathered up my things and headed for the airport to make the 1:00 p.m. flight to Port-of-Spain.

I sat beneath the large banyan tree in front of the Port-of-Spain airport, and time passed pleasantly until Pan Am 227 came in from New York. I boarded, and we took off on the last leg to Guyana. We rolled in at the usual midnight hour, and the smiling face of Sam Muhamad was there to greet me. After a smooth passage through immigration and customs, we were on our way down that long, potholed, smelly road to Georgetown.

At the Pegasus there was a welcome message from producer Bill Willson telling me he'd meet me for breakfast by the hotel swimming pool in the morning. I went to bed and to sleep and was back up in time to meet Bill, Clarence Gibbons, Ray Bribiesca, and Howard Brodie. NBC had been in Guyana for a week and had been to Jonestown and already had it on the *Today Show*. Willson had been unable to make arrangements for a Jonestown trip in the short time he had available. NBC had had a rough time of it, including running out of fuel and having to make an emergency landing in their small plane. Willson and I tried to nail down the ground rules for Monday's opening of the trial of Larry Layton. Mr. Barnwell, who was in charge of the Supreme Court premises, explained how far the cameras would be allowed—no further than the gate and the public street. Willson wanted to find the prosecutor, Nandrom Kissoon. After we tried everything else, I suggested we contact his brother, Latchman. We ran him down in his office, and there was brother Nandom. Paydirt!

We went to a back room where we hit upon exclusively that a plea bargain had been struck. The net effect was: the state would not prosecute on the murder charge in connection with the deaths of Congressman Leo Ryan, NBC correspondent Don Harris, NBC cameraman Bob Brown, *San Francisco Examiner* photographer Greg Robinson, and Patricia Parks. Willson in short order recognized that we should get this on the air the same day rather than wait until Sunday because we expected Monday's trial to last only a short while. Bill advised John Sheahan not to come down the next day as planned. We talked to Stanley Moore, one of the defense attorneys, and confirmed that the deal with his client was agreeable. We fed my voicers over the telephone to New York, one for TV and one for radio. We had a solid beat on NBC and ABC.

There was a "Tradewinds Show" at the pool at the Pegasus, and we attended. We invited Stanley Moore and his wife and Emerson and his wife. There were thirty-five "boys" in a steel band, making pans sound like Heaven. The leader of a separate musical group had written a song called "Brother Jones": "He tell 'em jump, they jumpin'…he tell 'em bump, they bumpin'…he tell 'em blink, they blinkin'…he tell 'em drink, they drinkin'."

The crowd danced happily to the haunting words on a moonlit night, three months almost to the day after the Jonestown massacre. Willson, the crew, Brodie, and I were smiling. We knew it would be only minutes after the end of the CBS Saturday *Evening News* that "rockets" from New York would be arriving for the NBC and ABC news teams because they did not have the story. We watched them, grinned at them, joked with them, and waited for the telephone calls. They came. Big time they came. The "rockets," the "sweat-seeking missiles" had landed, and the competition was no longer smiling, but we were, grandly. It was a small victory, but it sure felt good after so much that had gone so wrong.

I jogged along the Georgetown seawall. A few families were out there, splashing around in the filthy brown water. I felt good because after *Saturday Evening News* aired our exclusive report, *Sunday News* decided it wanted a feed, so I did an interview with Madame Minister of Information Shirley Field-Ridley. The day before I had interviewed prosecutor Kissoon. I did a standupper for *Sunday Evening News* and another for *Monday Morning*. With Bill Willson we took our pool charter corporate jet to Barbados. Joe and Mary Ann Carroll were waiting for us at the Cable and Wire office near Bridgetown. I remembered being in Barbados in the early '70s, when I went over to the loveliest and greenest of islands, St. Vincent, to cover a volcano rumbling, heaving up smoke and fire. Both *Sunday News* and *Morning News* decided, after all our efforts, to pass. We had shot ourselves in the foot, more or less, by the previous day's exclusive. The broadcasts were crowded with the China-Vietnamese storm, not to mention Iran. I went to dinner with Willson and the Carrolls at Alexandra's, where there was good atmosphere and not much else—like a location for a junior prom party of the '40s, but Glenn Miller and all the kids decided not to show up. Willson and I returned to the airport and rode the jet back to Georgetown, arriving about midnight at the Pegasus. I looked at myself in the mirror and said to myself that I did look a little older but that it was certainly nothing to worry about. I still felt younger than I had twenty years before.

I had set my alarm for 5:00 a.m., but I could not even consider running. Willson wanted to roll away from the hotel at 7:30. The Layton trial was scheduled to begin at 9:00, and we wanted to be at the Supreme Court building in ample time to pick off whatever fleeting picture we could of Larry Layton. It turned out to be not much. Our camera malfunctioned when the open truck appeared with the defendant, and all we saw and taped was a fast walkabout on the upper porch of the century-old wooden building. Right away it was apparent there was going to be a lot of last-minute bargaining, the end result of which was that Layton reversed field and pleaded not guilty on all charges. Rex McKay, the chief attorney for the defense, then asked for a postponement "to bring in psychiatric witnesses from New York," and the judge granted an adjournment until February 28. We did quickie interviews with the defense and the prosecution, fed radio, did a standupper, raced to the airport, and took the charter to Barbados. We fed a piece to *Cronkite* and a separate offering to *Morning News*, including the "Brother Jones" song. Willson and I signed in at the Hilton. I bathed and then went with Willson and the Carrolls to the Pisces on the cusp of the waters of the Caribbean, a sumptious setting with ambrosial food, first and foremost the island delicacy, flying fish.

Lalie gave her notice to Revlon de Venezuela and discovered that she would be recommended for a consultancy for Revlon International—for all of Latin America. She would be based in Dallas, and I was proud.

I checked out of the hotel, took the cab early to the airport, and checked in more than two hours before departure time of Viasa 981 to Caracas. I picked up birthday and anniversary presents for Scarlett—a made-in-England porcelain egg-coddler set and a replica of the first map of Barbados done in découpage. I also picked up a bottle of Old Grand Dad, took to the air on the first leg to Trinidad and Tobago, napped along the way, wrote in my journal, and worked on my expense account. I had benefited greatly much from Bill Willson on the trip. He had helped me to regain a measure of confidence, which had been spiraling downhill. I had sent specific instructions via New York not to have Paco meet me at Maiquetía in order to save CBS at least a little money, but when I stepped off the plane, there he was, grinning from ear to ear.

The landlord came by the office and signed the bureau termination-of-lease papers. I wanted to be entirely prepared for my first morning with Sorensen in quite some time. He was a man without a bureau, and Quixote was a man without a continent. We talked briefly and then I headed over to Centro Plaza to deliver to the CBS attorney the signed and sealed bureau lease-termination papers.

I was stunned, but I shouldn't have been surprised to hear it: Mr. Evans, the attorney, said he had done everything he could from the beginning to persuade CBS *not* to open a bureau in Caracas. He said he had told them it was next to impossible to operate in and out of Venezuela. But CBS had insisted: "Our people have done this sort of thing before; they'll be O.K." I picked up the crews' and my tickets for Georgetown on Monday and returned to the office.

The honeymooners were as relaxed as if they were floating on air. If we could just put about three more weeks behind us we'd be getting out of this hellhole. Maybe it wouldn't be going directly to Kentucky the way we had hoped, but one day we surely would, and until that day came, Texas would have to do just fine.

In the mail there was the nicest present a father could ever receive for his birthday—a sweet card from Nell and Cathy, a note from Nell with news of Pat, who had been lost for a night but had been found, and a marvelous letter from Cathy. She enclosed two enlarged impressionistic photographs, which she had composed with her camera, developed, and printed herself. The pictures were of herself and Nell. To me, they were priceless treasures.

I took inventory of all CBS property, other than electronic gear, and sent it in a telex to New York. I figured that the crew and I definitely would be going to Guyana the following Monday. The Layton trial was beginning to look like my last story as the CBS Latin America correspondent.

Later, when we returned to Port-of-Spain, the crew and I met Howard Brodie, who had again come down from New York. We continued together to Georgetown, where we did our midnight tap dance skirmish through immigration and customs.

Tuesday, February 27, 1979. I did not get a restful sleep because of the time change and the need to be up early to go to the airport to see off Jim Jones's natural son, Stephen, on Pam Am 228 to New York. We did an exclusive interview with him, and I thought it was rather good, but there was no charter available to take it to Barbados or anywhere else for that matter, so I was stuck with our little exclusive because there still was no satellite uplink from Guyana. I couldn't even feed any actuality to radio because the quality was distorted by background noise. It occurred to me that if the same story had appeared on the front page of the *New York Times* and I had not had it, CBS would have done a war dance of which Geronimo would have been proud.

I was up early to feed an all-purpose report to the *World News Roundup* and then, accompanied Brodie, Sorensen, and Moreno, to head to Guyana's Supreme Court for the long- and painfully-awaited start of the Larry Layton trial for conspiracy to kill Congressman Ryan. The trial had a jerky beginning. The brilliant, flamboyant, wily defense attorney Rex McKay moved to have the judge disqualify himself. Denied. McKay argued that the defense had not had time to prepare its case. Denied. He sought to prove a procedural error at the magisterial level, and on that one he seemed to have hit a promising vein of gold, the net effect of which was adjournment until the next morning so that the judge and the prosecutor could think about it. The judge reminded me of one of the Seven Dwarfs—Sleepy, or maybe Dopey. It was definitely the most entertaining show in town.

I had a decent night's sleep. There was much rain during the night and the tide from the Demerara River was running high again. Next day

I rode to court with Emerson, who got me a soggy egg sandwich and two cups of hot black coffee. It was a blithering roadrunnerday in court. I wrote in my reporter's notebook: "This is tomfool nonsense." The argument in court was whether the DPP, Director of Public Prosecution, had "sent" or "caused to be sent" the order to transfer Layton's case from the Port Kaituma Magisterial District to the Georgetown Magisterial District. "A very novel point...my learned friend's fascinating and subtle argument...a substitution of the indefinite article to the definite article." After more "novel" arguments, the judge announced he would rule next Wednesday, March 7, on whether there had been a procedural error.

I would not be around in Guyana for final decisions on procedural errors. Charles Beikman was later sentenced to prison. Larry Layton was acquitted in Georgetown, and a subsequent trial in the United States ended in a hung jury. After this, I lost track of him.

Friday, March 2, 1979. Go-home day. I had a good night's sleep and was up before my alarm went off to be ready to leave for the airport. My bags had been packed before I went to bed, ready to go at a moment's notice, like every good fireman, every good soldier, every faithful jack-in-the-box, every humming yo-yo. It was raining when Emerson and I pulled away from the Pegasus to go to Timehri. It was dark as sin, and there was not sufficient electrical power in the car to turn on the lights, or to blow the horn, or to listen to Ronnie Millsap on the tape deck, or to use the windshield wipers except now and then. Of all the conveniences, Millsap made the most sense. It was a rain-slick road, made all the scarier with the driving on the left side. We made it, but only after stalling and replacing the battery along the way. It was a generous slice of Third World life.

We took the Suriname flight to Port-of-Spain and connected with BWIA to Caracas. At Maiquetía, Roberto was arrested for climbing upon the baggage carousel to prevent $100,000 worth of electronic television equipment from being damaged by falling, as all baggage had to, and crashing into a steel wall. He was released with a warning.

Saturday, March 3, 1979. An important letter came in from Len Press. We had a crystal clear picture of where we stood insofar as

Kentucky Educational Television was concerned: We didn't have a leg to stand on. Len seemed reluctant to say what he really felt—that there was little justification for bringing me on board. Our friendship went back a long way, and he'd be willing to help bail me out of CBS, but it wouldn't wash. We were supremely fortunate that I still had my job and that the company had agreed to move us to Dallas. Revlon had asked Lalie to come to New York after our return to the States. She had worked really hard in Caracas and had earned the respect of the international office in New York. Soon she would inherit all of Latin America, and I promised to buy her new clothes.

President Carter had announced he was going to the Middle East, so Vice-President Mondale's recently announced trip to South America seemed in doubt. But the big downer for me was the news from New York that Sorensen could have the CBS Latin America Bureau office furniture, all new, including the safe, to be sold, given away, whatever.

My son Sam called to say he had been hired by the CBS affiliate in Lexington, Kentucky. It was Debbie's twenty-first birthday, and I was not there to watch her blow out the candles. I had missed many such occasions, and it dug deeply into my bank account of guilt feelings. In the other real world, I closed our personal Banco Mercantíl account, and in the afternoon the crew and I were wheels up via Aeropostal for Maracaibo in northwestern Venezuela, the country's principal oil exploration and export center. We were enterprising a status report for *Evening News*, but we weren't laying any bets on our success. At least the flight was smooth and pleasant.

I lay in bed, relaxing and thinking about letting the dead past bury its dead, even believing myself to be divine, protecting my health, loving Lalie simply and sweetly. I turned down breakfast with Carl to give the day a better chance to start. I checked out of the hotel and sat in the lobby and began writing the Venezuelan oil story. It seemed important in the midst of the global oil shortage. Typical television viewers had other priorities. I sat next to a couple of gringo tourists moaning about how they should have packed their bags before the lights went out the night before because maybe that way the cockroaches wouldn't have decided to hitchhike.

At eight o'clock our contacts from the Maracaibo branch of the Office of Information and Tourism picked us up at the hotel and drove us on the approximately one and a half hour trip to the Maroven Company's operation on the southeast side of Lake Maracaibo. A boat was waiting to take us out so we could have footage of the oil well rigs. I thought it would have saddened Lalie to see what companies like her former employer Sun Oil had built, and what the Venezuelan government had taken away from oil companies like them in 1975. If the Venezuelans were so smart, why didn't they do the job themselves from the beginning? If we were so smart why didn't we look for more oil in the United States? I worked on the script off and on all day and almost had it finished by the time we landed back at Maiquetía.

Sorensen and Roberto were to leave as soon as possible for Iran. Vice President Mondale was not visiting Brazil, as previously anticipated. I was to provide protective coverage for Mrs. Mondale, who was coming instead, and I would provide protective coverage when she stopped in Venezuela. Quixote couldn't have been given a nicer present. I completed the script for the oil advancer, recorded it with Roberto, and Paco dispatched it to be sent out on the following morning's Pan Am flight to New York.

Thursday, March 8, 1979. I turned over the combination and the keys to the safe to Carl, who also wanted the office equipment trucked out to his apartment. After he left, we asked Roberto and Paco to stay for hot dogs. It was an agreeable last evening together.

We were in the final, dying throes of the bastard Caracas Bureau.

Friday, March 9, 1979. Saying farewell to Roberto was not difficult because I knew I'd most probably see him somewhere again sometime— maybe on some street corner in Central America, maybe some evening when he was again sharing an abundance of laughter and Russian caviar. I had considered going out to jog to avoid Sorensen, but I didn't. I shook his hand and wished him a safe trip and good pictures. He had his usual smile to the end. If Will Rogers could like all network television cameramen, then Will Rogers was as crackbrained as I suspected he was. Carl and Roberto went out the door, the iron security gate clanged shut, and I would not see them again until the civil war in El Salvador, three years later.

Paco picked up the credentials for Monday's presidential inauguration, and he and Quixote would go together—Paco who would have made an excellent president of the country. Then I would go to Channel 8 in case my voice was needed for the *Evening News*. It wasn't.

Paco and Quixote went to the Gran Salon of the Caracas Hilton to watch as President-elect Herrera formally announced his ministers. I retreated to Apartamiento 4-M, recorded an inauguration folderol spot, and fed it to radio in New York. Lalie and I went to the swimming pool at the Caracas Hilton. There was not much sun. She was reading *Gulag Archipelago* and I was reading *Caine Mutiny*—the U.S.S. *Caracas* was beyond damage control.

Unborn child, I wrote in my journal, *your mother and father want you. Surely it won't be too much longer until you have your life. We promise to love you and be good and sweet to you. We want you to have a brother, Sam, and three sisters, Deborah, Catherine, and Nell. One day, we want you to know Rose."*

We fell asleep.

I had an impulse to call the U.S. Embassy concerning the arrival of Joan Mondale. I had second thoughts about ignoring it. I rode to Maiquetía on the embassy bus, and after our arrival I snoozed during the long wait for Air Force II. There was a jam-up of incoming planes carrying dignitaries and much confusion. Mrs. Mondale took a shortcut to a spot just inside Terminal Nacionál and said her "I'm so glad to be in your beautiful country" remarks (translated for her by her seventeen-year-old son). Then she headed into Caracas in a small motorcade. I knew I had sunk to the pits by my assignment to cover the wife of the vice-president, nice lady though she doubtless was. Martin Roman and I and a few other embassy people rounded up the spaghetti of unused microphone and speakers, piled them into canvas bags, loaded them into a station wagon, and headed back to Caracas. They dropped me off on the shoulder of the autopista, and like a wetback on the Rio Grande border, I squeezed through a hole in the chainlink fence, then crossed back over the autopista on the footbridge to return to Apartamiento 4-M. I called New York to tell them that Mrs. Mondale had arrived safely. The voice on the other end said, "Arrived where?"

Don Quixote bit his tongue.

Since it was inauguration day, Caracas was almost a bearable city because schools and many businesses were closed. The Caraqueños had fled to the beaches, and those who could afford it headed for Miami Beach. Caracas without people became a joy of sorts.

I was determined to show Scarlett a good time in the evening. We ate prawns, salad, mushrooms, and cake, and topped it off with coffee. Later, we snuggled on the couch and had a before-bed brandy. We read from my journals for this date, March 13, 1979, then 1978, 1977, and 1976. We talked about how happy we were.

I went to Candes and bought our tickets to the United States, Delta to New Orleans on Saturday, March 31. I called in Paco because there were several things I wanted him to do: first of all, to try to figure out a way to get permission to take our pericos to the United States. Stupid idea. Paco and I transported the last of the plants to Revlon, where Lalie distributed them.

While the office was giving Lalie a birthday- and going-away party, Paco and I ran around town trying to find giant-sized hot dogs and giant-sized buns. We finally succeeded, but only after talking the people at Le Drugstore into selling us some of the buns they used for their footlong monsters. We found some nearly perfect tomatoes at a street vendor's stand, large potatoes at another market, a big cake at a bakery, candles at another place, cold Zulia beer, and mayonnaise. Paco and I fixed us a little lunch at the apartment. Then I set up the dining room table and put out our best china.

Lalie opened the door, leaned against the iron security gate, and broke into tears. She said everybody had been so good to her at the office. They had given her a tailor-made caftan. My little birthday supper turned out well. When we extended our hands across the table to say the blessing, I surprised Lalie by holding in our palms the CBS belt buckle I'd brought back from Guyana. After supper I brought in the birthday cake with thirty-four candles burning, and I sang Happy Birthday to Scarlett. Then I brought her the gifts I had bought in Barbados, and last of all, her gift-wrapped one-way ticket to New Orleans.

I did not run on the morning the packers of Clover International came. Paco was there, and piece by piece, article by article, one more time, all our worldly possessions were wrapped and put into boxes. The men would return the next morning to complete the job. We were in a quandary still as to what to do about our little friends, June and July. We were thinking we might have no choice but to leave them in Caracas, but Quixote had not quite given up. Lalie worked extremely hard all day, and I insisted that she come to the park with me. While I jogged, she sat on the edge of one of the flower pools, reading Steinbeck's *Pastures of Heaven.*

I ran about four thousand meters. I was eight pounds short of my one hundred and fifty-pound goal. Lalie stayed away from Revlon in order to supervise the final packing. Each leather-bound book received special attention. The packers did not finish. Their two and a half-hour lunch may have had something to do with it. They would return a third day.

We received word that Vice-President Mondale was arriving in Caracas on Friday for a twenty-four hour visit, and we were invited to a reception given in his honor at the U.S ambassador's residence. Later we cooked a steak and baked two big potatoes for supper among the moving boxes. We made a picnic spread on top of the editing table, and there we ate one of our last suppers in Apartamiento 4-M.

Next day, the mover cleaned out the office/apartment and left me looking at the four walls. I began sweeping. Lalie came home to rooms stripped bare. I tried to console her and only partially succeeded. I was wondering how it was going to be, working in the Dallas Bureau, still following storms throughout the southeast, Central and South America, the Caribbean, and the Middle East. I told myself that maybe I could last out the final two years of my contract. I was tired in spirit as well as in body, and I didn't know how much longer I could cope with being a cannon fodder correspondent—the one who never folded his underwear and put it into a regular bedroom dresser, the Quixote who sacrificed birthdays, anniversaries, national holidays, the one willing to prance into whatever storm appeared, describe it, and slog back out of it again.

Vice-Pres. Mondale and his small party came in from Brazil. Paco drove to Revlon to pick up Lalie and bring her home. By telephone she asked me if I had "felt anything." I said, "No." There'd been a 5.5 reading on the Richter scale. She said desks had moved in the Revlon office and that some workers were crying. If God had decided to destroy Caracas like Pompeii, the worst part was, I'd have to cover the story. Without a bureau I would have had to report it, and I would have been a naked Moses on the mountaintop one more time. But there was little damage and the tremor didn't bring down any buildings. How ironic that with only one week till we'd be going home we would tap-dance with an earthquake. I fed my radio pieces, bathed, and dressed and was waiting for Lalie's and Paco's return from Revlon. Traffic was its usual Friday worst and even more so because of the heavy rain that accompanied the tremors in the eastern part of the city. We were able to leave on time for the home of Ambassador Lewis and the reception for Vice-President Mondale. It was a churning of the elite of Caracas in a setting high above all the problems of the city. What in reality were miserable barrios looked like stardust strewn by Melville's Cosmic Joker.

Vice-President Mondale came over, looked at the lights, and I allowed the opportunity to introduce him to Lalie to slip through my fingertips. The three of us should have stood together, and I should have said, "Mr. Vice President, Señor, those sparkling lights you see? Scattered like heavenly dust? Well, take it from Don Quixote, they're not what you think. You are looking at dragons' teeth, Señor, and from them armed men will arise, will arise. Innocent people will die, will die. Mr. Vice-President, yes, they will evermore die. Promises will remain unkept, will not be fulfilled. Please do something to stop it. But, excuse me, I realize there's nothing that you or I can do. I apologize for speaking in this untoward way."

The vice-president moved on quickly to a state dinner with President Herrera at Miraflores. Lalie and I swam a good distance in a river of Scotch. Paco brought us to the CBS office, and Scarlett and Quixote fell asleep one more time on the bare floor of Apartamiento 4-M.

Paco and I drove the short distance to the Caracas Hilton and waited for Mondale's motorcade to go to La Cason, the official presidential residence. While the vice-president had breakfast with former president Pérez, I sat in the coffee shop, ate a piece of papaya, and drank espresso. I doodled in my reporter's notebook: "Now, let's see—I will keep myself young all my life long. When I am eighty years old, only thirty-one years from now, I will have my brain functioning clearly and my heart beating in good health. I will be relaxed and unafraid of dying." There'd be no way of knowing that in only twenty-one years I'd be battling prostate cancer and in a few years more I'd be facing total impotence.

I went with the motorcade to La Casona where, after Mondale's final meeting with Herrera, there was a news conference. I recorded good sound, and then we hurried to Maiquetía for the liftoff of Air Force II, and I talked passionately to the rising plane: "Come on, Baby, get your ever loving wheels up and off the ever-loving runway, but whatever you do, PLEASE don't crash into the frigging mountains or the Caribbean Sea. Please get out of here, safely. Pleeeeease don't let there be a storm in the Bermuda Triangle, because Quixote might have to put on a diver's suit and go down there with Sorensen or somebody and take a close look at it."

This done, my formal duties were finished as the Latin America correspondent for CBS News.

It rained. We napped. Lalie read *Pastures of Heaven*. I went to CADA and returned with baloney, cheese, crackers, smoked oysters, and a bottle of J & B. At the Caracas Hilton we spent the evening in room 1328 playing gin rummy. We went to bed early and enjoyed being off the bare floor of what used to be the CBS News Latin America Bureau.

Las Pasturas de Ciego had brought me up from my miseries. I thought that in important ways, Steinbeck was a better writer than Hemingway because Papa seemed to revel in the simple act of being "Papa" and to be on a monumental ego trip, whereas Steinbeck had a touch as light as a feather and as sure as a whistling wind. I put on my running clothes but did not run. I went to the office to be sure the safe was O.K. We had about $13,000 in hard cash to handcarry to the United

States. I went to the attorney's office to sign my declaration of taxes. I took Lalie hers for her signature. She had about Bs3,000 coming to her and I had about Bs700 coming to me—a total of about $800. The attorney said that if we were fantastically lucky we might get it back in seven or eight years, without interest. In 2002, we were still waiting. What a way to run a country. So, O.K. Caracas, keep the frigging Bs3,700 and feed somebody.

I was persuasively advised not to try to hand-carry June and July into the states. I gave them to Paco. I cleaned out the refrigerator, giving some things to Paco, bringing the rest to our room at the Caracas Hilton. I went to the lobby to await Lalie's return. We went up to 1328 and ate some of the leftover birthday cake.

Thursday, March 29, 1979. I put on my jogging clothes and zipped up the $13,000 to go with me. My money belt resembled a well-fed anaconda. I was a mugger's merriest dream, but I didn't know what else to do with the cash I was required to take with me to the United States. I was too paranoid to put the money into hotel security. After I saw Lalie off to work for the next-to-last time, I went to Parque Las Caobas and ran two and a half miles. I went to Edificio Catuche one more time. In the mail was the official memo from Bud Benjamin at CBS News in New York announcing "with great pleasure" that the Caracas Bureau was being shut down "next month," that I was being reassigned as a correspondent to the Dallas Bureau, that Sorensen would continue to live in Caracas, and that Ed Rabel would be the new Latin America correspondent—"his base of operations to be announced at a later date."

For about thirty seconds Quixote lay on the bare floor and stared at the ceiling.

I put the memo away and its content out of my mind. I packed up the last of our odds and ends in three boxes, swept the place out, hauled out the last tomato plant, did a little more cleaning up in the kitchen, walked out, closed the door, turned the key, and never looked back.

I had a couple of drinks waiting for Lalie. I spotted her from the balcony as she made her way from the Anauco Hilton to the Caracas Hilton, and I was standing in the doorway when she stepped off the elevator. We had our drinks together after toasting ourselves. An old Abbott and Costello movie was on. The only thing in English was Johnny Mack Brown singing.

It was Saturday.

I put on my jogging clothes and went to Parque Las Caobas for the last time. I ran two and a half miles. My feet felt as light as wings.

By 1:00 we were on our way to Maiquetía. Paco was driving, and he must have been hurting. I saw it in his face through the rearview mirror. Lalie took one quick look back at the city just before we vanished into the first tunnel. Little did she know that in as few as four months she'd return to Caracas on her first trip as Revlon International's new Director of Retail Services for Latin America and the Caribbean. Without even thinking about it, I didn't look back, although I knew I couldn't shake the dust of the dragons' teeth off my shoes.

We were first in line at the Delta ticket counter four hours before the ETD of flight 955. After checking in we went to a restaurant for cervezas for Lalie and Paco. At 3:45 we cleared immigration, and soon the Delta DC-8 came in for its landing. We sat talking with Paco during the last moments in Caracas, and I tried to make him feel good, but I knew it wasn't going to be easy. In his own way he had struggled valiantly to help me be a Latin America correspondent. He had been infinitely patient with my unforgivably atrocious Spanish, but I would remember one word he had taught me—"tranquílicese"—which in Venezuelan vernacular is shortened to "tranquilo," meaning, "calm yourself" or "easy now." He had been a fiercely determined competitor in the battle of the traffic in Caracas, making all his airport runs without once missing a news shipment. He had endured Carl with a patience that could have withstood the fiercest Viking. He worshiped Lalie and was awed that any woman could be so tall.

It was time to board our plane.

When Lalie kissed Paco he stood as tall as he could in his elevated shoes. He was wearing the same black leather jacket he had had on when I first saw him. He still wore the cap that concealed his baldness. We embraced.

He cried. Lalie and I proceeded down the ramp, turned and waved, and Paco waved back. It was done. It was over.

We took our seats in the rear of the jet, and we felt the engines' roar. We were leaving several minutes earlier than scheduled. We kissed as the wheels left the ground. "O dragons' teeth, have you been sown again? Will you be in perpetuity? How foolish," Quixote thought, as we headed up the Caribbean to New Orleans.

We saw the lights of the oil rig platforms in the Gulf of Mexico, then the Louisiana coastline, and finally the unfolding brilliance of New Orleans. We kissed again when the wheels of the DC-8 touched down at Moissant Airport (later renamed for Louis Armstrong). We were, bless Pat, once more in the United States, and a short time later we had our feet on the railing of the oyster bar at Felix's on Iberville Street. We each had three dozen, the first ones slurped quickly from the shell, the others dipped slowly and sensuously in catsup, horseradish, lemon juice, hot sauce, salt and pepper, and decked out on crackers. We toasted each other with frosted mugs of beer.

Before we left New Orleans we visited St. Louis Cathedral on Jackson Square, where Lalie's Kentucky ancestors were married in 1840. No one saw us there. No one knew who we were. Only God. We went together to the rows of candles by the side of the sacristy. We each lit a candle, knelt, and prayed. We acted from love. We were not Roman Catholics, but we were true catholics in the sense of universality and the inclusiveness of mankind.

Our prayers were offered in memory of the five who had died at the Port Kaituma airstrip. We also prayed for Jim Jones and the more than nine hundred people who had died at Jonestown. We prayed for the innocent children who had died there. In only a few months we would be praying for ABC correspondent Bill Stewart.

In fifteen years we would be praying for the children burned to death at the Branch Davidian cult's compound outside Waco, Texas.

In twenty-two years, we would be praying for the thousands killed in the terrorist attack on the World Trade Center in New York.

CHAPTER ELEVEN

From 1979 to 1982, in the CBS News Southwest Bureau, there were many storms, and I followed most of them. I had wished to return to Kentucky in 1979 to live the simpler life of a writer, farmer, and teacher, but the Storm Creator had other ideas. There were hurricanes Frederick and David. The deposed shah of Iran was flown into San Antonio. Iranian students became news during the long hostage crisis in Tehran before the return of the hostages to the United States. There were the space flights of Columbia; Wayne Williams and the Atlanta murders; the royal wedding of Prince Charles and Lady Di; riots in Liverpool; and violence in Belfast. President Reagan was almost assassinated. Tornadoes touched down in and around the Southwest, the most devastating of these destroying much of Wichita Falls, Texas, my first assignment in my new CBS News bureau.

During the same period, Lalie worked for Revlon International. Every other week she commuted to Dallas from New York, except when she was gone on extended trips to the Caribbean or Central and South America. We had a small cottage on Flowerdale Lane in Dallas and an apartment on East 52nd Street in New York. We were examples of nontraditional married careerists, happy in our work and with ourselves. Time frames were not so much warped as compressed, so that each kiss was one to remember, each meeting at the airport a clock-stopping event.

One time, when she was returning from Argentina after a month away from me, I met Scarlett at Moissant Airport in New Orleans with a five-piece Dixieland jazz band I'd hired from the French Quarter to be at the gatehouse when she stepped inside. This was before the days of strict security, and a man said to me, "Who's the celebrity coming in?"

"My wife," I replied.

When she appeared, the band struck up "Hello Dolly" and blew into "When the Saints Go Marching In." Scarlett and Quixote trucked in front of the musicians, led by the local coroner, through the concourses to the main terminal. Those were the days of unfettered glory. We went straight away to Felix's on Iberville and had our traditional three dozen each at the oyster bar.

In 1982, Lalie decided it was time to come in off the road, to stop being a careerist from New York to Buenos Aires. She came to Flowerdale Lane to start our own family. She was sure she wanted to have a child. But 1982 was the year in which I would follow more storms than ever before. They were violent, and again I came close to "buying the farm." This time—El Salvador and Beirut.

We joined the congregation at the Episcopal Cathedral in Dallas, adding some foundation stones to the structure of our then basically unchurched selves. Still, we were leery of any preaching about "ultimate truth." After Jonestown, we'd not be the same. And rumbling off in the distance was a place called El Salvador. We feared it, greatly. One of the Hispanic priests at the cathedral expressed concern about our having anything to do with the place in Central America where dragon seeds had again been sown, the harvest cruel and dispiriting. An international television crew of four had been murdered and mutilated there. It could have been anybody.

"Praise the Lord upon earth: ye dragons, and all deeps; Fire and hail; snow, and vapours; stormy wind fulfilling his word," sang the psalmist. We listened, but many times there is simply no place to hide. There comes the time when shrinking back to imagined spiritual safety nets is unacceptable.

February 12, 1982, enroute to El Salvador. *My perspective is that of a journalist under fire. This is not intended as an apology, even as a*

184

defense. It is simply an honest, candid description of how it often is when a television and radio reporter is under intense competitive pressure operating within a small time frame. It is essential to deal dispassionately with issues and personalities, while at the same time not losing the basic need to be a sensitive, responsible human being. Tall order.

Civil war in Central America is old, complex, and as tragic as it is bewildering. Fighting pops up, sputters like spent fireworks, and flares again. North American interest in it depends mainly on national self-interest and, from time to time, U.S. television dabbles in coverage, the amount depending on the calculated need to improve audience ratings.

My commercial flight included one stop in Belize, which added another country to the list of places I'd visited, then on to the capital city, San Salvador. The sun was a fiery red ball that suddenly disappeared high over the volcanic mountains. I took advantage of TACA's free liquor in the hope of fortifying myself for the new, strange, and dangerous land I'd soon be entering. Nelson, a native driver, met me, and quickly we were on our way along the autopista to San Salvador. I checked in at the Camino Real, and soon I was embracing Roberto Moreno, smiling, affable, long-suffering Roberto from the days of wine and leprechauns and missed opportunities in South America, and nights of Nicaraguan rum in what was left of Managua. How had it been with Sorensen? I didn't ask. Where was he? I didn't want to know. Where was Roberto now in the network scheme of things? Well on his way to becoming a cameraman!

The next morning, my alarm went off at 5:30, and I was out of bed in a wink. One hour later I met another crew in the lobby. Mario Corvalho, who spoke seven languages, was the cameraman, and Shlomo Carmon, also of the CBS News Tel Aviv Bureau, was the technician. Shlomo had been with the Israeli army at Entebbe when commando forces rescued hostages held by Palestinian hijackers. Mario and Shlomo were a formidable but pleasant crew. We were given the number-one driver, Nelson. So we were a new team going down a new road on a new storm.

We headed southwest to Usulután province, which was believed to be controlled by the guerrillas. It was a long, exhausting trip. We forded

Mérida

MEXICO

Minatitlán

Villahermosa

Pichucalco

El Chichonál

Belmopan

Caribbean Sea

BELIZE

GUATEMALA

HONDURAS

Tapachula

Guatemala City

Antiqua

Tegucigalpa

San Salvador

Sensuntepeque

San Vicente

Usulután

NICARAGUA

EL SALVADOR

Pacific Ocean

COSTA RICA

one river where the bridge was out and crossed another on a railroad span because the guerrillas had blown up the motor vehicle bridge. I only *thought* I'd seen poverty and deprivation before, and I kept asking myself, what can we fortunate do to put a stop to this insanity that reduces humans to the level of animals and worse? Quixote had not a single answer.

After a long drive down a dirt road in ruts hubcap-deep, we found what we were looking for—a Salvadoran army artillery company. The captain politely refused to accept our credentials and firmly told us to leave. We did. He said we'd have to have special written permission from the area commander, who was at headquarters in Usulután City. We retreated to headquarters, and when we introduced ourselves, the second in command told us that his Número Uno was out in the field. It was Catch-22, but we said we'd return the next day.

It was a long, hard drive back to San Salvador, and shortly after our arrival at the Camino Real, Pres. José Napoleón Duarte came in and held a news conference. He announced that five of the six former National Guardsmen being held had officially been charged with the murder of four American missionaries in December 1980. Three of the four missionaries were Roman Catholic nuns, and CBS cameraman Bernie Nudelman had taken pictures of the uncovering of the remains. I did a radio spot. I felt coldhearted doing it, but it was my job, and I did it.

As I go to bed tonight, I say another prayer, thanking God for sparing me and getting me safely through this day and, I hope, another one tomorrow, I wrote in my journal. It was clearly life one day, one hour, one moment at a time, and I had a sobering feeling that God does not play favorites.

St. Valentine's Day, Sunday, February 14, 1982, I visited the National Cathedral in San Salvador. I will not forget the feeling I had when I saw its magnificent ugliness, its unfinished beauty, and the tomb of Archbishop Oscar Arnulfo Romero. On January 6, 1980, Archbishop Romero had called upon the people to "preserve the liberation process." On February 17, he denounced the "unscrupulous military." On March 23, he called upon the military to disobey its commanders. The following day, March 24, Archbishop Romero was assassinated while celebrating Mass.

I went to the National Cathedral on that Valentine's Day in 1982 to hear the acting archbishop celebrate Mass. I was on my knees in the back of the cathedral, my hands knotted tightly against my forehead, my thoughts extended toward the Great Creator, when I received word that a gun battle was in progress about twenty-five miles east of San Salvador. I was to go there with Roberto and Nelson, but we became separated and I did not go with them. Correspondent Gary Shepherd was already at the location with Nudelman and Born. They brought back footage of a head that had been freshly severed from a rebel soldier, a young man who, the day before, had been alive as I was alive, but now was no more than a horribly butchered thing. I was the only one in the editing room who believed the decapitation should be shown to the American audience, that not to show it was to sanitize the reality of an unholy civil war. I lost the argument.

Valentine's Day. *I miss you. Pray for me. And join me in prayer for the 560 children I saw today at the refugee camp in Santa Tecla. Can you imagine? A total of one thousand people living on one acre of land? And you and I have more than one hundred acres for the two of us? Until you have seen such a place you cannot possibly know the hurt I felt, and I think that those of us who are so wealthy must know about these things so close to our doorstep. It is numbing, just numbing, to see these dirty, hungry, crowded children, to see the sad, withered faces of the old men and women who have managed to survive another day of this sad, withering civil war. The shortage of water, the grinding of corn, the gruel for the babies, and those faces—oh, those heart-rending faces. Damn it, can't the killing stop? Can't the hungry be fed? Can't we brothers and sisters love and help each other?*

I wrote and recorded a spot for radio and then returned to the hotel with Mario and Shlomo, our interpreter Viviana, and Nelson. Straightaway we were turned around and sent to San Sebastión because there had been reports of another firefight there. If there had been one, it was gone as quickly as a Southwest dust devil. We secured footage of a funeral procession, the tolling of the bell in the church tower where the day before a guerrilla had gained entry and had fired upon the town. We taped the grieving people with their rosaries held tightly at the kneeling rails in the church. Nearby was the clump of ashes of a guerrilla who had been killed and set afire. We recorded the blackened corpse. For a time it seemed more fighting might begin, but it was as if echoes from Valentine's Day were reverberating. We hurried back to San Salvador. I fed the *World Tonight* and then wrote and helped edit a piece for *Morning News*

The piece I fed last night, the one on which I'd worked so hard, did not make air. It's ruthless to report a war, to dodge bullets. It's another matter to get shot down in this monetary game called television news, which we feel obliged to play.

As Mike Orloff was cutting our refugee piece for *Morning News*, I was assigned to go again to Usulután province to check out another report of a massacre that was supposed to have happened there the previous week. We knew in advance that we'd have to overnight. My cameraman would be the Dane, Carl Sorensen. It was the first time I'd worked with him and Moreno since Caracas, almost three years to the date. Sorensen and I observed a dubious truce, since he and I were no longer married to each other. We were only diplomatically dating. Roberto had grown in his role as lowly technician, and soon would be a shooter.

In Usulután, finding no one at the church, we went to the convent, where a priest was hearing confessions. When we talked with him, he could tell us nothing about a massacre. By then it was nightfall, and we didn't want to be caught out in it, so we checked in at a former whorehouse motel four kilometers out of town. I slept with my clothes on all night. It was not the whores I feared, unless they were wearing combat boots. I expected the worst because we were in the middle of no-man's land. I prayed. I was petrified. I smelled endangerment, and I loathed it.

My prayers were answered. The sun finally came up. We were not ambushed in the middle of the blackest of nights. We drove into Usulután City for breakfast, and then we headed on to the southeast in the direction of Jucuarán, where the road twisted into a Kafkaesque

189

labyrinth of stones, fallen trees, and craters. There was a nearly impossible detour because a bridge was out. We finally reached a point where I decided that to continue just wasn't worth it. We had no reason to believe there had been a massacre — everybody we asked knew nothing about it, or they wouldn't admit anything. On the way back down we ran into other reporters and crews, including Ray Bonner of the *New York Times* and an NBC crew. We returned to Usulután City and called CBS in San Salvador. As might be expected, because of the competitive factor we had no choice but to turn around again and go all the way back to the place where we had stopped before, then continue the rest of the way to Jucuarán. Several times, I didn't think our four-cylinder van would go one jarring foot farther. But we finally made it, and so did NBC, ABC, and the *New York Times*. Charlie Murphy of ABC was having his usual good old Texan time, treating almost everything with droll wit. The army was in town distributing food after the previous week's battle, and when we finally limped back to San Salvador I wrote a piece for next day's *Evening News*. I also fed radio.

As far as I could determine, there simply had been no massacre. UPI's John Newhagen sauntered across the hall from his room and solemnly announced: "The massacre was a hoax."

"Thanks a goddamned lot, John," I shot back.

Newhagen tried to excuse himself and UPI by saying *he* wouldn't have filed the rumor that was spread all over the world. Newhagen and I both knew that New York reacted to wire service stories like Plum Lick hogs to slop, but that often did not prevent the rumors from being spread from "sources." I went to dinner at Doña Mercedes, where the camaraderie among all the networks helped take minds off the possibility of being killed. I wanted to return to Lalie in one piece — one live, loving piece.

February 18, 1982. *Happy 52nd birthday! Another milestone. I called you after midnight and said, would you like to sing to me? You did. You sang the 'Happy Birthday song.'*

CBS personnel, led by Bernie Nudelman, surprised me with a birthday cake. Roberto gave me a bottle of rotgut champagne. Nudelman added a gallon of Nicaraguan rum. He, Steve Born, Mario, and Viviana treated me to a good Mexican restaurant. I ate and drank too much, but it was my birthday. I felt like hell when I woke up the next morning. It doesn't take much to get a fifty-two-year-old man hung over.

I went with Mario, Shlomo, and Viviana to the metropolitan cathedral to begin working on a picture essay for the following Sunday. I spoke with Shad Northshield, executive producer of *Sunday Morning News*, a Tiffany broadcast made famous by Charles Kuralt. Northshield gave me the go-ahead for about a four and a half-minute piece. It included Archbishop Romero's tomb, the cracked and soiled statuary, the protruding concrete reinforcement rods, the traffic noise echoing through the unfinished cathedral, the faces of the people praying, old women gripping their precious rosaries.

I lit a candle and said a prayer for you and for our first child.

As soon as I heard that Sorensen and Moreno were being sent east on the Pan American Highway, where some fighting had been reported in the area of San Felipe, I suggested that I go along, although I felt rotten. My gastrointestinal misfortune, Montezuma's revenge, had returned. I picked up some antacid, which straightened me out, somewhat. We found the Salvadoran army on the highway, and the lieutenant in charge told us, "No filmar." We didn't argue with him but continued down the road, and I heard one stray bullet's whine when we stopped to ask for information from a peasant. Two women ducked and hurried across the road. Farther on we found heavy-duty highway construction equipment burned by the guerrillas. But this time the army was not objecting to our taking pictures. It included some of the local residents who had returned to salvage what they could from their burned-out trucks. One of the men said the guerrillas had robbed him about twenty minutes before. I had the script written by the time we reached San Salvador, and we realized we would be leading the broadcast. I fed a separate piece to radio.

I went with Mario and Shlomo. Nelson was our driver, and we felt better when he was. He had the good sense to turn around and head in the other direction when the danger was unacceptable. Mario gave me some tablets to stabilize my body. I didn't know what they were, but the little pills made the reds redder and the blues bluer. They also made the body feel lighter. We headed down the Pan American Highway to San Vicente. We were looking for confirmation of ABC's report the previous evening that a Salvadoran colonel had "captured a Cuban." We went to the 5th Infantry Brigade, but nobody there knew anything about a Cuban. A colonel said "the man" had died but that there was no confirmation that he was one of Castro's own. A black beret and a darker skin do not a Cuban make, but it moved CBS back up the food chain to salivation.

We headed north to Sensuntepeque. At the military garrison there, same song, same verse, soldiers lounging around, people acting like stirred-up fire ants, the open market festering like a bad sore. As we came down a steep street, the crowd surged. Another poor, drunk Salvadoran was wielding his machete on a Sunday, having nothing or, perhaps in a deeper sense everything in the world to do with this prolonged civil war. We headed back in the direction of San Salvador, asking the campesinos what was going on. ¿Que Pasa? We accomplished absolutamente nada. Soldiers guarding a dirt road would not allow us to enter to check out an operation that UPI was reporting. When we finally reached the hotel, I fell into bed and slept.

February 22, 1982. We have a new interpreter/translator, Estela, superb and sexy, and I know from the beginning it's going to be awfully difficult to keep my hands off." She was willowy, dark-eyed, and spoke with a mellow voice.

My Spanish is improving more on this trip than ever before, and it is an exciting feeling. The sum total of CBS's efforts on this day was no runs, no hits, and no errors. We hardly came to bat. But late in the day an army colonel came by the CBS office in the Camino Real and talked with us for a long time. It was decided I would go with him tomorrow with Mario, Shlomo, and Estela to the colonel's post at Sensuntepeque to spend "a couple of days in the life of a colonel."

We rolled away from San Salvador at 3:15 p.m. the next day, arriving at Sensuntepeque one and a half hours later. We went to the cuartel of the Second Battalion and checked in to await the arrival of Colonel Ochoa Pérez. We had a get-acquainted session with the duty officer, and although my Spanish was muy pobre, I did my best to listen as intently as possible and to use as many Spanish words as possible. When all else failed, Estela supplied the right words. I was again committed to learning Spanish, motivated as I'd not been before in Venezuela, one of the countries where español is mostly manhandled.

We ate supper with Colonel Ochoa and visited with the troops as they carried out their final orders of the day. The colonel took us in his four-wheel-drive jeep on a ride around the town, which was peaceful and for that moment motionless. When we went to the top of a hill overlooking Sensuntepeque it was as if we stood beneath an inverted dish of silent stars. Orion, the Great Hunter, seemed closer to the ground, to the killing fields, than when he stood at the top of the hill in Kentucky. The alpha star, Betelgeuse, with its redness in the hollow under the arm of the Great Hunter, and Rigel, the double star, burned their images into the imaginations of the earthbound messengers staring at the heavens. From their light-year distances the Eagle, Charioteer, Flying Horse, Great Bear, Little Bear, and Fox constellations fixated on questioning and troubled mortal minds.

Estela's loveliness was troubling too. Our stolen glances were self-evident, but physical fulfillment simply must not come to pass. Every fiber of my being belonged to Lalie. Monogyny would mandate morality and with that would come increased understanding about ourselves, about each other, and about the world in which we'd been born.

Back at the cuartel we sat around sipping whiskey from the bottle Mario had thoughtfully brought along. He also gave me more pills to help stabilize my stomach. They worked a real miracle. Estela was given the colonel's hammock in which to sleep. He slept with the rest of us on cots in his office. He took his .45 automatic to bed with him. The lights went out. I felt secure.

The next morning, we taped the bugler announcing reveille and the raising of the Salvadoran flag with its twin stripes of blue separated by one of white, quite similar to the flags of Nicaragua, Honduras, and Argentina. We taped Colonel Ochoa jogging with his recruits around the plaza, past the gray-stoned ancient Church of Santa Barbara. The faces of the soldiers were childlike—they were officially no younger than seventeen, but surely some of them were fifteen or sixteen, and it was not uncommon for a twelve-year-old to slip through. A company of the troops marched off for a battle at Suchitoto.

We went inside the cuartel to have breakfast with the colonel, and afterward we met outside with a group of commanders of the Civil Defense. Colonel Ochoa told them it was their responsibility to help ensure that there were free elections on March 28. We traveled with the colonel all day, from San Isidro to San Ibisco and as far as the "Fifth of November" hydroelectric dam in an area almost equaling the remoteness of Jonestown. In El Salvador there was at least a narrow and rocky winding road up and down the mountains. I interviewed the colonel in his jeep on the side of the road when we stopped to rest.

At the "Fifth of November" dam we photographed an example of what was wrong with the Salvadoran army. Sights for mortars that had come from the United States had parts that did not fit. The sights were held together with tape. We returned to Sensuntepeque, where I did an on-camera with the street vendors behind me. We drove back late into San Salvador, and I went to dinner with Bill Moyers, who was gathering information for a documentary. He was comparing notes with Warren Hoge and Ray Bonner of the *New York Times*.

The Sensuntepeque piece was well received in New York, and Moyers said his researchers had complimented it. There was also a telex message from CBS with kind words about it. Praise was appreciated as much as money, yet I remained ambivalent. My work was love and loathing.

I set out from San Salvador with field producer Larry Doyle and the Mexican crew, Roberto and James. We went to an old sugar refinery, where we were expecting to be transported by army chopper to the battle area around one of the volcanoes. Night closed in and the army had no intention of taking anybody anywhere. We ate a Salvadoran supper that gave me a stomach problem, but I fought it with Mario's miracle pills. It was a strange, forbidding place, and I wondered what in the name of God I was doing there. I finally settled down to sleep on a thin mat on a concrete floor alongside Doyle, Timothy Ross of ABC, and the

Argentinean "fixer," Viviana. She made things happen, and in time she would become the technician for Roberto when he finally replaced Sorensen as cameraman. Viviana and Roberto became inseparable. Later they would marry.

Dogs barked. Roosters stirred. Cats meowed. Soldiers mumbled. Doyle snored. Thoughts of Lalie finally soothed me into sleep. But I woke up about 3:45 a.m. and about 6:00 everybody else scrambled up off the floor at the sound of the first incoming chopper bringing in six wounded from the fighting on the distant mountain. As the day wore on, the number of incoming wounded tapered off, and so did our chances of being taken into the area of the fighting. Harry Madison, photographer for *Time* magazine, described his experiences of the day before, his helicopter ride with the dead. Quixote was prepared to go and risk his life, but it was not to be. The commander of the operation was relieved of his leadership. That only confirmed everybody's suspicions that the Salvadoran army had lost a major encounter, or at least that the guerrillas had slipped away again, demonstrating their determination and their fighting ability.

As we lounged around waiting to see how the day would end, NBC producer Don Critchfield came from the telephone to announce the resignation of Bill Small as president of NBC News. Almost to a man and a woman, both in the field and back in San Salvador, the feeling was the same on the part of those of us covering the war for U.S. television. It appeared that Small had paid a dear price for his style of management—arrogance and intimidation, employed by many who maneuvered in the stratosphere of the front office. But Bill Small had hired me at WHAS in Louisville when no one else would give me a chance. He had hired me at CBS and again had gambled heavily on my talent. He had come close to firing me on more than one occasion, and the announcement that he had left NBC after leaving CBS gave me pause to wonder. What else was there about the man that caused some to dislike him so much while others believed he was a remarkable moment in time? I don't know.

Years later, after I had left CBS to teach at the University of

Kentucky, and after Small had left United Press International as its president, we sat rather forlornly together one evening at a minor league baseball game in Portland, Oregon. Small was on the faculty of Fordham University, and we were among those attending the annual meeting of the Association on Education in Journalism and Mass Communications. It seemed ironic: after Caracas, Jonestown, Managua, Buenos Aires, and Beirut, Bill Small and David Dick were still survivors amid ankle-deep academe and peanut shells in a cold, wet stadium where the Trappers were playing the Beavers.

When I came up for promotion to full professor at the University of Kentucky, it was Bill Small, then Dean at Fordham University, who wrote for me an unusually enthusiastic letter of recommendation. Through all the good times and the bad, it had been Small as much as if not more than any other one person who was the mentor who had mattered most.

Larry Doyle and I hurried back to San Salvador and fleshed out with new material the soundtrack and tape I'd sent to the capital earlier in the morning. We led the broadcast! Having a first-rate producer like Doyle didn't hurt one little bit. There was hardly anything more satisfying to a correspondent's ego than to lead the broadcast. I talked to Lalie on the telephone, and we agreed to meet one week later in Mississippi for some much needed private time.

I was up almost all night. I was sick from the food I'd eaten and the water I'd drunk. It was shortly after 2:00 a.m. that I began to feel some better. I read from *Matanza*, the story of the 1932 massacre, when the army exterminated more than thirty thousand people, about 4 percent of the population of El Salvador. The leaders of the campesinos were hanged in the town squares. People do not forget a "Matanza."

As I was beginning to feel better in the early morning hours of February 27, I resumed writing in my journal: *There was no "Matanza" to report on this day, but there was a murder.* I had gone with Mario and Shlomo up the road in the direction of Suchitoto. We were stopped at a checkpoint north of San Martín. Two civil defense guards were stopping all traffic—one guard was twelve years old and the other was fifteen, their cigarettes and their G-3 rifles almost bigger than they were. When a twelve-year-old Salvadoran kid with a cigarette in his mouth and a G-3 cradled in his arms tells you to stop, you stop if you have any sense at all. We stayed at the checkpoint for lack of something better to do. I was still fighting my stomach problems and managed to buy more medicine at a drugstore in San Martín.

Down the road from our position, we could hear automatic gunfire, and the best I could piece it together the army, fresh from having its nose bloodied, was roaming up and down the road ahead of us, shooting up the countryside with relatively little effect. Psychologically it had to be intimidating. There was no way of knowing anything for certain. We did a lot of guessing, but we kept it out of our scripts.

I have tried diligently since I've been here in El Salvador to report only what I've actually seen with my own eyes, heard with my own ears, I wrote in my journal.

We returned to San Salvador, and just as I was resting a bit, we had another wild rumor of thirty civilians killed in San Sebastíon. Mario, Shlomo, Nelson, producer Phil O'Connor, and I rushed up there. We found no massacre. A massacre would have meant large numbers. We found no large numbers. We found one body beneath a foul sheet on the sidewalk. Her name was Maria.

This woman, Maria, had been on her way to sell her bread on the streets of San Sebastíon. She, an unidentified child, and three National Guardsmen had been killed in a guerrilla ambush. The bodies of the soldiers were hauled away, the child was quickly buried, but Maria was accorded a special honor.

Her body was stretched out on the concrete pavement. Her small red purse was alongside the body, and her bare feet protruded from the end of the unwashed white sheet. Maria's toes were large, a peasant's toes unaccustomed to shoes. The bystanders were willing to pull back the sheet and expose Maria's face. They did it politely, automatically. They must have thought it was important that as much of the world as possible should look into what had been this woman's kind eyes. I looked only for a moment.

Maria's red purse was used to collect donations for the cost of the flimsy box in which she would be buried as quickly as possible.

The story of Maria was on the *CBS Evening News*, and it was on radio. I had dinner with Bill Moyers, and we talked about the civil war in El Salvador. I told him about Maria. To me, she represented the inhumanity of all wars.

On the first Sunday in Lent I had to go chasing after another massacre report, this one in San Salvador. We could find only a crying woman who said her two sons had been taken away at gunpoint. She said they had been "on the list." I was concerned that we might have been set up for an ambush. We didn't push our luck too far and returned to the Camino Real.

There was a flap involving a media columnist for *Newsday*. He was off and running to make us all look like a bunch of blockheads, if possible. Maybe we were, but I told the guy I didn't want to talk to him, and I didn't give any reasons why. "The truth is I came down here to do the best job of reporting that I know how to do, and I don't need to do any extra tap-dancing with media columnists. I get my satisfaction from the pieces I do, and they speak for themselves."

It felt good to be alive just one more day. There were gunshots during the night and sometimes they mingled with war dreams I was having. I ate breakfast early and was ready to roll away from the hotel by 7:00. Manny Alvarez, Jim Forrest, Phil O'Connor, Estela, Nelson, and I went to a part of San Salvador called El Prado. We were following up on an incident the day before in which eight or more young people, including a fourteen-year-old boy and a fifteen-year-old girl, were hauled away by gunmen in civilian clothes. No one knew whether or not a death squad had scooped them up. The teenagers were not likely to be seen alive again. We found nothing.

I received confirmation that I would be leaving El Salvador on March 5, returning with Lalie on March 20. John Lane gave his permission for me to bring her on the next trip, which I considered to be relatively safe, as long as she remained inside the Camino Real. I wanted her to have the experience.

The days go marching on on this Texas Independence Day. Friday is coming into view. I was up early and wrote, recorded, and fed a spot to the *World News Roundup*. It was used on an hourly. Correspondent Dick Wagner gave me a couple of uppers, and the blues were bluer and the reds were redder before we were out of San Salvador.

Mario, Shlomo, Estela, and I went to the airport to meet the LACSA flight coming in from Mexico City to see if we could find any deportees who'd been denied political asylum. There were twenty-seven deportees, but no one was willing to admit being involved in the story Mike Wallace was working on for *Evening News*. We had all kinds of problems with the authorities at the airport, and they finally told us to leave the terminal. In the afternoon Estela and I were driven to La Libertad. President Duarte was making a campaign visit to El Salvador's city by the sea, the one to which the U.S. missionaries had been returning when they were murdered.

We met the Moyers crew in the town plaza, which was filled with a hot, sweating crowd. Estela, whom I was then calling "Corazón," which was as close as my Spanish could bring me to "Sweetheart," treated me to a tapped coconut with a straw to draw out the sticky-sweet milk. I didn't particularly like it and gave most of it to the kid with the sweatiest face in front of the speaker's stand. Duarte and most of the ruling junta showed up almost on time, and everybody was treated to a fairly typical Latin American stem-winder. After his speech, El Presidente, his arm around me, perambulated down the main street and answered my questions:

"What do you want to say to the people of the United States?"

"We need their support."

"Why do you need more aid from the United States?"

"To win the struggle over communism."

His answers had been heard since 1979, and during that time an estimated fifty thousand Salvadorans had been killed. In the following year another one thousand would be killed at the hands of death squads. To my way of thinking, it was another "Matanza."

That evening, Estela dressed up in her finest—a pale green gown that accentuated her willowy figure, her long black hair, and her pleasantly framed light brown face and full, dark eyes. When she appeared in the lounge of the Camino Real, I saw her without her combat fatigues. I admired her beauty, her courage, her love for her country that was being torn asunder.

"Nos veremos por la mañana, Corazón." My own heart ached as I said it, but I desired to be true to my corazón in Dallas, so I went to my room alone and pulled the covers over my head.

The assignment the following day was to go with Estela and Manny ("The Wild Cuban") Alvarez, who would have a bit part later in the movie *Broadcast News*, in search of "Nellie with the sad, sad face." That was the name I'd given to one of the deportees whom we'd found at the International Airport. Estela was in her combat fatigues again. Our trip took us to the western part of El Salvador, entirely different from the eastern area. Campesinos were working in the fields of coffee, watermelon, and sugar cane, and the two-lane road was about as good as any in the United States. We stopped at pre-Columbian ruins, and I bought souvenirs.

We drove to the village where "Nellie" was supposed to be, but we only found her mother and son. I interviewed them and went on in search of "Nellie," who was supposed to be selling shoes in Ahuachapan. We went almost to the Honduran border—no Nellie. We came back to San Salvador. I began working on a five-part radio series. Ed Fouhy, who was playing the game of musical chairs in the office of the CBS Senior Vice-President for News and who had advised me not to go to Latin America in the first place, called with some words of praise. He expressed concern that we be as cautious as possible and "not get hurt down there." Almost instantly after his call, an exploding mine wounded two journalists. I had just taken two stay-alert pills. We covered the medivac rescue of the two still photographers. I carried the TV sound recorder with Manny, and we beat the competition.

I was up by 5:00 a.m. and was filled with joy that tomorrow, tomorrow, thank God, tomorrow, I'm coming home! As I was writing these words in my journal, as if to show me, a mortal, that He is still running the show, THE EARTH SHOOK.

¡Terremoto! Earthquake. I wondered where in hell I could hide, but there were no hidey-holes. The lights went out in the Camino Real. I threw on my clothes and went downstairs. Harry of *Time* magazine said it could have been a pre-shock and that in an hour all Hell could break loose. I advised New York to look at somebody's Richter scale. It was a 5.5 centered about one hundred miles off the Pacific coast of Central America. I was lucky one more time—there were no more tremors in El Salvador. Less than a year later a 5.5 earthquake killed 250 in Colombia.

Friday, March 5: *Let us pray for peace and the brotherhood of man. Let us pray for El Salvador.*

I took a fast shower and was downstairs, bag and baggage, by 6:15 a.m. Corazón wasn't anywhere in sight, so I called her in her room to tell her goodbye. I knew I was going to miss her. I didn't want her to be killed in this maniacal civil war. She wished me a safe flight. I told her to be careful. There were no kisses—not even one blown from the palm of a hand.

Ricardo and I pulled away from the Camino Real at 6:25, and by 7:00 we were at the airport. I was first in line at the ticket counter, first to arrive in the waiting room, first in the heart of the woman I truly loved and who would be in my arms in only a few hours. I was wheels up from San Salvador at 9:07 a.m.

At 11:57 we began our descent through the Louisiana clouds to the Crescent City. At twelve noon I saw Lalie's favorite river. At 12:04 p.m., TACA 110 touched down at Moissant Airport. Thank God.

After I cleared immigration and customs, I smiled through the door, and there were Lalie and her mother. Out by the car I broke an egg filled with confetti on Lalie's head, and later at Uncle Jimmy's house we broke two on his head. We went to Bozo's in Fat City, where we had our oysters and two pitchers of beer. We said goodbye to Jimmy, and then with a "dressed" oyster po-boy each, we headed north toward Mississippi.

March 7, 1982. The congregation at St. Paul's was a sparse one this second Sunday of Lent. I thanked God I had returned to Wilkinson County safely, and I prayed for our safety on our return trip to El Salvador. I thought a lot about the poor Salvadorans and the rich Woodvillians, but I reached no conclusions, not even any resolutions.

Father Whitney Barnes quoted a line from Bishop Jeremy Taylor, a seventeenth-century poet I'd not read since my earliest college days at the University of Kentucky thirty-four years before. "Beware that the branch removed from your tree be not the handle for the ax with which the Devil chops down the tree!"

Dallas, Sunday, March 21, 1982. I went downtown to pick up the Sunday New York Times. *Coming back, as I passed over the spot where Pres. John F. Kennedy was assassinated, the view of the Hyatt Regency, its glass exterior was awash in the deep blue of another Texas sundown.* Later that night I read all the Salvadoran stories in the *Times*.

Monday, March 22. The space shuttle Columbia launched without a hitch. And then came the phone call from New York to the Dallas Bureau. "Tell David to take the first available flight to El Salvador." I called Scarlett and told her to start packing, made reservations for us to Miami, where we would overnight, made car, motel, and plane reservations to San Salvador the following afternoon. We lifted off from Dallas at 8:00 p.m. When we stopped at the front desk at the Marriott near Miami International, there was a message to call John Lane in New York. We both knew what it meant before we dialed the number. John had decided it was too dangerous for Lalie to go with me to El Salvador.

Tuesday, March 23. *It was a painful disappointment to have to terminate your trip with me in Miami. We decided you would return to Woodville to be with your mother as long as I am in El Salvador. I told you I didn't want to talk about being killed, only that if anything did happen to me, you would know what to do.*

I wanted to be buried on a ridge at Plum Lick in Kentucky. There was a spot I had picked out many years before. I knew that country burying grounds in time became unkempt, unnoticed, unappreciated, but that didn't matter to me. I wanted my body to be a part of the Plum Lick soil, and as much as possible, I wanted to be a little encouragement for the bluegrass growing there.

I was paged in the Miami airport and told there'd been a coup in Guatemala and for me to try to take a flight straightaway for Guatemala City. I tried but was told the flight had been canceled because the airport in Guatemala City had been closed. CBS told me to continue to San Salvador. At 2:15 p.m. I was on board TACA 311, and Lalie was scheduled to leave at 3:00 p.m. for Baton Rouge via Atlanta. We kissed a lot before we became airplanes passing in the afternoon.

The scene at the airport in San Salvador was the beginning of a major downer. I was disillusioned by the influx of media upon media. The Camino Real had become a zoo. People were sleeping in the lobby, rooms were packed, and the air tasted stale because there were so many lungs breathing in the same small supply of oxygen. Cigarette and cigar smoke didn't help. And it was hot, hot, hot. It was fortunate that Lalie had not come with me. You can't go home again, not even to San Salvador. There was much tension, and Doña Mercedes seemed lifeless compared to the first trip.

Estela was beginning to look tired, gaunt and hollow-eyed. Not only the civil war itself but also the demands of the CBS office in the Camino Real were taking their toll on this fine, good-looking woman who'd be forevermore a spiritual Corazón to me. When we talked, it was not the same. Her voice was strained. Her nerves were on edge. We were still friends. We were good friends. But the flower of our friendship had been crushed by the war, which seemed not a bit nearer to a peaceful resolution.

By 5:45 a.m. I was in front of the Camino Real to join Ray Bribiesca, Richard Wagner, Phil O'Connor, and Nick Bourne to go jogging. I made it to the sports stadium, a distance of about one-half mile. Once inside, I alternated walking and running quarter-miles for about one and one-quarter miles, and I ran once up and down the stadium steps. Quite a number of Latinos and gringos were up and about. So were the guerrillas and soldiers on the eastern edge of the capital, from where automatic weapons fire could be heard.

Why can't we all be joggers and live in peace?

Corazón was my interpreter at President Duarte's news conference, and when it was over I filed a radio report and prepared to leave for Guatemala City, which Gary Shepherd and Larry Doyle had been able to reach overland the day before. They shot footage and filed the first CBS report on the coup for *Morning News*. Gary was being sent back to San Salvador, and I was to replace him. German Bonefont, an editor from Los Angeles, accompanied me. There was a thickheaded incident involving correspondent Steve Kroft and *my* typewriter, which he didn't want to stop using. I had left it behind while I was on R and R, but when I returned to El Salvador I had to commandeer my own frigging typewriter. Kroft got even by parlaying his aggressiveness into a position on *60 Minutes*. By 2002, I got even by watching or not watching him from Plum Lick. "Way to go, Kroft, way to go. But I've got the damn typewriter! And I'm the president of this here company, Plum Lick Publishing!"

The airport now open, Bonefont and I took the five p.m. TACA flight to Guatemala City. Guatemala was the thirtieth country in which I'd set foot. The atmosphere following a "bloodless" coup has a strange, disquieting calm, like the way it feels along the Gulf Coast of Texas, Louisiana, Mississippi, and Alabama. You know the storm is out there, but it hasn't yet gathered itself, hasn't made up its mind about which direction it'll take, is toying with the idea of killing six thousand people, as at Galveston in the hurricane of 1900.

March 25. I was up about 5:00 a.m. in Guatemala City to begin day three of the golpe, the coup. Larry Doyle was the producer for CBS, and a young man from Los Angeles, John Vincent, was the interpreter. He was a non-Spanish-speaking correspondent's dream. John, who called me "Dad," could waltz through Hell itself, and if the Devil were a Latino, John could have him feeling good about tying a knot in his tail. We went with the crew, Born and Nudelman, to the presidential palace, where everything was calm, on the surface at least. We were in position to shoot footage of the new junta jefes, the maximum leaders, when they made their first official appearance. The new Big Guy, Ríos Montt, didn't help matters by fueling speculation that he might be having trouble getting his act together and that there might be another golpe at any time.

Larry and I went with the rest of the journalists to the U.S. Embassy at 11:00 a.m. for a "deep, deep backgrounder" with the ambassador, meaning nothing could be quoted or attributed. It was a fascinating session, and we came away with a treasure of useful information that would become the underpinning of the report we offered to the *Evening News*. We went back to the palace, where I did an on-camera closing for our piece, and we picked up some more footage of the "surface calm." I did a radio piece for *World Tonight*, but *Evening News* passed. They said they were too jammed up. We fed the piece to *Morning News* via the satellite. At the feed point I watched some of the amateurish, sophomoric, inane, inept, inaccurate, exaggerated pieces being put together by the horde of reporters from local stations all over the United States, while still more of the same kind of thing was being fed to the bird from El Salvador. They had crashed in there at ratings time to hype their visibility. It was another reason why I was glad I was in Guatemala—the media zoo in El Salvador was a disgrace.

I did not go dancing. I ate a little supper alone, went to bed, and fell fast asleep. There was a dream that involved the proper use of the brain, allowing a free flow of impressions to come in, be synthesized, and then utilized as needed. When I awoke I recommitted myself to fluency en español. I told myself to recognize the different levels at which humans operated best, to know my own, then to excel there.

I wrote in my journal: *I will write books about Kentucky. I may teach courses at the University of Kentucky. I will operate Plum Lick Farms until the day I die. I will not do anything to encourage a move to Miami or anyplace else. Today, I bought you a nice silver bracelet, a matrimonial hammock, an oil painting of a Guatemalan peasant boy's face, and a colorful tablecloth with eight napkins.*

"John Boy" Vincent, the crew, and I attended church services on the fifth Sunday in Lent beneath the "Bible Outreach" tent near the Camino Real in Guatemala City. We went as reporters, which means we were neither saints nor sinners. Yes, I know, the clergy will say that's not possible, you have to be one or the other. The clergy doesn't usually appreciate messengers when they report philanderers and pedophiles.

The new head of the junta, Gen. Ríos Montt, showed up and was warmly embraced by the Pentecostal congregation. He whooped it up with the faithful, clapping hands, joining their swaying bodies, while some fell down in swoons. He spoke with his brothers and sisters in

Christ, but he had nothing to say to me.

We had our driver take us to Antigua, where we spent a delightful afternoon. *I must bring you here for a vacation. It is beyond belief. The volcanoes are majestic, the air is cool, the marimbas and their players are from a storybook, the macaws are brilliant, the Lenten processions are from another world, the people are incredibly gentle and friendly, the food and drink are good and inexpensive. We taped the Lenten procession and wound our way back to Guatemala City.*

When I talked on the telephone to producer Jim Ganser in New York, he told me I had been mentioned in a *New York Times* story as "a television correspondent who knew how to let pictures tell a story." It was the only Pulitzer Prize I would ever need or covet. I spoke with Latin American Bureau Chief John Harris in Miami and laid the groundwork for my return to the United States. I told him I wasn't busting my buns to get back to El Salvador to clean up the crumbs left by the junior stars, the wannabe "Big Feet." I told him I wasn't feeling so keen about following up a babysitting job on the "coup that was" in Guatemala with a babysitting of the post-election scene in El Salvador. I suggested the possibility of returning to Dallas. It was duly noted. I thought I'd probably return to El Salvador. That was before we were notified of a volcano that had erupted in southern Mexico.

CHAPTER TWELVE

At 4:30 a.m. on Tuesday, March 30, 1992, I was up and ready to roll. Our charter flight out of Guatemala City, over Antigua and the mountains in western Guatemala was spectacular. We landed at Tapachula, Mexico, and cleared immigration. Born and Nudelman were the crew, and we were allowed to proceed ($50.00 to the immigration officer) in our own plane north to the volcano. The mountains of southern Mexico were grand, except El Chichonál—it looked like a decapitated Gulliver.

The eruption had blown off the top of the mountain and reduced the countryside to powder. Desolation was total. At 8,000 feet, as we circled the volcano, Born and Nudelman took the pictures and I began making the notes I would use to write the story on our return to Guatemala City. I knew there was neither time nor the possibility of landing the plane to do any reporting on the ground. By the time we were touchdown in Guatemala City, I had both the television and radio scripts written and the *World Tonight* piece recorded for radio. We fed *Evening News* after incorporating a new paragraph to cover ground footage obtained from Mexico City. I resisted the temptation to be godlike, but the view from the small plane had made godliness tempting.

I had psyched myself for a return to El Salvador, but I received word that we would probably go back to Mexico to do a piece for *Weekend News*. The story was the huge numbers of people displaced by the eruption of El Chichonál. I spoke with Larry Doyle and Estela in San Salvador about shipping to me money, clothes, and other personal things left behind. (I still had the typewriter!) The crew and I were at the airport three hours ahead of our Aviateca flight to Mexico City. There was time for newsmongering about how much more passionate Latinas were than gringas. I smiled. It's an advantage to know more than you're willing to tell. Best sex, Quixote thought, is more mental than physical. Playboys, playgirls, and hanky-panky littered the roadways from top to bottom of network news coverage, but when final scores were tallied, what mattered most was the mind. Yep, T and A would come and go, but everlasting life would evolve from wisdom. But beware of the hormonal part of the brain!

We checked in about midnight at the Holiday Inn near the airport. Don Blessor came in from Miami, a most welcome pigeon with $2,500 in cold, hard, gringo cash. We laid it out among the four of us, and on the bed the greenbacks looked like a mafia spread at Vegas. "This for you, this for me. This for you, this for me." I had a third whiskey in Don's room, and we talked about CBS, about El Salvador, about erupting volcanoes, about the meaningless myth that Latinas are more passionate than gringas.

¡Te amo, Lalie. Te amo mas y mas cada día. Tu eres la mujer para mi. Tu eres mí esposa hermosa. Espero a verte muy pronto. Te necessito. Buenas noches, mí corazón!

April Fools' Day began like a real dandy. The hotel receptionist called me at 4:45 a.m. (fifteen minutes late), and there was a blue-ribbon Mexican standoff at the courtesy bus to the airport for what was supposed to be our 6:30 Mexicana flight to Villahermosa. We quickly concluded it had been canceled because of the volcanic ash in the area. We scrambled and tried to make a flight to Veracruz with the idea of driving six or seven hours to the disaster zone, but the flights were full. We limped to the hotel and licked our wounds, advising Miami and New York. We were told to try to line up a charter, but all those we contacted refused to take us, telling us they were forbidden to fly into the area. So we were back to square uno.

We booked out on a Mexicana flight at 11:30 bound for Veracruz.

I learned today that the U.S. Embassy in Guatemala City came under attack by terrorists—bombs lobbed, gunfire exchanged. Here in Mexico, El Chichonál erupted again, killing an estimated fifty people.

There were all the hassles anyone would expect at the Veracruz airport. It was impossible to make a phone call to the United States. Even bribes fell on their funny faces. We rented a car and drove into the city, still unable to get through to give a status report or to receive any possibly helpful information. We stopped for lunch at Las Brisas del Mar on the beachfront at Veracruz, then headed off on what we estimated, if we were lucky, to be an eight-hour drive to Villahermosa. The odyssey seemed interminable. Born and Nudelman and I took turns driving. It was pitch black on a two-lane Mexican highway jammed with trucks, buses, and other vehicles. About 10:15, we rolled into Villahermosa, literally a "beautiful town," elegant and proud, but since the eruption of El Chichonál, everything was covered with powdered white ash.

We were up at 6:30 a.m., and after confirming that our car rental had given up the ghost and refused to go one more mile, we rented a mini-van and headed toward the disaster zone. Soon we were driving past sprawling banana plantations, the trees drooping beneath the weight of the volcanic ash, the bananas cooking in the sun. The farther we went in Tabasco State, the worse it became. We stopped at Pichucalco, where there were many refugees from the outer villages and the army was milling about aimlessly, while workers were trying to clean up the monumental mess. I interviewed a British volcanologist who said the worst was over.

We drove the tortuous road to the village of Nicapa, destroyed by the eruption. Powdered gray-white ash lay ankle deep throughout the town. The buildings looked like rattling skeletons. The roof had fallen in on the pews and altar of the Church of San Andres. Houses of worship may be ridiculed, but to see a holy place torn asunder is to be torn at the heart, the questions becoming, "Will you want to build it back?" "Who will undertake the construction?" "Who'll pay for it?" "Who'll be in charge?"

After the people of Nicapa heard the rumble from Chichonál, they retreated to the church because the priest was ringing the bell. When the people came inside, the priest wasted no time in giving the Benediction. "Go in peace to your homes," he warned. A few minutes later, the roof fell in. Three people were killed in the church. Two were children.

Hungry dogs wandered through the deep dust shrouding the streets, enveloping everything. The confused animals were looking for something to eat, anything to eat, but there was nothing. People said they thought it was el fín del mundo. And so it seemed. We drove back down the mountain and took with us some of the refugees who otherwise would have been forced to make their way on hot, aching feet. We returned to Villahermosa and checked in with Miami and New York. We were told to drive to Minatitlán, where a charter would meet us the next morning. I slept some on the hood of a car, some on the floor of the airport. I kept waking up. John Donne's poetry prowled and penetrated the closeness of the night: *"Any man's death diminishes me, because I am involved in Mankind, And therefore never send to know for whom the bell tolls; It tolls for thee."*

Saturday, April 3, 1982. *With a whole lot of luck I'll be in Miami later today, editing our volcano piece. The airport at Minatitlán this morning is a menagerie...we are awaiting the arrival of our chartered jet...what a way to make a living.*

The most refreshing sight of all was the twosome Bill O'Neal and Rusty Barnes, who landed in the Lear ahead of the president of Mexico. Bill and I recalled our flights together almost four years before at Jonestown, all the runs we made from Guyana to Trinidad and Tobago, Barbados, and Puerto Rico. John Boy Vincent and I settled back in the lap of luxury and felt the Lear roar down the runway and lift for the sky. Quixote poured himself a generous shot of whiskey, held it high in tribute, then bolted it. By the time we took off I had the script for the *Evening News* piece roughed out, and by the time we landed for fuel in Merida I had the script typed. John Boy made some good suggestions, and I incorporated them. We cleared immigration in Merida and headed up over the Gulf to Miami, from where we would feed our volcano story up the line to New York. John Boy and I drank beer and screwdrivers while crossing the Caribbean and Cuba. "Here's to you, Fidel, Baby." We had Jimmy Buffett on stereo, "Margaritaville," "Miss You So Badly," and "Banana Republics."

It was John Boy's first ride in a Lear, and he thought he had died and gone straight to Heaven.

Instead of knocking on St. Peter's door, John Vincent and I the next day, Palm Sunday, rose above the towering Florida clouds and headed for Buenos Aires. Argentina had invaded the Falkland Islands, a storm John Boy and I could not resist. We were wheels up from Miami International at 11:00 p.m., streaking back down the Caribbean in search of the story of the year. There would be many big stories to come in 1982—a 737 commercial jet crashed into the Potomac at Washington D.C., killing seventy-eight people...John Belushi died of a drug overdose...Israel invaded Lebanon...a 747 jet crashed in New Orleans, killing 149 people...Ingrid Bergman and Princess Grace died...Gen. William Westmoreland sued CBS for $120-million...Soviet leader Leonid Brezhnev died...and Barney Clark became the first recipient of a permanent artificial heart. But on Palm Sunday, April 4, 1982, "John Boy" and Don Quixote, a.k.a "Dad," were off to see the sorcerer in a scorched place on the underside of the world—Comodora Rivadavia.

Un de mis sueños anoche comprendió nuestro hijo. Él fué muy hermoso. Gracias, Lalie, mí corazón, para su amor. ¡Te amo, siempre!

After we landed in Buenos Aires, it was necessary for John Boy and me to fly across the Río de la Plata to Montevideo, Uruguay, to obtain visas to Argentina. Montevideo was gray and grim. I remarked to John Boy: "In Argentina, there are a lot of little men going around picking up little pieces of dirt. In Uruguay, there is hardly any need for any such little men. It is that clean."

Uruguay, with its then high standard of living, appeared even more distinctly Old World than Argentina. Thanks to John Boy, we obtained our visas. Moral: when dealing with Latin Americans—be patient, be persistent, cajole, flatter, smile, but above all, *do not*, repeat, *do not* lose your temper. New York City and Rome cab drivers need not apply.

By 7:30 in the evening we were back in Buenos Aires, where we finally cleared immigration. I took John Boy to La Mosca Blanca for Argentina's finest steaks. It is quite possible that most North Americans never in their lives will experience the incomparable flavor of natural, pampas-fed Argentinean beef. No hurry. Nothing artificial. Steroids and growth stimulators don't count. Aging meat is an art form and a passion, and the waiters serve as if they care. After our feast, we returned to the Sheraton and turned in for the night.

We juggled charters and commercial flights most of the next day trying to reach Comodoro Rivadavia, the jumping-off place for the Falkland Islands, which the Argentineans called Las Malvinas. About 4:30 p.m. we departed B.A. on Aerolineas Argentinas, southbound for Rivadavia on the lip of Patagonia, a city of almost a hundred thousand — dry, dusty, and windy. The South Atlantic moon was full and the Southern Cross was shining, but we were ordered to close the shades on the windows of the plane so that we could not see the military buildup on the ground. The army had the airport under tight wraps. We took cabs into the city and checked in at the Austral Hotel, simple and European.

It appears we will be here until there's a war or until diplomatic negotiations save face on both sides of this little piece of idiocy. From the Argentinean perspective, it seems they are damn well determined to claim Las Malvinas come hell or high British.

I quickly wrote a script, and we went to the highest point overlooking Rivadavia and the Gulf of San Jorge, where we recorded the narration, and I did an on-camera "bridge." We shipped what we had to Buenos Aires. I went to bed at the Austral, thinking more about Dallas, Texas, than a war over the frigging Falkland Islands. But in Miami, John Boy and I had asked for it, and here we were. We had nobody to blame but ourselves. We had met the enemy, and it was us.

It was becoming increasingly difficult to enter the airport. Soldiers were checking all passports. I saw helicopters, C130s, supplies, and troops, but there was no way, without being arrested, to take a picture of any of it. There was nothing to do but go to dinner. There was an excellent seafood restaurant with a fine view of the sea beneath a bright full moon and my first widened view of the Southern Cross. Close by,

Centaurus was a reminder of man's dissatisfaction even with himself.

Control of the Falkland Islands had been in the hands of the British for 149 years, although Argentina had historically disputed the claim. The shepherds and kelpers of the Falklands, with their 4,700 square miles on 200 islands, needed the Brits and the Argentineans about as much as any peaceful people need a remote, self-serving patriarch. The major industry was raising sheep, the major export was wool. The British were 8,000 miles distant and the Argentineans were 250 miles away. There was trouble in paradise.

Good Friday in Comodora Rivadavia, and I woke up missing you, mi corazón. I rested well last night, wished I might have reached you on the phone, but accepted the fact that I could not.

John Boy came rushing in with the news that a funeral would be held about midday for a nineteen-year-old marine killed April 2 during the Argentinean invasion of the South Georgia Islands, the 1,450 square-mile dependency of the Falklands almost 1,000 miles to the southeast. In 1775, Capt. John Cook claimed South Georgia for Great Britain. Formerly a whaling port, it had become a jumping off place for Antarctica, a place Quixote would have loved to see.

John Boy had obtained permission from the military to photograph the funeral, where family and friends were grieving. It was U.S. network television's meat and potatoes. The mother of the youth cried, "¡Mí hijo! !Mí hijo! Don't take him away!" We watched and we listened and we took pictures. We were unquestionably desensitized, but so was the audience in the United States.

I did an on-camera as the funeral procession headed for the cemetery, and I slipped in all I could about the military buildup in Comodoro Rivadavia, all the things we weren't permitted to photograph with our electronic tape. I was able to do it with the camera in my head. We made our phone calls to B.A. and N.Y., cut the soundtrack, and sped to the airport. Later I would learn that my funeral story had been shoehorned into a Bob Schieffer piece. I forlornly rationalized that if I had to be big-footed by somebody, it might as well be Bob, who'd been a friend since the day I met him when he first came to work for CBS in Washington. That was during the Vietnam War protest rally in November of 1969,

BRAZIL

ARGENTINA

URUGUAY

Buenos Aires

Montevideo

CHILE

Atlantic Ocean

Comodoro
Rivadavia

San Jorge Gulf

Stanley

Tierra del
Fuego

FALKLAND ISLANDS

when 250,000 people demonstrated from the Capitol to the Pentagon.

Saturday in Holy Week, 1982: *We were told that starting today, all phone calls made outside Argentina would have to be approved by the national police. As I write these lines in my miniature room on the 5th floor of the Austral Hotel, it is not difficult for me to feel as if I am an inmate. It is colder today, not an especially cheerful Easter eve. Only thoughts of your love keep me warm. But what I want most of all is you and our child and years of peace and happiness together in Kentucky.*

I attended the 11:00 a.m. mass at the Catholic Church in Comodoro Rivadavia. Soldiers were attending the services, and we were permitted to take pictures of them being the good little religious soldiers they allegedly were. It is wrong for Quixote to be so judgmental. The soldiers had their own relationships with the Almighty, did they not? Who was I to lord it over them? I was reminded in a prophetic way of the television documentary I had done at WHAS in Louisville in the mid-'60s. It was titled "My Son, the Soldier." It was a primitive attempt, but it was to a great extent prophetic of the relationship of children playing war with guns and young men fighting and dying in real combat.

I called my son Sam in Lexington as he and his wife were preparing to leave for his new job at WCBS-TV in New York. I was glad I had attended the wedding, and I was relieved that the priest had permitted me to be best man. I didn't know whether Sam had discussed my "impediments" with the good Father, and I didn't ask. I was not herded into the confessional, and I didn't push my luck. Sam said his traditional Easter party included a lot of tears concerning his leaving Kentucky. He could not then know that his time in New York would be short, or that he would join the NBC affiliate in Orlando before returning to WKYT-TV, the CBS affiliate in Lexington, Kentucky.

April 12, 1982. *Had trouble sleeping last night. Wish I could even come close to describing the horrifying dream I had night before last. It was the human equivalent of the process used in the poultry industry of converting chicken offal into chicken feed and shoveling it back down the long-necked throats of more hungry chickens. In the dream, two of the biggest chickens were George Orwell and Franz Kafka.*

I read up my script to producer Jennifer Siebens in Buenos Aires and heard her unyielding opinion that the Monday *Evening News* would not go for our footage of Easter services, which I had thought so graphically demonstrated the melding of church, military, and poor mortal chickens. I wrote an alternate script, but I was bloody tired of being chopped to pieces, when what I was saying was important and timely—or so I believed.

April 13. *The word from B.A. now is that the recent optimism about a settlement of the Falkland Islands issue has been solidly and thuddingly replaced with a deep case of pessimism, so we're back to saber rattling and the sowing of dragons' teeth. This begins our fourth week apart, and I need you desperately."*

John Boy drove the crew and me south down the coastal highway from Comodoro Rivadavia. We had not gone far before we encountered, going in the opposite direction, a long military convoy, including anti-aircraft guns. It appeared to be communications and other support equipment and artillery shells by the truckload. I had John Boy make a U-turn, pass the entire convoy and find a high hill in Rivadavia, where we pretended to be taking pictures of soaring seagulls. When the convoy passed through, we captured it all on tape. I called coordinating producer David Miller in B.A., and without going into specifics (calls were monitored by the national police), I told him we had some "good stuff." We could not ship the tape on a commercial flight in time for the *Evening News*. Out in the street, I did an on-camera, which happened to be directly across from a record shop. The owner came over and gave me a copy of a record called "Las Marchas de Las Malvinas." We shot pictures of soldiers loading up a truck with contributions from civilians to the Argentinean occupation force on the Falklands. We were in a rush to script and record narration for the last evening flight to B.A. in time for *Morning News*. This led to an argument with David Miller over who would get the convoy footage, *Evening* or *Morning*. The peeing contest was resolved by the Good Lord, who changed the airline schedule. *Evening News* would be the first to have the piece the next day.

I placed a call to you in Woodville, and we wished each other happy anniversary. You said you looked across the street to St. Paul's and found it hard to believe that we were married there four years ago today.

I was up at 7:00 a.m. to rewrite the script for our offering to the *CBS Evening News*. Before recording, I checked with Jennifer Siebens in B.A. She said ABC had blown us away with footage from the Falklands two nights in a row. Here they come. Duck your head. Rockets from New York. Wounded animals in B.A. Dead meat in Comodoro Rivadavia. All of our effort to try to reach the Falklands from Rivadavia had fizzled. ABC had figured out a way. *I'm ready to get out of here. Oh, God! Let's make love, not war.*

If I thought feces had hit the fan, I hadn't seen anything yet. Some worthless no-good at the airport had either forgotten or willfully failed to put our convoy footage shipment on the plane, and we didn't hear about it until B.A. called down in a panic. I sent John Boy back to the airport, and he found the shipping bag still sitting in the Aerolineas Argentinas office. He stayed to watch it go out on the next flight, which, of course, left late. The footage I thought was, as the Brits like to say, so tickety-boo, added up to about ten pathetic seconds in Bob Schieffer's story. My piece did not air. That wasn't all. When we returned to the airport late in the afternoon to interview the Minister of Defense and a group of Anglo-Argentineans just returned from a one-day visit to Las Malvinas, who should step off the plane but—you guessed it—the National Biscuit Company. We deposited more of those little shiny green goat marbles on the floor of the airport. I commiserated with the mortally wounded animals in B.A., took a hot shower, enjoyed a most delightfully hot, prolonged bidet, ate a little supper, went to bed, and dreamed of Plum Lick in Kentucky.

Just had a call from Vincent at the airport, who said the military had taken over the flight to B.A. and that we could not ship on it. He also said he heard on the radio that British journalist Simon Winchester had been arrested and charged with espionage for taking pictures of a military installation down near the southern tip of Argentina.

There was a dog-and-pony show (also known in textbook journalism as the "feeding of the goats") on the second Sunday after Easter. Even crumbs of news were suspect. We were invited to come to the airport at

217

Comodoro to take pictures of what Quixote described as a kind of
M*A*S*H unit, a mobile medical facility hurriedly set up, giving a half-
hearted impression that it might actually be needed. I interviewed a
brigadier general who said you never could tell, you've got to be ready.
Much to our surprise, the military authorities decided to give us
permission to take pictures of planes and other war materiel at the
airport. We were taken around, like children by the hand, and we were
repeatedly warned of the dire consequences should we sneak a shot of
something we shouldn't, whatever the hell that was.

"You will take pictures only of what we tell you."

If that didn't satisfy the military mind, an officer spot-checked our
tape cassette through the camera's viewfinder before we could leave. I
quickly wrote a script, and we recorded it on the spot. I sent John Boy as
pigeon to B.A. with our shipment. Access to the airport had become
even more Orwellian. *And I say to myself, don't cry for Argentina.*

We retreated to the Austral and watched a movie provided by the
American Biscuit Company. It was Richard Pryor in *Stir Crazy*. "We
bad, we bad" was the sweetest of comic relief.

The next day we were escorted on another dog-and-pony escapade,
this time to the Ninth Logistical Brigade north of Comodoro Rivadavia.
We saw tanklike personnel carriers, camouflaged anti-aircraft guns, raw
recruits cleaning automatic weapons, and food supplies being taken from
storehouses and loaded onto trucks. I did an on-camera, then the crew
and I headed back to the city. I wrote a script and read it to Susan
Zirinsky, who in turn read it to N.Y. The decision: "Broadcast too full
tonight, write it so it will work for *Morning News*." I already had.

I became aware, in all its bloody-minded detail, how there had been a
capacious screwup in the CBS office in Buenos Aires. After receiving
waves of rockets for days because we "had no pictures from the
Malvinas," John Vincent pointed out the two cassettes we had dubbed
from the local television station in Comodoro Rivadavia the first day
we'd made our beachhead. The world's greatest communicators had
completely overlooked them—the first two tapes in their library right in
front of their beady little eyes. John Boy said everybody had been
"sworn to secrecy" never to reveal it. Talk about Richard Nixon's tape

cover-up! On the way to the airport to ship, we met Vincent coming from B.A. We turned him around and sent the poor devil right back. I was too fed up with the crowd of reporters to go to dinner with any of them. Instead I found an excuse to eat majestically alone in the coffee shop at the Austral Hotel—medium-well steak and regular Coca-Cola, topped off with chocolate cake and vanilla ice cream.

I had a good, sharp, fertile feeling that in four short years I would retire from CBS to love you and to raise our family in Kentucky. It's been one month since I said goodbye to you at Miami International Airport. In a telephone conversation with Miller in B.A., he said Dan Rather had called to tell him to tell me how much my work was appreciated. It was the "Rather touch" that was cherished when it was earned.

Word was passed down to me that my son Sam had been on the air a number of times at WCBS-TV in New York, conspicuously in the story of the murders of three CBS technicians. They had been leaving the Broadcast Center about 6:00 p.m. and, in a parking structure, had come upon a man holding a woman hostage at gunpoint. The technicians had tried to be Good Samaritans, but the man killed them and the woman. Somehow, the killer wound up in Kentucky, and Sam was sent there to continue the story. This one was no dream—it was reality—and my child was beginning his own career of following storms.

Argentina's President Galtieri made a refueling stop in Rivadavia, but we missed it. It was just as well. The only TV cameraman who got it (*VIS News* from Colombia) was arrested later in the day for taking pictures in the city, nothing more that street scenes, and he would spend time in jail until his film was processed in B.A. and returned to Rivadavia. It was the kind of intimidating circumstances under which we were working, yet it was all immaterial. New York had put us on the back burner because of Israel's four-hour bombing of Beirut.

Friday, April 23, 1982. I was told in a phone conversation to B.A. that someone other than myself was going to the Falklands, and I accepted it. Before you could say Jack Sprat, I said to David Miller: "When do I go home?"

He said, "How about one week more?"

"Fine. *¡Muy fino!*"

President Galtieri came through the airport at Rivadavia on his way back to Buenos Aires, and we attended his news conference. Physically he was impressive, likened by some to Juan Perón. Bob Schieffer came into town with cameraman Domingo Rex from Mexico City, and the grand strategy was for them to go with two from ABC to the Falklands. CNN went into a total tailspin and NBC sulked, even though it had already kicked butt by being the first to get to the islands. Later in the evening, somebody, we didn't know who, threw a monkey wrench into the whole business—the Argentinean military authorities canceled the trip. There was speculation that the British Navy was too close for comfort and that there might be a war "this weekend." I had my doubts, but I was wrong. The fighting would begin on May 1.

Since I'd been repeatedly big-footed, and since I'd been gone from the United States for over a month, I started my own war to get the hell out of Dodge. Schieffer and Rex were heading back to B.A., and I was told to make sure "we don't get aced out of a trip to the Malvinas, in case it's back on again." What shittiness. What goofiness. What gratitude! Quixote took a nap and left a few more claw marks on the walls of his room.

On this third Sunday after Easter, I thank God I am alive, and I pray there will be no war between Argentina and Great Britain, and that I will be on my way to Baton Rouge in about one week. I pray, selfishly I pray, the Lord will let me live these next four years so that I might come in off the road, stop following storms, and retire—to love you every day for the rest of my natural life.

To David Miller I repeated the crew's and my desire to return the following Saturday to the United States. He foresaw no problem and hoped to have a clearer idea the first of the week. Fine. Muy fino. I asked him if he would be leaving too. He said: "I cannot walk away from the number-one story in the world." The Brits *might* call that "toffee-nosed."

"I don't want you to think that that's what I'm doing, but I'm in my second month in this sorry sack of a place," I enjoined.

"I spent four months in El Salvador and went from there to Tel Aviv for four months without going home to Rome," Miller shot back. He said that CBS was his "whole life" and without it he "had nothing." There was a time when I was saying pretty much the same thing. Not anymore. The Millers could have it.

I didn't pursue the conversation any farther. *But, I'll tell you this* (Quixote wrote in his journal): *CBS News is no longer everything I have….I have riches beyond measure…. I have a future outside CBS….I am not a corporate machine that one day will grind to a dizzy stop…. Neither the David Millers nor the Dan Rathers will decide my fate. I'm not bitter. I know what I want and where I'm heading. Oh, God, we've now begun getting reports of military action in the South Georgia Islands, apparently some activity involving British helicopters and Argentinean submarines, perhaps some injuries. CBS in B.A. is becoming as hyper as you might expect. Good God, help us if CBS News is ever called upon to run a government or fight a war. Can you imagine a President Cronkite or a General Rather? The first thing they'd proba-bly do would be to lock up all the Quixotes.*

Reporters went to Comodoro Rivadavia's rendition of the "Five O'clock Follies" (a highly structured and questionable news briefing), which was livelier than usual because of the rumors piling up on top of rumors that the Brits had now captured the South Georgias—and there had been casualties. No comment in Comodoro. I talked to B.A. and heard that the two fine scripts and the excellent footage we had sent up had been "overtaken by events." Most probably none of it would ever see air. *And so it goes in elegant downtown Comodoro Rivadavia. There's supposed to be another blackout tonight. Shucks, folks, I think I'll just cozy up to the bidet, jump into bed, play a game of Pac Man on Manny's miniature computer, and pull the covers over my head. If I'm lucky, I might have a sexy dream.*

Our new field producer, David Caravello, was turning out to be what we feared he would, a super "go-get-em," "let's-get-this-story-NOW" type, and Quixote calculated that it was going to take a few days to quiet him down. *Nothing much new on our little war—the Brits say they've secured the South Georgias, but everything remains roughly the equivalent of ho-hum in Disney World Comodora Rivadavia.*

The thing that strikes me most of all is what I perceive to be the Argentinean mentality, if there is such a thing still residing in the average man so unconditionally dominated by the military regime. Authoritarianism is stultifying, devastating to the spirit, which ought to be the basic nature, the soul of every human being. It's as if the people don't comprehend what they've lost. This country, like any totalitarian regime, could produce its own Hitler and there might be a lot of folks unaware that one day they may pay with their lives.

The Argentinean military's paranoia about cameras was absolute. We were denied permission to take pictures of the school in Comodoro. ABC was stopped from photographing workmen repairing the sidewalks. I paused to smell a rose, but there was no fragrance. There must be justness here — but I hadn't found it. I decided to buy a ticket for B.A. for the next day and if possible make arrangements straight away to Miami. I would only have to pay my hotel bill in B.A. and gather up my belongings in the Miami bureau.

We were informed at the Five O'Clock Follies that there would be a big night rally in the Plaza de San Martín, so we covered it, and it gave good pictures. Manny did a yeoman's job of shooting it, holding the camera high above his head like a tennis racquet, and I hustled up a script using my typewriter on the hood of our car. We raced to the airport and producer Caravello barely made it on the last flight to B.A. John Boy and I returned to town and telexed Miller that Caravello was coming in with a "good" story and needed an editor at midnight to cut the piece for *Morning News*. I ate dinner with NBC, CNN, and *Newsweek* at Ronstrol Restaurant and ascertained that all newsmen south of Comodoro had been ordered to leave. Quixote prayed to the Lord that he'd be next.

April 27, 1982. *Happy birthday dear old boy, Ulysses S. Grant, one hundred and sixty years old today! A southerner salutes you. What is past is past, and we are one nation now.* What Grant had done to Vicksburg, surrounding it and capturing it, Britain's Iron Lady, Margaret Thatcher, was about to do to the Falkland Islands. She imposed a blockade on this date.

I had a call from Jennifer Siebens in Buenos Aires bringing me up to date on what CBS knew there. She said that Argentina's military appeared confused and divided as to how to respond to the British takeover of the South Georgia Islands, and Dan Rather had said that the Brits might be soon attacking the Falkland Islands, or might already have commandos landed there. If all this was true, Argentina might be about to have its butt kicked, and who knows what then would happen to the junta headed by President Galtieri? How about reform school? We seemed to be headed for a juicy time. I was told to prepare for our Tuesday night offering, a "paragraph or two" on "what we know and what we don't know" (Dan Ratherese) in Comodoro, along with any wallpaper footage we could find. As Dan would concede, this'd be like trying to hang Texas deer gut on a doorknob.

We found out there would be a special noon news conference at which I would not be surprised if we were told we'd been ordered to leave the area. Quixote's bags were packed! There was no surprise. Col. Esteban Solís announced that all foreign journalists had forty-eight hours to get out of Comodoro Rivadavia. I could have kissed his big fat, Machiavellian bald head. But I only sighed a deep, silent breath of relief. I did a quick on-camera, a little lead-in to the news conference, and rushed John Boy and the cassette to the airport, bag and baggage. I telexed B.A. concerning what had happened and got into another low-level peeing contest with Miller about when the crew and I would be heading back to the States. Foreign Editor Peter Larkin was not even acknowledging our requests, and I received a micro-sermon from Miller about newsmen being newsmen and staying with the Big Story. Bullshit.

We were told to go north to Puerto Belgrano, wherever in hell that was—I was betting my bottom peso we were persona non grata there too. Even Argentineans know that wherever you go, there you are. Our plan was to stay in Comodoro until the last possible moment of our forty-eight hours and then head north, more than likely to Buenos Aires. The high point of the final Five O'Clock Follies was Colonel Solís re-reading the get-the-hell-out-of-our-town communiqué, which he had read at noon. John Boy called from B.A. to tell me "they," the Rather wannabes, were down on us in Comodoro, mainly me, because they said we had been doing little if anything the past several days.

Just somehow, dear Lord, get me through the last four years of my contract. There will be no more CBS except retirement checks after 1985. In the meantime, I will take as few chances as possible.

As I look back on it from my 2002 view from Plum Lick, the most important thing that happened to me during my entire time in Comodoro was my stumbling upon eighty-five-year-old Jimmy MacLeon Robertson, who'd come from Scotland to Patagonia when he was sixteen. He had stayed. He made more sense than anybody I'd talked to in many years. Jimmy and I rattled on over robust cups of espresso about how he married when he was fifty-seven years old a woman twenty-one years his junior. He told me about their three sons who grew up on the camp on their 20,000 acres about 400 kilometers west of Comodoro in the Patagonia heartland. He told me about his 200 cows and his thousands of sheep, and about how freedom used to feel good in Argentina, but how it had fundamentally changed under an authoritarian regime. I told him about my retirement plans. Jimmy smiled when I described Lalie, and he talked about his wife who, he said, also anticipated his every need. He acknowledged that it felt good to be eighty-five years old, knowing well Bobby Burns and "The Cotter's Saturday Night":

> *His clean hearth-stane, his thrifty wifie's smile,*
> *The lisping infant prattling on his knee,*
> *Does a' his weary kiaugh and care beguile,*
> *And makes him quite forget his labour an' his toil.*

April 28, 1982. *I am into my sixth week away from you, and I feel almost helpless to do anything more to speed up my return, so I'm going to hunker down and make the best of the damn situation. Our day is coming, as surely as I know anything in this tired old warring world. When it's done, I'll take my leave from CBS a free man to do as I wish without idiot-box shamans on my butt about anything.*

Fabulous news! We would shoot on this day a "Goodbye Comodoro" piece for Thursday's *Evening News*. We would say our fond farewell to Rivadavia on the next afternoon's flight to Buenos Aires, the crew and I to go on to Miami on Friday!

I'm sitting in the coffee shop, while Manny 'The Wild Cuban,' gets pictures of the ABC crew packing it in and leaving the hotel for the airport. At the last Five O'Clock Follies, I shook hands with Colonel Solís, gave him a big old smile, and told him, Adiós. The look on his face was a blend of "good riddance" and "where did they dig this one up?"

We—Caravello, John Boy, the "Wild Cuban," Irv, and I—spent most of the final hours working on our last little piece of tap-dancing in Comodoro Rivadavia. We toured the city, picking up street scenes, and returned to the top of the high hill overlooking the Gulf of San Jorge. When we had finished all our shooting and were parking in front of our hotel, two policemen advanced on us. They took John Boy and me to the police station. We were told to wait. They took away our credentials. It was eerie to be led down a narrow corridor to a dark, cell-like room where there was a small desk and two small chairs, and a soldier's face that looked into your face and wanted to know if you were a spy. If it was only an attempt to chill journalism, it worked. We had no desire to be thrown into a prison cell on trumped up charges of espionage. Untold numbers of journalists in Argentina in the twentieth century had been killed, their bodies dumped out of helicopters flying over the South Atlantic.

The soldiers sat sober as judges behind the little table. There was a large stick nearby. It bore its own silent message. Questions were asked slowly and coldly. After taking our names, they wanted the names of our colleagues. We had to prove that our Ford Falcon was rented as we said it was. They wanted to know what we were doing at 12:40 p.m. John Boy smiled his confident and charming smile and told them exactly where we'd been. He'd kept a time code. Someone had turned us in at that precise moment. We were asked if we knew that we were in the vicinity of a fire station. It was hard to believe they'd try to put us away on something so transparent. The only thing that saved us was John Boy's calm, non-menacing, unafraid aspect. He politely told them that we had permission from Colonel Solís to do what we were doing. They cleared their throats, looked at each other, and backed off. We were released. Simple as that. Quixote made a mental note to dance at John Boy's wedding.

We booked on a heavenly flight leaving two hours before the

deadline for all foreign journalists to be out of the area. We did an interview with Tony Hillman of the CBC. He would not be leaving until a court decided what to do about the spy charges brought against him and his crew. I had a long talk with Joel Halderman of the brand new CNN, who wanted to go to Chile, head south, rent a boat, and go through the Beagle Channel in order to sneak back into southern Argentina. *Have at it, fellow, and tell the frigging penguins, hello! I've got my lover to woo, and I don't need to look back over my shoulder one time. I know where I'm heading and whom I want to see when I get there.*

April 29, 1982. The day we were to leave Comodoro Rivadavia, twenty-three days after we had come upon the scene. I wrote another draft of our television script and by 7:20 was in the lobby of the Austral, bag and baggage. I paid my bill, but not one word in Spanish or English from the cashier at the front desk, such as thanks, Gringo, for your business—not a smile—not a farewell of any kind. But, hell, maybe the feeling was mutual. Argentinean Air Force pilots, their hair combed straight back like Valentinos, .45-automatics smartly in their holsters, paced back and forth. It was still dark outside. I did an on-camera bridge on the street at the corner near the hotel, and then we headed for the airport, where we ran into another thorough scrutiny. We weren't strip-searched, but it was the next thing to it. Soldiers went through my attaché like doctors looking for germs. No smiles. They read my scripts, wire copy, even my expense accounts. It made me anxious, but John Boy had schooled me well in smooth shit-eating grins. Sancho Panza's words also returned—Paco's "Tranquilo, tranquilo."

At 10:10 a.m., Aerolineas Argentinas vuelo 625 started moving down the runway. The music on the intercom was "The Way We Were." Quixote felt the start of tears, but they didn't come. I remembered Bobby Burns and "The Cotter's Saturday Night." As the jetliner skirted Patagonia, the thought returned of old Jimmy MacLeon Robertson— would his sons and their sons forget not the dream of freedom, nor choose to sow more seeds of authoritarianism?

In Buenos Aires, I right away bought my ticket to Miami. Miller, in his usual flurry of motion, told me I was going to do a live debriefing on the next day's *CBS Morning News*. Muy fino. I signed into a room at the

Sheraton, confirmed my reservation for the next late evening flight to Miami, and took my first deep, hot bath in weeks. It was tempting to help the cause of working girls, for they were stacked high in Buenos Aires—Big Apple! They needed the money as much as returning journalists ached for release of bottled up passions.

No, Señora, I'm leaving B.A., that is to say if the Brits don't liquidate ten thousand Argentineans or the Argentineans don't vanquish ten thousand Brits. Yes, I know you need the pesos, but you really should go back to your family before it's too late. Are there no more silver spoons to sell?

April 20. *Happy twenty-sixth birthday, Sam. Your father wishes you every success at WCBS-TV in New York. Here I am in Buenos Aires, and if I'm the luckiest man in the world, I'll be heading for Miami tonight.* I was up before 6:00, read some more, and at 8:18 was doing a live two-way debriefer with Bill Kurtis on *Morning News*. It was over so quickly I hardly had time to say anything. I knew all about sound bites, now I was one. Without hesitation, I went back to work on my airline reservations—Pan Am to Miami, American Airlines through Dallas to Baton Rouge. I called Lalie to tell her it seemed possible that I would arrive by 3:00 the next afternoon. In the CBS office, Miller kept making remarks about my walking away from a story. I was determined not to let it get to me or to make me lose my temper. But I was right close to giving him a royal piece of my mind. Look at it this way: there are junkyard dogs and there are mild mannered Labrador retrievers. Each has a different job to do. Miller was doing his, and I was doing mine.

Secretary of State Alexander Haig announced that if push came to shove, the United States would side with Great Britain over the Falkland Islands. I nuzzled up to my friend Mr. Miller and told him that the "Wild Cuban," his soundman, Irv, and I would work in any way possible to help. So we were sent to a stakeout in front of Casa Rosada just in case President Galtieri had anything to say to reporters. He didn't, of course, and I don't know why he would. We picked up footage of people practicing the art of sidewalk dialogue and there was a Venezuelan demonstration, which was pro-Argentina. When we moseyed back to the CBS office, Manny and Irv were told to leave for Miami, and I was told unceremoniously to report to Montevideo, Uruguay, that evening. I was too numb to commit hara-kiri. But anyway, I liked Uruguay, no matter what the liberals said about it, so I'd take what most likely was going to be a last look.

I said goodbye to John Boy. We gave each other a warm abrazo, and I wished him well as he continued his rambling life through Latin America. He wished "Dad" a good life back in the States and eventually on Plum Lick in Kentucky. John Boy was youth at its zenith, energy at the bursting point, enthusiasm unbounded, imagination thrown open, the leading edge of life at its sharpest. Humanity loved him, and so did I.

Quixote, one of the new old farts, bit his tongue and shook hands with David Miller and wished him a happy Falkland Islands war. I caught the 9:30 shuttle across the Río de la Plata to Montevideo. It was good to be out of Argentina. My driver took me to the Colombia Palace Hotel, where I checked into room 701. The first thing I did was to call Lalie: "Te amo, mi corazón." I asked her to watch the Kentucky Derby the next day, Saturday, May 1, 1982. I asked her to watch it for the two of us. At day's end, Gato Del Sol wore the roses, and a few weeks later in the last leg of the Triple Crown, Conquistador Cielo would capture the Belmont Stakes. Maybe it was Latin American poetic justice.

May 1. *The view of the mouth of the Río de la Plata from the Colombia Hotel in Montevideo is peaceful, pleasing in its gray Old-Worldness. Sailboats glide by. People fish with long poles. Feelings seem reserved. Somber. Conservative. Deep. There is a caring about antiquity. Preservation is a given. Values have accumulated in people and things. It's not the disposable society of the United States or littering cultures throughout the world. Uruguay is rhapsody in blue—a mood piece, slow to the touch, aging like fine wine. Freedom has an Uruguayan definition. Freedom, too, is in the eye of the beholder. Benign dictatorships are not necessarily oxymorons. Democracies can be malignant. Even slavery has degrees of definition. Some free people are slaves without ever knowing it.*

We heard on the radio that the Brits had staged an air attack early on the morning of May 1 on the airfield at Port Stanley in the Falklands, but understandably there were conflicting reports. Argentina claimed it had shot down two British planes, but the Brits denied it. The CBS News branch office in Montevideo, installed as a backup to the one across the river in Buenos Aries, represented a typical tactic for following a storm: straddle the target, hedge all bets, stay flexible. I had my own plan to avoid being ground into any finer cannon fodder. The edge of enthusiasm for more risk-taking was dulling. Or had I fallen deeper into moaning and groaning, the whining and whoring stage, as Roger Mudd used to say? Whatever the characterization, the desire to be with my wife had deepened, and the next day I received permission from CBS to leave Uruguay and return to the United States.

I flew back across the Río de la Plata to Buenos Aires, and I was first in line to board Aerolineas Argentinas 322, a jumbo 747. It was the best feeling I'd had in six weeks.

I've been marveling at the ability of the brain to recover and reroute and put on display certain memories, certain categories of memories. I believe that it is true that the brain has an infinite capacity, does not forget, and does not delete anything. Later, looking back at it from my view from Plum Lick, I was unsure about what causes Alzheimer's disease, oblivious of the reality of alcohol killing brain cells. Surely there's a reason why certain kinds of thought are readily retrievable and controllable by the conscious part of the mind. I have a self-incriminating category, and it works counter to my best interests. I should hit the delete button for this category and open up a new document called "'Be Good to David."

The 747 approached Río de Janeiro, and the lights of the city shone like diamonds. I looked for the Christ of the Andes, but I didn't see it. We landed and were told we must deboard while the plane was being serviced. The female Brazilian voices coming through the terminal's intercom system were Portuguese-sultry, rich, melodious, awfully sexy. A salivating Don Quixote sat down and made his lonely journal entry:

The Argentinean paper I've been reading claims eleven British planes have been shot down—if that's so it would be a disaster for Maggie. Let's hope it's not. C'mon limeys, let's kick some butt!

I was back on the Aerolineas Argentinas shortly before midnight, and I didn't say anything about my loyalties. *We're now backing away from the terminal at Galaño International Airport in Río. So long, Brazil, it's been good to know you, all of one hour. You girls of Ipanema missed your big chance. Lalie is the star I'm tracking!*

Monday, May 3. *I'm wide awake after midnight on this flight from Río to Miami, looking at myself in the mirror of el baño, telling myself no one receives engraved invitations to become fulfilled, physically, or spiritually—it's something which must, and rightly so, come from within. Are you listening, David?*

Corazón, I feel winged sweetness in the writing of these words as I fly in the early hours of this day, high in a 747 somewhere over South America, maybe over what is left of the People's Temple, Jim Jones's cabin, the pavilion, the dormitories reclaimed by the jungle. Port Kaituma airstrip stained with death. Suffocating heat. Sounds of gunfire. "She went over and sat down and gave herself the poison. I didn't know how a mother could do that." At last, over the Caribbean, Quixote waited patiently for the eastern horizon to brighten with another madrugada. Listening to stereophonic music, the lyrics of Buffett's "Margaritaville" spiral from a shelf in the brain, where there're love and restitution of contentment.

The Gulf of Mexico between Miami and New Orleans was blue and a welcome sight. I crossed my fingers that I would make the next connecting flight to Baton Rouge, as I had from Miami to New Orleans. *I'm now down to my last twenty minutes before I see you again, maybe another ten minutes until I'm in your arms.*

And here we are, finally, back at our airport, Ryan Field. And there you are as I open the door of the waiting room and step straight into yours arms for the first time since March 23, 1982.

CHAPTER THIRTEEN

Plum Lick. May 29, 1982. We're on vacation in Kentucky, respite and reprieve from following storms. *We went over to Billy Wayne's to be there at the 8:00 a.m. starting time. The rest of the non-television, non-media, non-career-driven crew was already at the tobacco beds, and soon we were on the mechanical setter, working steadily and methodically back and forth across the patches of rich, freshly harrowed and dragged ground. We'd come over past Bunker Hill to Montgomery County to help Billy Wayne Gilvin and his family. They in turn would come to Plum Lick in Bourbon County to help us. Two jet setters had become pretty good Kentucky tobacco setters. The two more experienced men on either side of us had to do a heap of filling in for us whenever we got to tripping in our underwear. Every once in a while, we set the plants upside down, a reminder about best-laid plans.*

We broke as usual for midday "dinner," prepared by Nancy Gilvin. She'd cooked a juicy and tender roast, steaming corn pudding, and two kinds of pie. While we ate, there was the distant muffled sound of thunder. It had been quite hot, and we knew there was considerable likelihood of an afternoon thunderstorm. Local wisdom said to listen to the weatherman, then look up! We did, and it turned out to be a lot worse than we'd thought.

We'd begun setting plants again when there was a buildup of clouds to the west. It passed us to the north, but then there was another coming at us from the south. Lightning began to play around with our apprehensions, and soon the big drops of rain began falling. We bent our heads before it, and Bill took us to the end of the row before he turned off the tractor's motor. As soon as he did that, we all jumped up and ran to the trucks and piled in just in time. Hail began hammering us with stones about half the size of black walnuts. Scarlett would never let me forget that on that day, chivalry died. The only female working on the tobacco setter that day in Camelot did not have a hand extended to her, and when she reached the cab of the pickup truck there was no more room for her there.

An exceedingly wet Lalie and I drove toward Plum Lick, where not a drop of rain had fallen. I headed up through the pasture to have a look at our cows and calves, but a wet southern belle was concerned about the lightning as well as getting dry, so we came down from the hills. We'd not lost our fascination for the sound and fury of storms and the gentleness that followed.

June 6. *I was up and about at Mt. Auburn, in my boyhood room, before the morning fog had lifted. I gave you a kiss and headed for Plum Lick. The sun was shooting shafts of light through the slowly thinning fog. Stone Road was like a large impressionistic painting—the canvas of Camelot washed through my consciousness. At the same time, the hydrologic cycles of moisture watered and fed both the good and the bad in many parts of the world.*

June 15. *Lord, time is flying by. Quixote heard on the radio this morning that the war in the Falkland Islands is over. Great Britain has claimed the surrender of the Argentinean forces at Port Stanley. The World's Greatest Story has come to a merciful end, but now comes the aftermath, which of course will go on and on and on. And the New War in the Middle East continues unabated, and of course will go on unceasingly.* The toll of the storm over the Falkland Islands: more than 150 sons of Britain dead; more than 700 sons of Argentina dead; approximately 14,000 Argentineans taken prisoner. Argentina's president Galtieri quickly resigned in disgrace.

It had begun to rain again in Camelot. It began with gentleness. It steadily increased in intensity, so that when I was driving up to Wallace Taylor's house on the Thatcher's Mill Road to talk to him about building a board fence, a mighty storm rolled over the headwaters of Strode's Creek toward Stoner Creek with lightning, thunder, wind, and heavy rain. I made it inside the house, and after a few minutes, Wallace, veteran of World War II in the South Pacific, received a telephone call that a tornado had hit to the southeast in Clark County and was headed in our direction here in Bourbon County. Luckily, the twister didn't touch down again. When the storm had spent itself, I drove to Plum Lick and found the creek cresting after a flash flood. Our tobacco was safe; but in places the fields looked like brown water Finger Lakes. Our bulldozing had done its work and our crop was high and relatively dry. I drove over to the Judy crossroads to look at the tornado damage there, thankful that we still had our barns and our houses.

There were tears in your eyes as we listened to the tape of Camelot one more time as we crossed the Bourbon County line on our way back to Dallas. In late afternoon we were finally on our way to the Bluegrass Parkway, then south on Interstate 65 out of Kentucky to Nashville, then I-40 to Memphis and Little Rock, and finally I-30 to Dallas.

June 21, 1982. *A new summer, a new moon, a new man with a new love. A new rain was falling in Dallas and, yes, there was new lightning and there was new thunder.*

June 26, 1982. *I said goodbye and boarded American Airlines 227 for Los Angeles. If all goes well I'll see you when I return to Dallas tomorrow.* The flight on the DC10 was letter-perfect. Quixote had a little breakfast, read from his space shuttle press kit, and filled another page in his journal.

The approach from the mountains and the desert toward Los Angeles was like coming in on a magic carpet to Hollywood. But not long after arriving, reality set in—yahoos in all directions, hunks of motorized steel posing as cars and buses.

I rented a National car, my own personal hunk of steel, and headed north on the freeway, I-405, to its intersection with Interstate 5. Listening to the CBS Radio affiliate, I heard pollution warnings: "Unhealthy for sensitive people." I continued northeast toward Lancaster, and after a while the air began to clear as it usually did upon leaving the Pompeiis. I signed the register at the Antelope Valley Best Western.

June 27. *The drive at 3:30 this morning from Lancaster up through the spindly little Joshua trees to Edwards Air Force Base put Quixote to thinking, which could be a dangerous thing: But hey, I've set my own priorities. Remember how invigorating it is to be up and about one's business before dawn. How important it is to be thin and healthy. The need to be in charge of my own desires, my own ambitions; the importance of not allowing anything or anybody to cause me the slightest discouragement. To be in frigging control! It is I, Don Quixote, who is all the time making overtures, visits, explanations to others, so seldom repaid. They represent the mountain. Well then, I'll simply become the mountain. No acrimony or disharmony. Simply recognition that what I need now, most of all for my fulfillment, is to be myself.*

Shortly after 4:00 a.m., I drove through the gate at Edwards and began getting myself organized. That's what I called it. At 6:15 a.m., I did my first live insert into a radio special anchored by Reid Collins at the Kennedy Space Center in Florida. All went well. I did my next live insert at 7:30 and described wind conditions as they might affect an emergency landing—the AOA—Abort Once Around. But the launch of Columbia IV with its crew of Mattingly and Hartsfield and its combination commercial and military payload went off smooth as silk.

As soon as I received my "goodnight" from the CBS News producers at the Johnson Space Center in Texas, I headed south from Edwards to Los Angeles International Airport. I toyed with the idea of dawdling— going for a swim at the beach at Malibu, visiting the old piers at Long Beach, stopping by the Pasadena Playhouse and auditioning for a part. I could drive down past San Juan Capistrano, San Clemente, and La Jolla—but I knew in my heart of hearts that what I wanted before all else was to be on Flowerdale Lane in Dallas and as soon as possible. I stood by for two flights and managed to make the second one at 4:00 p.m.

After we took off and headed briefly out over the Pacific Ocean we made the usual turn back to the left. For a moment I remembered that other life, had a clear view of those many things lodged in my brain and unalterably connected to my marriage to Rose almost thirty years before. There'd been the first kiss in the Palos Verdes Hills...the anchorage at Long Beach, where I first boarded the U.S.S. Manchester *in 1951...St. Anthony's Catholic Church where Rose and I were married in 1953...She had made her own wedding gown...Ocean Boulevard, where the first apartment was...the dark, Spanish furniture...the day I almost drowned when I was caught in a Long Beach undertow—I fought it, overcame it, returned exhausted, and fell down on the sand. "Oh, Rose" I sighed to myself. "Was it all a dream? Remember, I'd wanted to go to Mexico and write? But it was the early '50s, and there were pressures to be conventional. Lawrence Welk was music of decency. 'Father Knows Best' was the way families should be. The churchly Fathers had warned of the 'wages of sin'—venial sin, like gossip and laziness—mortal sin, like fornication and adultery. The good Fathers and the Sisters too had forewarned against 'falling away' and, worst of all, the horrors of excommunication. But life in the last quarter of the twentieth century was not meant to be so simple."*

Then the memories were gone, just like the marriage that had lasted twenty-five years, gone as quickly as it had come. No regrets, no tears—only that unavoidable looking back, no more. There was Huntington Beach of the 1960s, Palm Springs of no year thus far, the mountains whose name I did not know, the desert and then the Imperial Valley, the Colorado River, Henry Fonda and the Joad family crossing over at Needles into the glory land.

July 3. I thought I might have to go jumping off to northern Arkansas, where a band of religious loonies had hijacked a Continental Trailways bus and warned of the deaths of one passenger every half hour until a Missouri television station permitted the fanatics to broadcast a second-coming/end-of-the-world speech. I didn't have to go. Thank God, I didn't. The hostages were released and the hijacker was killed.

Memories of Jim Jones wouldn't go away.

July 6. There was a historic eclipse of the moon, but I was too busy sleeping to go out and look at it. I'll just have to wait another couple of hundred years. Word came down from New York that if Quixote was willing he might be asked to go to Israel to help cover the war with the Palestine Liberation Organization. I talked it over with Lalie, and she gave me her support. I was drawn to the excitement and maybe, more importantly, somewhere deep down inside of me, I wanted to experience the Holy Land.

I booked on flights to New York, London, and Tel Aviv. But the next day the Middle Eastern trip was off again, and I was on my way to Arkansas to do a story on illegal aliens allegedly forced to pick tomatoes. I continued reading Ambrose Bierce. The tomato story turned into a turkey.

July 8, 1982. As we passed the Pine Bluff cemetery, I asked our technician, Arnie Jensen, to stop because he had covered the funeral and burial of Martha Mitchell, the wife of President Nixon's attorney general, and I wanted to see her gravesite. We couldn't find it. How soon we forget!

Not long after we reached a telephone back in Little Rock, the call I'd been waiting for came in at our affiliate in Dallas. Southwest Bureau Chief Travis Linn simply said: "Tel Aviv."

The flight into Gatwick south of London was as silky as most magic carpet rides—tassels unfurled, colors undulating, hair blowing free. Quixote took the "Airlink" helicopter to Heathrow, giving him an outstanding view of the English countryside: the green enclosures, rich pastures, handsome and practical hedges, works of art in their own right, something we've largely lost and maybe something we never realized we had in the first place in the United States.

Our British Airways Tri-Star took off about an hour late. It was 2:30 when we passed over Dover, the English Channel, then Normandy. About ten minutes later, we were crossing in an east-southeast swoop above the continent of Europe. *Our path took us over the Alps, leaving no doubt as to their awesome height. I should like to go there with you and our child and roam the valleys of Switzerland.*

We flew east of Italy in a downward arc across the Yugoslavia of 1982, then over parts of Greece and Turkey. By the time we reached the Eastern Mediterranean shore the sun was setting the world on fire behind us; the darkness in the east allowed the lights of Tel Aviv to show off spectacularly when we came in for our landing at David Ben Gurion Airport.

I turned to the Israeli woman sitting next to me and asked her if she was concerned.

"Concerned about what?"

"Terrorism in your homeland."

"No more than you should be concerned about terrorism in America."

A CBS driver met me and drove me into Tel Aviv. We stopped briefly at the CBS Bureau before going on to the Hilton, where I checked into room 1445. Quixote took a hot bath, ate some good Israeli fruit, hung up his clothes, and watched Paloma defeat Francia in the World Cup. Olé, olé!

Lalie called the next morning to tell me about the Pan Am flight that crashed into Kenner after takeoff from Moissant Airport in New Orleans. It had gone down about the time I said goodbye to her and took off from Dallas to London. More than 150 people had been killed, the kind of news that shook me to the soles of my feet. One part of Quixote said, "Life is such a roll of the dice." Another part said, "Thank God for good odds."

In June, Israel had invaded Lebanon. The tanks, the guns, the Israeli hounds of summer leaped across the border and headed north to Beirut, chasing the fox, Yasir Arafat, Al Fatah, and the forces of the Palestine Liberation Organization. Fierce fighting was like storms beating with their lightning and thunder and killer winds along the eastern coast of the Mediterranean. The storm raged through the old cities of Tyre, Sidon, and Damour to the doorstep of Beirut. On the eastern flank, Israeli jets streaked across the skies of the Bekaa Valley, and tanks filled with young smiling Israeli faces rolled through the Lebanese villages, swirling the dust of the centuries.

*I thank God that after living fifty-two years I have stood on the
Mount of Olives and looked down on Gethsemane and the place where
Jesus was condemned to die, the way of the cross, and the Church of the
Holy Sepulchre. I was awestruck and grateful that I'd been so fortunate
as to see these places with my own eyes. I won't be the same as the result
of it. How could I be? I'll return to the old walled city of Jerusalem and
stroll along the streets slowly and breathe the air.*

I bought the book *Jews, God, and History*, and I thought, "How
important it is to be filled with ideas rather than to pile up property.
Knowledge cannot be taxed, is infinite, can set men free."

July 12. 4:00 a.m., from the fourteenth floor of the Tel Aviv Hilton.
*The sun rises early here, providing a pinkish, brown, dusty distinction.
The Mediterranean is a robin's-egg blue.*

At 5:00 a.m., I met my driver, Danny, and we headed north in CBS's
rented Peugeot toward the Lebanese border. We went along the coast to
Hadera and then swung up northeasterly through Afula. When I saw the
road signs to Nazareth I was dumbfounded. I hadn't expected to see a
biblical name from my childhood treated in such a commonplace
manner. We turned north again, east again, and then I had my first view
of the Sea of Galilee. It was as if I was dreaming. Or had I died in the
Laurel, Maryland, shopping center? or on the street corner in Estelí,
Nicaragua, or on the Port Kaituma airstrip? or after swallowing the
chicken bone at theTimehri Airport in Guyana? Now St. Peter was
taking me on a personally guided tour of the Promised Land.

We proceeded north again until we entered the border town of
Metulla, where I met my cameraman, Amnon Eventov. In much the
same way as Carl Sorensen and other prototypical cameramen, Amnon
did not know what fear was. He too could get a correspondent killed.

We had a breakfast of bread, cheese, and fruit before joining our
Israeli military guide, Zohar Arnon. Then we crossed over the border
into Lebanon and continued north as if we owned the country. *Hot,
dusty, and dangerous as hell on the narrow mountain roads with Israeli
tanks and trucks coming at us head-on, and we, like trout going
upstream to our breeding grounds, dodging, lurching, leaping along with*

sheer drop-offs yawning at us with mouths as wide as hungry bears. We finally reached our destination, a rare grove of Cedars of Lebanon high in the mountains where the Israeli soldiers and we rested. The grove of cedars was called Dahar Meshra El Bakara.

We stopped for lunch at Ein Mishki, where there was a grotto with a waterfall. *Thank you, God, for the little oases of our otherwise desert lives.*

We returned to the border, where I again met the driver Danny, and we backtracked to Tel Aviv. There, we edited our Cedars of Lebanon piece and, after the Israel censors approved it, fed it to CBS News in New York.

The strains of Janis Joplin's "Bobby McGee" were floating through an open door in the building where the CBS office was located in Tel Aviv, bringing back memories of Memphis, Baton Rouge, Houston, Los Angeles, and the San Joaquín Valley. An interview with opposition party member Abba Eban was set up for me in the afternoon at the Knesset. I had long admired his eloquence, but I'd not expected to meet him, much less talk with him. The interview went well with the suave, articulate Mr. Eban. He argued convincingly for the Israeli dissent in the debate about the Israeli army's invasion of Beirut, particularly military action against West Beirut.

Many fine books will be written on the complex and highly emotional subject of Israel's place in the Holy Land, the Palestinian homeland, and the surrounding Arab world. Not once have I presented myself as knowledgeable, much less expert in the ongoing debate. At the time I was in the Middle East, Thomas L. Friedman was the Beirut correspondent for the *New York Times*. Two years later he was reassigned to Jerusalem. Friedman's serious and superb print journalism led to his writing of *From Beirut to Jerusalem*, published five years later and winner of the National Book Award. His work exemplifies a level of dedication and professionalism seldom seen in the sound bite land of broadcast journalism. It will be argued that there's a place for both, print and broadcast, but we ought to be honest about the difference.

I went to dinner with CBS's chief European correspondent, Tom Fenton, at the Singing Bamboo restaurant. Fenton and correspondent Ike Pappas were ending their tours of duty and leaving the country.

Correspondent Richard Roth was also coming out after two weeks of intense combat. I looked into their tired faces and wondered how well I might acquit myself. Quixote was going in, come hell or high water—there was no turning tail.

July 14. A divine thing happened just before I went to sleep. Reading of all the bloodshed in the history of mankind, I sighed, "Oh, God, help us." I looked up and out through the window over the Mediterranean. At that moment I beheld a small cloud with a glimmer of light behind it. As soon as I said the words, "Oh, God, help us," the light began to glow brighter and brighter. It was a crescent moon, but without my glasses on, it appeared to me as an epiphany, a definite spiritual presence. I was never one to claim that I'd had anything but one-way conversations with the Great Creator, but on this occasion it seemed there might be a message coming back if I'd only listen more carefully.

I read from *Jews, God and History* until 1:00 a.m. and before 6:00 I was reading again. It was relatively quiet in Beirut after the previous Sunday's shelling. I had made up my mind that I would go into Beirut if asked, but I was not going to jump up and volunteer for it. At day's end I was given my assignment—to set forth from Tel Aviv at 5:30 the next morning with a driver heading north up the coast to the Lebanese border to meet one of the CBS crews there and to go on up through Tyre and Sidon to Beirut. Our objective: look for "targets of opportunity." Without thinking twice, I said I would go.

Thoughts of Plum Lick keep surfacing—the development of more springs, vegetable gardens irrigated by them, the end to growing tobacco, the building of fences and a tight barn lot. A sturdy facility for handling cows and calves. A place for ewes and lambs. A dry place for blocks of salt. Thoughts such as these kept me from jumping from the fourteenth floor of the Tel Aviv Hilton.

I was up at 4:30 and by 5:30 I was in front of the hotel awaiting my driver to take me north. *I pray I come out of Beirut alive. I'm all right in my mind and heart. I pray for our soul child. Am I scared? I'd be lying if I said I wasn't.*

My young Israeli driver took me up the coastal highway as if it was a runway and we were in an airplane. If our Volvo had had wings we would have been airborne and headed for the Swiss Alps. The CBS drivers played a game to see how many Volvos and Peugeots they could tear up. I held on for dear life, and so did chickens, ducks, and pigs. Finally we jolted into Nahariya, where we met our crew. Ed Mullis, a freelance cameraman from London, who formerly worked for the BBC in Beirut, was good company. After an unfulfilling cheese and fruit breakfast, we went to the nearby kibbutz, where we were assigned our military escort, a young government economist in civilian life. He had a Germanic air about him, but all in all he seemed potentially useful. His Uzi, his automatic weapon, was well regarded and sincerely appreciated.

We cleared the border at Kefar Rosh HaNigra and headed up the coastal highway of Lebanon. The view of the Mediterranean was sweeping, and it brought back fantasies of college days at the University of Kentucky. A young and callow Quixote would be a fisherman throwing out his nets or mending them, perhaps he'd be eating a loaf of bread and drinking from a jug of red wine with enticing bouquet. He'd be writing poems to young ladies wearing low-cut white cotton blouses, revealing plentiful breasts. *I saw no fishermen today. I saw just indecent destruction and devastation from Tyre to Sidon to Beirut.*

Tyre, captured by Alexander the Great in 332 B.C., destroyed by Moslems in A.D. 1291, was in ruins again in 1982. The ancient Phoenician capital looked like a dynamited rock quarry. Sidon, the other early Phoenician city farther north, was pulverized too. Nothing made sense, at least nothing made sense to a Kentucky boy who had first heard of Tyre and Sidon in his North Middletown Christian Church Sunday School lessons. They'd been painted with silken images of striking color, not heaps of cracked and ashen rubble.

An article appearing in the July 13, 1982, issue of *Newsview*, the Israeli weekly newsmagazine, admonished journalists, including gringo graduates of U.C. (University of Caracas, CBS branch): "Less than one month before the Israeli invasion some $420 million worth of damage had been caused in the city [Sidon] by fierce battles between the PLO and the Shiite-dominated militia known as the Amal."

At the last Israeli checkpoint on the edge of West Beirut near the abandoned international airport, we were routed around, up, and through

241

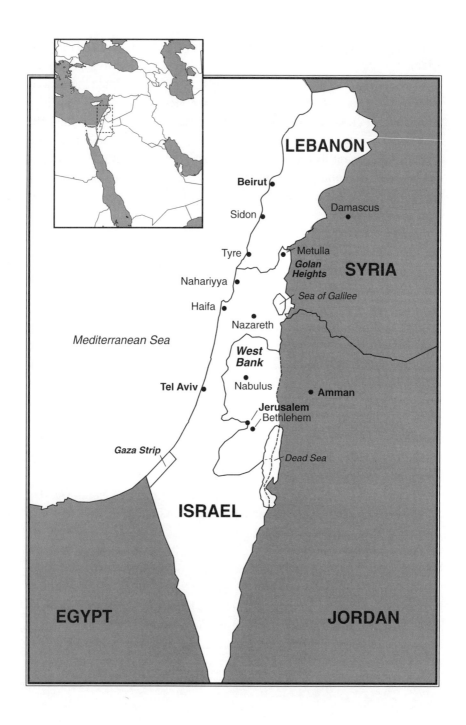

242

the mountains on the southern edge of the city lying beneath us like another of the world's impossible urban hellholes. East Beirut was seething with traffic. I had a brief peek over the "Green Line" into West Beirut, where an estimated five thousand to six thousand PLO guerrillas were trapped by the Israeli bombardment. I stopped briefly at the Alexandre Hotel and said hello to Rich Cohen, CBS producer, who was getting some sun on the roof. It had been several days since the bombing of Beirut had halted for negotiations. Everybody knew well the meaning of "cease fire." It was what in the twinkling of an eye preceded a resumption of fighting. We went to the restaurant serving as the pickup point for all networks' material heading south. On our way out of the city we took pictures of the long lines of refugees, and I did a standupper. Back in Tel Aviv that night, we made our offering to New York, but we were passed. Whenever CBS said the words, "We pass," there was no opportunity to say, "How come?" or "Why the hell not?" Passed was passed and that was that, like excommunication.

July 16. I was hungry early in the morning, so I put on my walking shorts, slipped into my new Holy Land sandals, and went shuffling off to Dizengoff Street in Tel Aviv. I found a little sidewalk place and treated myself to a Hungarian mushroom-cheese blintz and a glass of lemonade. I was playing roulette with terrorist bombs, but you simply couldn't live in a state of paralysis. The CBS Bureau beeped me and told me I did not have to go to Lebanon the next day unless I wanted to go; a CBS crew would be going as pool for all the networks. I said that dying for CBS would do nicely—I had no desire to die for ABC and NBC as well, and since I had a choice, I would not be going, thank you very much. I had one of my rare chances to "pass" and I took it. Later at the hotel, I called the office and requested a driver to take me to Jerusalem the next morning and another driver to return me to Tel Aviv when my personal pilgrimage was concluded. I finished reading *Jews, God and History* and began reading *Yasir Arafat*.

July 17. *I consider this to be one of the most meaningful days of my life, for this is the day I go to Jerusalem to explore with my mind and my body the foundations of faith. I thank God for the opportunity. I thank you, Lalie, for your continued support in all I do. I'll try to be your eyes and ears as well as your feet. I wish you were here with me, but since that is not to be at the present time, I'll do my best for us both.*

On the way to Jerusalem, I passed within fifteen kilometers of the place where David slew Goliath the Philistine. Quixote imagined himself to be the new David, but wondered whether he'd have the courage or the desire to stand up to giants, having nothing more than a sling and a single stone. I knew, instinctively, that that force was not yet in me. I would continue for a while to be only a good follower of storms.

At 10:24 a.m., I passed through the Jaffa Gate to Jerusalem. I set my unplanned course through the market center and the Jewish quarter, up and along St. James Road, where I'm writing now in my journal at the corner with the Armenian Orthodox Patriarchate Road. I keep saying, I must bring you here. I can't begin to describe it. Narrow pathways filled with people, merchants, people, merchants, holy men, some. At 11:00 a.m. I stood and marveled at the entrance to David's Tower. I climbed the steps to the top of it and proceded around the parapet overlooking Old Jerusalem. I was filled with a sense of peace and a greater appreciation of the realness of Christianity, Judaism, and Islam. Do you understand? Not just one of the three but all three along with the rest of the religions of the world.

At 12:00 noon I reached the Western Wall, the last visible and touchable part of the second Temple. I was told to put on a head covering. I did as I was instructed. When I touched the Wall it felt as if it were a piece of velvet. I kissed it. I silently prayed for you and our families. I prayed for Rose and the children. I prayed for our unborn child. I prayed for peace. I thanked God for the experience of touching with my lips the Western Wall.

Just as I wrote these words I was scolded by one of the wizened keepers of the holy place and warned to refrain from writing so close to the Wall. It pricked like a pointed example of fanaticism, but I accepted it and moved on to a cool spot where I wrote this thought. I respectfully made my way to the entrance to the Dome of the Rock, the Islamic holy place, site of Mohammed's ascent into Heaven. The gatekeeper said it was closed. I imagined it had a little something to do with the look of

Christianity written all over me. I trod up the passageway called El Wad, through the crowded vendors hawking everything under the sun. By 1:00 I was passing out of the old city through the Damascus Gate. I traveled on foot down Nabulus Road to the American Colony Hotel, where I rested and had a too-expensive buffet lunch. It is now 2:45 p.m., and it is 7:45 a.m. in Dallas. I send you kisses.

I plodded along Salah El-Din to Herod's Gate and entered the Old City again. For the next two hours I was one damn tired Quixote with powerfully aching feet. I wound up in a tight, forbidding, menacing section where there were children and more children, filth and goats up and down tortuous cobblestone corridors. I made a large circle and brought myself back to the Damascus Gate. I set my sights on the Church of the Holy Sepulchre, and when I finally reached it they wouldn't let me in because I was wearing shorts! Give me a holy break. Soldiers inside with guns, but no shorts. Lord forgive them, for they know not what they do. I was so tired from walking, it didn't matter. I went through the passageway called Suq Khan Ez-Zeit to the point where it merges with El Wad Road and then, thank the Lord, back out through the Damascus Gate. If Christ died for all these heathens, then that was some kind of generous spirit he possessed.

I went to a telephone to make contact with the driver the bureau had scheduled to bring me back to Tel Aviv. When he found me, he pointed out something I'd missed—The Garden Tomb.

When I went in, only ten minutes remained before closing time (5:30). I could only pause for a few moments and look at "Golgotha," realizing I might be looking at the exact place where Christ was crucified. I also went into the tomb where Christ's body may have been placed, although the "Place of the Skull" is enshrined within the Church of the Holy Sepulchre. I think it's ironic that I was not allowed in the latter because I was wearing shorts, while they were acceptable at the Garden Tomb. There the Church of England representatives were cordial and helpful.

First thing I did at the Tel Aviv Hilton was to take a hot bath in a valiant effort to remove all the holy dirt I'd accumulated this day, a day I'd not soon forget. I ordered ice cream to the room.

The seventh Sunday after Pentecost, July 18, 1982. *Had a call from the office last night telling me that a driver would pick me up at 7:00 a.m. here at the Hilton to take me to Jerusalem, where I would meet a crew and go on to Bethlehem. A man had been shot there yesterday and reaction to it was anticipated.*

Danny drove me over to Jerusalem to the CBS office, where I met the Moshe Ben-Dar crew. They drove me to Bethlehem. The city was peaceful, so I excused myself and went directly to Mass at Holy Nativity Church. I didn't wait. I didn't ask for permission or measure the height of the little doorway. I didn't ask the good padre if it would be all right to take communion. I didn't go to confession. I just got in line, slinked to the altar rail, and left the rest to the Almighty.

Later we went in search of a new settlement of Israelis on the West Bank. The area made West Texas look like the Garden of Eden. It was my first experience with a "wilderness," and after this occasion when I'd see the word in the Bible, I'd know it did not mean trees. It meant huge boulders, sand, and weeds blowing with crackling sounds.

...the desert shall rejoice, and blossom as the rose...for in the wilderness shall waters break out, and streams in the desert.

The words from Isaiah would have richer meaning with the viewing of Solomon's Pools, where I rededicated myself to the development of the springs from the hills at Plum Lick in Kentucky. These were the first drops of water in the subconscious pool of an understanding of the oneness of humanity and the water cycle, a fundamental idea to be developed after much introspection, fervent prayer, reading, and sustained writing.

I bought for us in Bethlehem today two large brass vases, a brass bell, and the figure of a man carved from olivewood. It speaks to how I view my approaching old age: slouched hat, hunting bag slung over shoulder, pipe touching lips, slight inclination of mortal body in the direction of immortal soul.

July 20. Danny picked me up at the Hilton at 6:00 a.m., and we headed up the long series of roads to Metulla on the Lebanese border. We met the Ed Mullis crew in Metulla, hooked up with our military escort, and then drove into Lebanon. A Christian charismatic, a true loony tune, told me, in what was supposed to be a serious interview, that a prophecy would be fulfilled. He declared that God would take a hook and pull Russia into this valley and destroy it with hailstones and pestilence. Other than this mumbo jumbo it was a relatively quiet day.

On the way back to Tel Aviv I had Danny drive me along the Sea of Galilee through Tibernias. It became my favorite body of water. I could not decide why this was so. I had visited many other seas and lakes in many parts of the world, including Kentucky, but the Sea of Galilee had a unique essence, as if at any moment Jesus would appear during a storm to calm the fears of his disciples.

July 27. I received my assignment for the next day: to go to Lebanon and visit a Syrian prisoner of war camp. I went out to a fruit and vegetable stand and purchased all I needed for a couple of meals for under two dollars. I watched on Israeli television the footage of the destruction in West Beirut. Horrifying. No matter what one's judgment is about it, Israel was destroying a city. *May you never have to see a war.*

After Israeli jets completed their bombing mission on a single day in the summer of '82, the dead numbered at least 120 in West Beirut, and the injured totaled more than 230. The target was 6,000 PLO fighters. But again and again it was the civilian population—women, children, and the aged—who were caught in the bombardment, pulverized along with the concrete.

July 28. Danny picked me up at 5:00 a.m. He said when he's not driving for CBS he's an apiarist, a tender of beehives, an avid collector of honey, and I can well believe it, for his driving and his manner are smoothly and sweetly confident. On our way up to Metulla I asked him if he'd please take us into Nazareth, the boyhood beginnings of Jesus. It was quite early in the morning. I went into St. Joseph's Catholic Church, where there were no more than three women attending Mass. *I knelt and said a prayer for you, our unconceived child, and for me.*

We entered Metulla about 8:00. On the radio we heard that the air and sea bombardment of West Beirut had continued another night and that there had been many casualties. *Most Israelis I talk to either don't want to believe it or don't want to talk about it.*

I visited Beaufort Castle in Lebanon, a fortress built by the Crusaders about AD 1100-1200. From its height, in 1982, it seemed possible to view eternity. I was there only moments, for at 2:00 I was looking into the cheerless faces of five to six thousand men behind wire fences in an Israeli prisoner of war camp. We had pictures, but they didn't add up to a story. The gloomy faces would go into the deep end of the CBS archives pool. The view from Beaufort Castle would live in the expansion of personal discernment, defying imprisonment.

Danny drove me down the valley of the River Jordan, and it restoreth my soul! For me, the Jordan and the Sea of Galilee had become essential parts of the water cycle, the unity of humanity. Within that understanding would grow an improved appreciation for what awaited me in the Commonwealth of Kentucky—rills and rivulets and runs, branches, licks, creeks, and rivers flowing toward the Gulf of Mexico. Along the way, there would be people to visit and to write about.

There was another "cease-fire" in Beirut. I ate roast lamb in Tel Aviv. Late in the afternoon, I bought a Bible and a Bible Atlas and went to the balcony of my room overlooking the Mediterranean. I wanted to become absorbed in the reading. I had completed *The West Bank Story* and *The Jerusalem I Love* and was continuing to read *O Jerusalem!* I had also begun Leon Uris's *Exodus*. Reading from Genesis on the edge of the Mediterranean at Tel Aviv was a marvelous experience. I ate watermelon in my room and retired for a peaceful night's sleep.

The latest cease-fire was broken, then followed by a new "All Quiet." It was time to look for the dead and wounded. I waited in Tel Aviv to be sent back to Beirut as soon as the fighting resumed. I bided my time by counting the seeds in one watermelon: there were 589. In one honeydew melon, 576. The project made more sense than counting human casualties. Did it not?

I proceeded with my reading of Exodus, the second book of Moses, and then switched on BBC for the 7:00 a.m. news. Naturally the cease-fire in Beirut had been broken again early on the morning of the first day in August 1982. Israel was pounding the western sector of the city. I called the bureau to check on the situation in "the Jewel of the Mediterranean" and was told there had been heavy action, with Israeli ground troops seeming to be on the move. PLO positions were under attack at the airport. I wondered if this is the real start of the final assault on the trapped PLO. *My assignment tomorrow is to go with the Naim Mor crew up the coast to the area of the fighting.*

I took a long ramble in the afternoon along the beach, south in the direction of Jaffa, thinking I might be able to make it the whole distance. The hot sun and my feet aching in my sandals turned me around a little more than halfway there. Coming back I saw what seemed to be a sexual assault, or the beginning of one, a rape in the back seat of a speeding car. If I'd been closer to the crime, what would I have done? Probably nothing. The rapists would have killed the woman and me. As I approached the front door of the Hilton, an attractive hooker smiled and said: "Hello—come here."

"No thanks," I said, and passed her by.

I went out to cover a speech by Defense Minister Sharon. He wouldn't hold still for an interview. I began to feel as unwanted as the hooker. Someone in the crowd threw a Coca-Cola can at Sharon, but it missed. Assassination and assignation were constant threats.

August 2. I was awake at 4:30 a.m., reached for my Bible, and read Chapters 18, 19, and 20 of Exodus. Verse 13 of Chapter 20 contains four unequivocal words: "Thou shalt not kill." But when does unequivocal become "sometimes"? Israelis may take seriously the Ten Commandments of their Torah, but they're not alone in modifying this one to read "Thou shalt not kill, *unless*...or, *until*."

My new driver, Norman, took me up through Haifa at the foot of Mount Carmel. At Nahariya we met our cameraman, Naim Mor, and his technician, Gabriel. We drove on up to the rendezvous point with our military escort at the Rosh Hanikru kibbutz, where I bought *In the Footsteps of Moses*, a book of exceptional pictures and a text both scholarly and readable.

I believe my brain is more susceptible to ideas now, new and old. It comes with maturity. I don't feel any hardening of the veins in my brain, not yet anyway. I feel fresh, young, and vibrant because of you.

We made a successful approach by highway to Beirut International Airport and picked up some good footage of the destruction in the aftermath of the Israeli takeover of what at best had been a no-man's land. There was artillery, mortar, and small arms weapons fire a short distance from the airport grounds. Quixote picked up a small piece of shrapnel and felt the razor sharp edges, musing about how it would feel if it were to strike a chest, an arm, or a leg. He lined up with a mushroom of smoke over his shoulder and did a Hollywood on-camera. Then we sped through the war zone, holding down our heads below the windows as our driver zipped through sections where sniper fire was unpredictable, the lulls leading the inexperienced and the naïve to false feelings of safety. It was like a shooting gallery at a county fair, and we were the ducks. We stopped, unscathed, at the Alexandre Hotel in East Beirut to check on our CBS colleagues there, and then we made the madcap dash south to the border. I had hoped to have my first piece on the *Evening News* since I had been in the Middle East, but it was not to be. I wasn't a Big Foot, only a nine and a half D. We edited for *Morning News*, and I fed radio a piece I had done in Beirut.

August 4. 7:00 a.m. On the way north to the Lebanese border I heard on BBC that there was heavy fighting in Beirut. It sounded as if the Israelis were beginning the "final assault." I recommended that rather than returning to the prisoner of war camp at Anzar, both Tel Aviv news teams should be in Beirut. Maim Mor had gone on ahead. I went in with Amnon Eventov.

The shelling in the city was heavy. The blue sky and the high, thick white clouds counterpointed the storm on the ground. The thunder and lightning were near the earth, or in it. The streets of East Beirut were empty. Amnon turned left at the top of a hill and started down it with his foot floorboarding the accelerator of the Peugeot. The avenue was completely deserted except for us, and that should have told us something. Any Moses should have known: Thou shalt not go down deserted streets. We were heading straight and powerfully as an arrow toward the bull's-eye, which was the Green Line separating East Beirut, controlled by the Christian Militia, and West Beirut, occupied by the PLO.

The "swoooooosh" of a rocket-powered grenade passed over our car. The launcher had slightly miscalculated Amnon's speed and, for a microsecond we were like missiles passing in the night. I knew the next shell would be closer because the PLO launcher was "straddling" our Peugeot. As the Israeli storm tightened the noose around the necks of six thousand PLO guerrillas in West Beirut, one of the six thousand had in the cross hairs a CBS News car. In seconds, the straddling would have a noose snuggled down tighter around the necks of journalists, and the Peugeot would pop open like a can of beans. There wasn't time for me to tell Amnon, for God's sake, make a U-turn and go back up the hill. He wouldn't have listened. We were committed to our trajectory. To turn back would have been certain suicide.

When we barreled up to the Green Line, the unmarked border cutting the bleeding city into two wedges on a chopping block, Amnon spun the car to the right and slammed on the brakes. The PLO rocket-powered launcher had us dead to rights. As my hand reached for the door release, the last RPG sucked the air off the top of the Peugeot. The "swoooooosh" had a finer whine. The paint on the car top singed and screamed like cold water sprayed on a branding iron. The launcher had missed again, but only by the barest.

Quixote slithered out of the car like a limp bean after the lid of the can had been popped open. He hit the ground and began propelling his body as low as possible. The memory returned of the day on the street corner in Estelí, Nicaragua, but Beirut was worse. Estelí was a single bullet. Beirut also had heavy machine gun fire. As I ran, I heard the bullets peppering the air already hot and choking from the August sun. As I churned my legs, I wondered why the bullets had not punctured my legs and why blood was not spurting from the holes. I was disoriented. The machine gun fire was Israeli outgoing, not PLO incoming. I stumbled through a small archway and slammed myself against the side of a building, which then was a barrier between the PLO positions and me, wanting only to survive.

A grinning Amnon joined me there with his technician, two drivers, and one more journalist. I was told it was Terry Anderson, whom I had not met before. There was no time to talk, because Israeli bombardment was encircling the PLO positions as well as us. The building that was our safe haven for the moment quivered with the concussions of the aerial bombing. Machine gun fire intensified. People were in their basements. I did an on-camera on the building side of the archway. I wore a helmet and a flak jacket, but I was not ashamed to wince as the RPGs continued to "swoooooosh" past me, seeking anything that moved.

We knew we *had* to move. We were those frigging sitting ducks again. We had to waddle across the boulevard on the edge of the Green Line in plain view of the PLO positions. We would go one at a time, Indian file, as through a gauntlet. The journalist described as Anderson of the Associated Press went first. Just as he safely reached the other side, I began to waggle low to the ground, but fast—not in a straight line but with sudden movements to the right and the left. There was one driving force—survival. Survival was everything.

We all made it safely to the other side. An Israeli tank looked like a mother welcoming a stray duckling to her folded wing. I thought about embracing the tank, but its crew would probably not have understood, or cared. I saw a face. It was CBS correspondent Bob Simon. His cameraman was taping our crossing, and if I had died, I would have made it onto the *CBS Evening News*. The obituary would have lasted about fifteen seconds, the picture would have gone to black, and there would have been a pause—then the commercial. Maybe a deodorant. Maybe dog food.

I had survived another dance with death, but for a time it was anticlimactic. I wandered inside a partially destroyed building on the East Beirut edge of the Green Line. I peeked inside a room. There in the darkness were two young Israeli soldiers playing Ping-Pong. We gave our tape to Bob Simon and Bob Faw for their *Evening News* pieces. I settled for *Morning News*. And I didn't duck radio.

August 5. *On this day I come to the end of sixteen years with CBS News. Tomorrow begins the seventeenth.* I could not know that my actual retirement date from William Paley's Tiffany Network would be almost three years later. I celebrated the seventeenth anniversary of following storms by having one of my finest efforts on the *Morning News*. I had a call from the Foreign Desk at CBS in New York: "Everybody is coming up and talking about the piece," I was told, which was a warm feeling. *Morning News* was not *Evening News*, but little down and dirty ducks can't be finicky.

A car bomb exploded outside the Alexandre Hotel in East Beirut today, wounding three. I was there yesterday. There are few safe places left in Beirut. It has been turned into a hell on earth. I pray for my safe journey tomorrow. I want to come home safely, and I want to begin our family.

August 6. *Amnon and I are returning to Beirut. We must be bonkers. But, we are messengers. Loony messengers. Well-paid loony messengers.* I read Exodus to take my mind off the insanity of the traffic on the coastal road. If it were possible for Tyre and Sidon to look more miserable, they managed to do rather well. I breathed a sigh of relief when we reached Beirut and realized there was no bombardment today. It wasn't necessary to put on our flak jackets. When we reached the main Green Line checkpoint, people from the West Side were pouring out to the east. I sat down, watched it, wrote and recorded a radio piece about it. I called it another Exodus.

We delivered two boxes of new flak jackets to our colleagues at the Alexandre Hotel, where I gawked at the damage left by yesterday's car bomb. I had stepped on the exact spot the day before. I was thankful to be alive. On the way back down the coast, I had Amnon show me more of the ancient city of Tyre. I stood in wonder at the ruins—ancient and modern. With the passage of centuries, little had changed. "Thou shalt not kill" had remained as much of an enigmatic beast as any of the other nine commandments.

Sunday, August 8. *El Dad met me at 7:30 and drove me to Jerusalem. I innocently sauntered through the portal at the Garden Tomb just as the service was beginning. How I wished you were there to share it with me.* The marvelous sound of the English language was an oasis in a wilderness of babbling foreign tongues. Next, I had El Dad drive me to the Garden of Gethsemane, where I marveled at the ancient olive trees, and I thought of Jesus there in his agony. I went inside the Church of All Nations and joined a group of tourists as they kissed the rock on which He may have made His plea to God in Heaven. I kissed it too. Then I hiked up to St. Stephen's Gate to climb the Via Dolorosa to the Church of the Holy Sepulchre. This time I was admitted, but I was appalled by the throngs of tourists taking pictures of themselves at 'The Place

Where ___." Once again, I tried to gain entrance to the Islamic Dome of the Rock, but for the second time I was told it was closed to the Christian likes of me. That's fair.

August 9. Michener's *The Source* was a companion to me going and coming from Beirut. We lucked upon a fruitful little story in Sidon— fishermen going out in their boats. I hope I captured the mood of it. With the sound of more bombardment up the road in Beirut we decided we'd better put in an appearance. We went high up on a hill and got some cover-our-butt footage. After our second and final battery ran down, we decided to call it a day.

August 10. *Up at 3:30 a.m. Read chapter 9 of Matthew concerning miracles of healing. I will take our little Bible with me today.* El Dad was on time to pick me up promptly at 4:30, and I was able to nap from Tel Aviv to Haifa. We had breakfast with the crew at Nahariya and were progressively an hour early as we passed the usual checkpoints at the border, Tyre, Sidon, Damour, and finally Beirut. It was, in many ways, a dangerous child's game we were playing in covering this war, which made it all the more cockeyed. Television crews and correspondents were everywhere competing for that precise moment when the story would reach its climax—in this case, when the PLO would make its exodus from West Beirut, or the Israeli army would make its final assault. Everyone seemed sure one or the other would happen that week. Bob Simon, the heavy hitter for *CBS Evening News*, received an ignominious gash on his head in a traffic accident. The doctors shaved the front part of his hair and sewed him up with four stitches. Just what he didn't need for his standuppers. At 2:00 p.m., the Israeli air force began bombarding the southern and western parts of the city—a sad, tragic anthill, honeycombed by the shelling. It lasted for about an hour. I did a radio spot from the top of the Alexandre Hotel. There was no way to tell how many people were dying because of the Israeli assaults.

We visited a church in Damour on the southern edge of Beirut, the site of the massacre of Christians by Palestinians in 1976, a pogrom avenged in September of 1982 when Phalangist forces murdered hundreds of Palestinian men, women, and children in the Sabra and Shatila refugee camps.

The church in Damour was as bare as the Church of San Andres destroyed by the volcanic eruption of El Chichonál in Mexico, as gutted as the Church of Virgen Pilar de Zaragoza in Nicaragua, as filled with deathly echoes as the Metropolitan Cathedral in San Salvador. Only in Damour the rear wall of the sacristy where the altar had stood was painted with a large bull's-eye. Armed men had target practiced there.

The drive back to the border was the most anal it had been since I began making those trips. The road would simply not hold all the Israeli military men and equipment heading north and all the refugees and regulars heading south. There were many hair-raising close calls, but we made it back safely long after dark with the infinite patience of a Lord who must wonder how much longer his children are going to behave like pathetically deranged ducks. Supper in Nahariya and then back to Tel Aviv where I fed radio, read from *The Source*, and fell soundly asleep.

August 11. When I talked to Bureau Chief Travis Linn in Dallas, he told me he and his crews were covering four mass murders in the state of Texas. I told him I didn't know whether I wanted to rejoin him or not. He said if I did to be careful. I thought for a time that I would be joining an Israeli army unit for three days, but the plans fell through, and the next day I would travel again up the coastal highway to Beirut.

August 12. *The ride, or chase, or race, or suicide mission—whatever you choose to call it—from the border to Beirut, was as scary as ever, and I'll be damn glad when the last trip is made. Today there were only dry holes in Beirut. There were also dry bones.*

August 13. *The passing of Henry Fonda will leave us the poorer. But while he was here on this earth he was superb. I am grateful to have lived to see another day and pray that I'll make the utmost use of it. Perhaps you and our friends who may in the future read these pages will marvel, as I do that at this moment, my hand can use the pen in the fashion it does. The talent for simply making longhand characters in any language is a miracle in itself. I did forty sit-ups this morning, and I began, one week in advance, packing my bags for Dallas. There's another cease-fire in Beirut—the eleventh. President Reagan has warned there'll be dire political, diplomatic, and economic consequences if the Israelis continue their bombardment of the city. It comes close to being an abomination. There was bitterly acrimonious debate in the Knesset yesterday.*

This trip has had the profoundest of effects on me. I'm grateful to you for helping me to complete my destiny, to run my distance, to be more gentle, more patient, more understanding, more courageous, more determined to take one earthly life and make the most of it. I promise to be good to you, to be by your side when you bring forth our child.

August 14. *I sent you kisses across the Mediterranean. I felt yours coming back. Tel Aviv sparkled in the sun today. How long will it exist? How long will America live? New York City? Woodville? Plum Lick? I want to live my remaining years at Plum Lick with you. I want to read, to fill my mind. But no, not just fill it, to adorn it, to increase the power of it, the capability of it, the spirituality of it. What miracles we are. What a miracle is every living thing. To think we are living now in these flashing moments of millions of years. The mystery of life is so deep, so unfathomable. I keep reminding myself that no one can ultimately help me but myself.*

You told me on the telephone that you cried when you heard that Henry Fonda had died. You said the CBS special closed with the words of Ensign Pulver from Mister Roberts— "Mr. Roberts is dead"—the line I delivered when, as a University of Kentucky student, I played Pulver in the play at the Guignol Theater. Then it was only a play. Now it was real. The stage was real, the players were real. People were birthed and people were dying. Storms were real storms.

August 15. *The mind is an unfathomable well where the water is sweet, and Quixote wondered if he might become a saint. Thomas Merton once was told that the first step to sainthood was to want it. I'll not dare to presume too much. I will return to you a man rededicated to making the most of life. There's much work to be done, but I promise to be unpretentious about it—not to shout from rooftops, but neither to hide my candle beneath a water maple.*

August 16. El Dad was the driver, and we headed up to my Sea of Galilee. As we passed the point where the Jordan River flows out and begins its journey south, El Dad said, "Jesus was baptized over there." The casualness of the remark was startling. I had El Dad take me to one of the loveliest spots in the world. I stood for a few moments, silently looking at it.

I did two hourly radio pieces after it was revealed that Prime Minister Begin was studying the final draft of the peace proposal worked up by U.S. envoy Phillip Habib. Peter Larkin, the CBS foreign editor in New York, asked if I would stay a few more days past my scheduled Saturday exit for the United States, in anticipation that the PLO would be evacuated from West Beirut early Saturday morning. I said I would.

Norman was my driver up to Nahariya, where I had breakfast and met the Eventov crew, and we continued to Gesher Hazio to meet our military escort. The drive up the coast was only a little less hectic until the driver of an army truck in front of us decided to back up and knock out one of our headlights. We found an infantry company near the airport and took pictures. It was a relief to see Beirut not being bombarded and beginning to resume some normal life again. "Normal" was the Christians fighting the Moslems in a civil war.

August 20. Danny drove me to Metulla where we had breakfast and met the Eventov crew. We went as far as possible up into the Bekaa Valley to the Israeli frontline at the village of Mansura, where there was a funeral for a young farmer who had stepped on a land mine that morning. It was a heartsick scene inside St. George's Church. When they opened the coffin, the family became hysterical. I felt profoundly sorry for these people, the Lebanese caught in the middle in the otherwise magnificent Bekaa Valley. As I stood at the altar I wondered if someday I might become a priest. I actually felt as if it would be a good thing to do. After the coffin had been taken to the cemetery and I had done my stand-up and a radio piece, I went back inside the church. There was no one there except God and me.

"You can't be a priest because you can't sing," Quixote wailed.

"Is that your excuse?" I answered myself.

I raised another objection and gave myself the same response. So I made a simple prayer. I prayed for peace.

I would not return to Beirut again. I would not witness the exodus of the PLO. I would not report, the following year, the bombings of the U.S. Embassy, when 40 people died, and the U.S. Marine barracks, where 216 marines were killed.

I was the lucky one. I was going home.

August 24, 1982. *El Dad was right on time at 7:45 a.m., and off we went to Ben Gurion Airport for my flight to London. The young man and I talked some more about Israel, present and future. I knew I'd never again be willing or able to dismiss Israel as a noisy nuisance. Much of the heart of America and Christianity is rooted in this little country. It is for us a source as real and as necessary as the springs on our farm in Kentucky. The springtide is, therefore, a beginning of a new life. I feel sound in body, mind, and spirit as I speed across the continent and the Atlantic to you.*

August 25. *This could be the day of the creation of David Charles Dick or Ravy Bradford Dick. You gave me new life when you first loved me. Now we are ready for the commingling of our bodies, minds, hearts, and souls, and with the miraculous power of the Great Creator, without which we could do nothing—to bring another new life to this earth.*

The English sky was a deep, passionate blue. I took a hot bath and when I emerged, BBC radio was playing "Way Down Yonder in New Orleans" and there was a smile on my face as wide as the Mississippi.

By 6:45, I was ready to head to the terminal and catch the 11:10 American Airlines flight 51 to Dallas. On the news, the first contingents of U.S. Marines had taken up positions in Beirut. *It is now 1:47 Dallas time, and I hope you're dreaming sweet dreams.* At 11:18 a.m., London time, 5:18 a.m., Dallas time, our 747 backed away from the gatehouse. Our flight path took us south of Iceland, then over the southern part of Greenland.

It's now 12:50 p.m. Dallas time, and I'm so excited I can hardly write in my journal. We started our descent into D/FW airport at 2:48 p.m. Won't be long now...It was shortly after 3:00 p.m. that we landed and I cleared immigration and customs, and then I was walking through the doorway and we were smiling and hurrying to each other. We were in each other's arms for the first time since July 9, 1982.

You told me to park in front of the house on Flowerdale Lane. You wanted us to enter through the front door. When I stepped inside the house, I saw what you had done while I'd been away. Fresh paint and wallpaper. A new sofa. A new beginning in every room. You opened the gifts I'd brought you from Israel, and not long after, our eyes met and they would not look away.

In the evening by candlelight I read to you Chapter 4 of the Song of Solomon: "Awake, O north wind; and come, thou south; blow upon my garden, that the spices thereof may flow out. Let my beloved come into his garden, and eat his pleasant fruits."

CHAPTER FOURTEEN

Ravy Bradford Dick was born June 15, 1983, almost ten months after my return from the Holy Land—a war baby and no mistake. Lalie and I had decided that such a love affair as ours should not be childless—there should be a direct descendant of our flesh and blood, a progeny to pass the torch of soul mates.

Wednesday, 1:30 a.m., Presbyterian Hospital, Dallas. *I changed as fast as I could into strictly enforced delivery room clothes. At first I tried to put my feet into the sleeves of the top part and my arms into the legs of the bottom part of the flimsy green two-piece scrub suit. A smiling nurse helped to straighten it out. A few minutes later I was at your side in the delivery room. Everything was happening so fast. At 1:53 a.m., by looking into a mirror, I could see Ravy being born. The doctor cleaned her mouth, there was a soft cry, and the nurses put her on your breast. You and I were beside ourselves with joy.*

Dan Rather sent a beautiful arrangement of flowers on this turning-point day, and so did the Atlanta bureau of CBS News—I was a new father at age fifty-three, Lalie was a mother at age thirty-eight. The hand that rocks the cradle may rule the world, but my clock was ticking, and I had visions of being in a wheelchair upon Ravy Bradford's graduation from college.

The final two years with CBS News (1983-1985) in the Southwest Bureau in Dallas had been a period of more run-and-jump assignments, occasional soul-searching, and more than my share of deep-seated foreboding. There were long days and nights at the Johnson and Kennedy Space Centers, where I lived in absolute fear there'd be a disaster on my watch and I'd have to be an instant expert, live, coast-to-coast. I interviewed astronomer Carl Sagan and fearfully asked him, "Are there other civilizations out there?" He replied, "Hundreds." *Cosmos* had a weary, long-suffering look on its face, and I felt overwhelmed. A gaggle of Martians might land at Houston Intercontinental, and I'd be expected to ask, "How do you feel?" There were so many calamitous possibilities. But I was spared the unforgettable Challenger disaster that happened six months after my retirement.

I'd gone to the University of Alabama the day Paul "Bear" Bryant died, January 26, 1983. I did interviews but Bernie Goldberg reported the story from New York, and therein was a hint of handwriting on the wall—my career as a network correspondent had probably peaked. On the stage of no-business-like-show-business, Bernie's and many others' stopwatches were ticking faster than they knew—Phyllis George Brown, Connie Chung, even Dan Rather.

On trips to New York that year, Lalie and I had seen *A Chorus Line, Chicago,* and *Evita,* but then there was that nasty little oil spill on the Texas Gulf coast in 1984, the year Johnny Weissmuller died. I'd interviewed "Tarzan" in his retirement in Florida and, just for me, he'd uncorked the famous yell one more time. I was beginning to feel like a real senior citizen when I interviewed ninety-one-year-old Bob Hope, so deaf he could barely understand the questions.

One of the most memorable last stories in my nineteen-year career with CBS was David "The Bubble Boy," the Houston child who suffered a defective immune system and spent most of his twelve years inside a plastic bubble. He died Feb. 22, 1984. The *CBS Evening News* aired my report, and *Travis Linn called from Dallas to say, "David the Bubble Boy" was one of the finest things he'd ever seen. He said, New York was "elated."* David's parents were devastated. We honored their request not to put a camera in their face at the burial service.

Other assignments during this two-year period included the execution of James "Cowboy" Autry, the monster tornado at Morris, Oklahoma, and an anti-drug campaign in Arkadelphia, Arkansas. Seven and a half tons of dogs and cats were put to sleep each week in Houston, and when we reported the grim details the switchboards went crazy. Willie Nelson's annual birthday party reached fever pitch near Austin, and we were there. These and other happenings laid the foundation, I believe, for my nonfiction writing career in the last years of my life.

On a trip to Kentucky in April 1985 to deliver the Joe Creason Lecture at the University of Kentucky, my aging stepfather, Mr. Bill, invited us to dinner at Mt. Auburn. I looked again at the winding stairway, rubbed my hand along the railing, top to bottom, and remembered the man in the white coat. I peeked into the room where I often awakened to watch through the window when storms rolled in, and I went out to the barn where I recalled that day I took Lady for a ride.

In the summer of 1984 I flew to New Orleans to be with Lalie and Ravy Bradford at the Louisiana World's Fair: *One of the highlights of the day was our ride on the giant gondola across Ole Man River and back again. We had lunch together at Pete Fountain's Reunion Hall—red beans and rice and jambalaya and bread pudding. We shared the water exhibits and added to our growing knowledge of the greatest resource we have at Plum Lick and throughout Earth—water. In the evening we stopped back at Pete Fountain's place and listened to the old master in person. You had Bourbon, I had Scotch, and Ravy Bradford had her bottle of milk.*

On the way to our second day at the World's Fair, we talked about the possibility of having a second child. Lalie declared without qualification or reservation that she did not want to become pregnant again. Although I'd wanted us to have a son named David Charles, I told her I didn't want to have another child just to assuage my ego. *We love you, Ravy Bradford Dick—we'll not spoil you, but you are our flesh and blood, you are our love child, and we pray you will have children and they will have children and through these pages they'll know that they came from two loving, most imperfect people—David and Lalie.*

Van Gordon Sauter, when he was president of CBS News, was quoted as saying: "Running CBS News is like running a baseball team; if you've got a bunch of old overpaid .260 hitters you trade 'em off and get some cheaper, younger .260 hitters, in the hope that they become .300 hitters." Well, at age fifty-five I'd played on the team, hit a few home runs, could be counted on to steal a few bases, but I wasn't what the front office called a heavy hitter. My voluntary early retirement was timely because my lifetime batting average was about .250.

I didn't lust to become a whistle blower or a kiss-and-teller, but there were a few stories I think deserve to see the light of day.

August 16, 1984: Correspondent Jerry Bowen and a crew were hustled off in a Lear jet to the Rio Grande Valley to check out a story about a town putting up a "No Bums" sign at the dump to discourage the hungry from eating there. Dan Rather wanted it the instant he heard about it. His Republican detractors would say (and they would, in some measure, be right), that Rather wanted this story because it was in Dallas virtually on the eve of the G.O.P. National Convention. Trouble is, there was no story evident when the correspondent and cameraman arrived (the sign was gone), and that led to a whole lot of gnashing teeth in and around The Big Apple. "We got fucked," was the most frequently heard battle cry.

August 21. I thought it was unforgivable that tonight at the convention, CBS was conducting interviews during the Pledge of Allegiance, the National Anthem, and the opening prayer. If this makes me a conservative Republican then I guess that's what I am.

I shook hands with Van Gordon Sauter, who had risen to become executive vice-president, broadcast group, CBS. He might've been trying to remember my batting average, but more than likely he was more concerned about Rather's ratings.

August 23. I was awakened about 4 a.m. by a phone call from the newsroom at the Convention Center. The old School Book Depository was on fire, a five-alarmer—get down there and join the crew for a Morning News *piece. Visions of flames and the ghost of Lee Harvey Oswald danced across the countryside of my mind. So did the possibility of a "live shot" into the network and a lot of ad-libbing about something going back twenty years. It's the kind of scary stuff that I intend to include in my courses at the University of Kentucky next year. I made it down to the fire scene, met the crew, talked to the newsroom at the Convention Center, determined I had about one hour to get everything done, hurried over to the Convention Center, quickly wrote and recorded a one-minute piece, fed radio the same spot over the phone directly to New York, and was debriefed. I was spared having to do a live on-scener.*

When I walked out of the Convention Center on the final night of the Republican National Convention, I had a sense of one of those major passages of time, but I walked straight ahead, never once looking back. I thought CBS coverage of this GOP love feast was awkward and lacking in good judgment. Tonight I attended the post-convention party given by CBS at the Adolphus Hotel. Everybody got a cowboy hat. I spoke with Rather and Cronkite, but I didn't stand toe to toe with them and tell them what I really thought. Outside in the parking lot, I said "No" to a hooker.

August 30, 1984. University of Kentucky Chancellor Art Gallaher tells me he is enthusiastic about my coming to UK to teach. *There seems to be no doubt that I will be a college professor next year.* Gallaher called again on September 12 and told me he and President Otis Singletary had authorized a position on the faculty for me beginning in the fall of 1985! I'm going home at last! *I can truly begin to prepare myself for the four seasons of Kentucky. I consider it to be the most wonderful time of our lives together. It seems natural and sweet and uplifting—a reward for having worked so hard out here on so many roads from one end of this country to the other.*

I received our early retirement benefit numbers from our agent, Stu Witt, in New York. He confirmed that many heads were about to roll at ABC, and he said CBS was also in a head-counting mode. He agreed that our timing may have been well-crafted.

October 17. *Phyllis George Brown, former Miss America, former First Lady of Kentucky, fixture on* CBS Sports NFL Today, *will be given a two-week tryout on the* CBS Morning News. *She looked good and was as polished as the professional she has come to be—but professional in a Miss America sense, a smashingly beautiful face and voice-quality sense. It must make many sensitive female journalists want to go out and throw up their toenails. This is the direction journalism is heading, another clear confirmation of my judgment to cash in chips, fold tent, and head for our old Kentucky home.*

In late October the news leaked out that I was leaving CBS as of June 30, 1985, to begin teaching at the University of Kentucky. *I'm committing myself to being a creative writer for the next twenty years— then I'll do it all over again from age seventy-five to ninety-five. I'm looking forward to writing what I want to, when I want to, where I want to, how I want to, without having some frigging producers in New York or anywhere else in the world pickin' nits like they don't have anything else better to do.*

On November 13, I received a personal letter from Rather. *It was a good and warmly written letter, and I'll treasure it.* Dan was supportive of me during my rookie year (1966) in Washington, D.C., and there were many times when he could have pushed my exit button but didn't. To this day, in 2002, I view him as the hardest working broadcast journalist I've ever known, but there've been many times when I've questioned his emotional manner, and I'm troubled by the charges of political bias. A day of reckoning will one day come for every player—even Babe Ruth (.342 lifetime batting average) was finally reduced to coaching the Dodgers.

November 13, 1984. I was sent to El Paso. *About 9 p.m. I took one of our car rentals out to the airport to meet my old friend, John Boy Vincent, who was arriving from Los Angeles. He looked almost the same as I remembered him the last time I saw him in 1982, during the Falkland Islands war. John Boy is married now to an Argentinean, and they live in Santa Monica. He has become a field producer for CBS!*

November 14. To Chihuahua City, Mexico, to do a story. *Thousands of peasants fleeing marijuana fields where they've been forced to work under slave-like conditions. We went right away to the train station, where Mexican army soldiers were heavily armed and walking up and down the platform. As if on cue, nine cattle trucks pulled up. As I said in my script for the* CBS Evening News with Dan Rather*: "But they were not cattle. They were people. Nine-hundred people." The people were unloaded, some falling to the ground. The soldiers urged the people to run to the waiting train—Correle! Correle!—and they ran. There were so many faces, the ages ranging from fourteen to seventy. They were being shipped back to their villages from where they had been lured "to pick apples" but instead had been forced under armed guard to work in a massive marijuana harvest deep in the mountains of this vast, mostly desert state. We taped from every conceivable angle, including getting on the train with the peasants. John Boy was invaluable in helping with the interpreting. We were like kids in a candy store. Wherever our cameraman pointed his camera there was a portrait of a face—furrowed foreheads, brown eyes dulled, mouths drawn in moodswings.*

We raced back to the border at speeds of eighty-five to one hundred miles an hour and fed the network. *We received rave reviews from New York.*

November 16. *When I checked in with bureau chief Kathy Moore from the El Paso airport this morning, she was most appreciative of last night's piece. She told me, "You look and sound as if you have the world by the balls—and you do!"*

Well, maybe so. I wasn't so sure.

November 23, Dallas. *I lay in bed awake between 6:00 a.m. and 7:00 a.m. thinking about my human condition, hoping to be able to live not only a long time but a long quality time. I thought about snows to come on Plum Lick and how we'd cope with them.*

November 25. On Plum Lick briefly: *We will take care of the farm, and it will take care of us. It is more precious than jewels. It is God's creation, and how well we care for it is a measure of our self-worth and self-respect. I thank God that we have such an opportunity. Money itself means nothing to me—what matters is the precious, irreplaceable land. There is much to do and a short time in which to do it. All we can do is to work every day, to love every day, and never to lose faith.*

November 28. We postpone our planned trip to Hawaii in order to save money and increase our chances of buying the farm of our dreams.

Our attorney tries to discourage us by telling us the dismal realities of farming in 1984 in the United States and the "impossibility" of operating a farm for profit.

November 30. *I went out for a little walk over to the giant sycamore trees on the old Jim Crouch place. I wondered how many before me had stood on this spot looking up at these giant creations. I walked over to the water gap to watch the flow of Plum Lick Creek, wondering how long it would take it to get to New Orleans.*

December 3. A full day of stripping tobacco. *After work today we borrowed Bill and Lena's four-wheel-drive pickup and drove across the Rock Ridge Road and on through North Middletown to what used to be Mt. Auburn but, to me, is no more since Mr. Bill sold it. We found him, his Martha, and their Matt in their new 72- foot trailer on the ridge on the other side of the road. Mr. Bill was sitting in the corner with household effects stacked up to around his ears.*

December 7. We realize that we have to sell our 221 acres called "Little Springs" in order to buy the adjacent Windley Place, which we will rename Plum Lick Farms.

December 21. I'm told to go to Utah to cover a coal mine disaster. *I departed Dallas at 3:40 p.m. on Western Airlines. The mountains of north central New Mexico were snow covered and most pleasant to view from 32,000 feet. Somewhere down there, there must be a nice log on a fire, a loving mate, and a handsome dog.*

December 22. *Departed Salt Lake City before sunrise, heading on a southeasterly course. The mountains were well covered with snow and we flew just over and along the rim of the highest peak. Our pilot pointed out Robert Redford's cabin retreat. I'll always remember the grandeur of the mountains: Mt. Olympus and the Wasatch National Forest, Lone Peak and the Lone Peak Wilderness area. We landed on a little snowy strip outside the community of Huntington. It was zero degrees and looked like Antarctica.*

The networks and local stations are all set up with their editing gear in the union hall directly across the street from the Emery Mining Company headquarters. The fate of fourteen miners is still unknown. The bodies of thirteen others remain in the mine while rescue attempts continue. We have an "earth station" available to us...It was 8:42 p.m. when the company spokesman made the official announcement: no survivors. Twenty bodies found so far, the search continues for the last seven.

December 23. *It was announced that the Wilberg mine would be sealed with the bodies of the twenty-seven miners still inside. The fire in the mine is still burning and spreading, a threat to rescue teams. There was a total evacuation of the mine area because of high levels of methane gas. Executive producer Jonathan Rogers called from New York and called my script "lovely." At church services we had sound bites from the lone survivor of the tragedy and the wife of one of the dead miners. There is disagreement as to whether there was a causal relationship between the deadly fire and the company's pressure on the miners to set a new all-time, one-day production record.*

December 24. *We the living are so conscious of our well-being, while the dead are so dead. We should be grateful every day of our lives for every breath we breathe, for every sensation, every thought process, every act of love—the ones we receive and especially those we originate. We should be the embodiment of love.*

CBS sent Christmas dinner, and we feasted.

December 25. *The wind is God's breath, the snow is God's garment, the rain is God's tears, the sun is God's smile. And I wrote in my script for the Evening News: "Perhaps the tragedy that occurred here, that robbed these coal mining communities of twenty-seven lives, has increased the meaning of Christmas—the celebration of a birth, but at the same time, the knowledge that in birth there is death and in death there is birth."*

December 26. *Seventeen hundred people came to the memorial for the coal miners and there was a chorus of two hundred. The word had gone out on Christmas day for people to come and sing, and sing they did, beginning with "A Mighty Fortress Is Our God." I pondered deeply, life and death, and I became calmer and less fearful about my own mortality. We drove to the landing strip just north of Huntington, Utah, were our twin-engine charter was waiting to take us to Salt Lake City. A low ceiling became a problem, so we could not land in Salt Lake City. Passage through the mountains with Utah's tallest peak off to our right was spectacular. We came down for our landing in Provo, having radioed ahead for a helicopter to pick us up there and bring us on through the fog to Salt Lake City. We landed on the chopper pad on the roof of KSL-TV. The* Evening News *producers sent their praise for the work we'd done.*

February 11, 1985. I travel to Valentine, Texas, to do a Valentine's Day feature.

There's one thing you might say about Valentine, Texas, population 328. It's one of those little places with hearts as big as the sky. Nothing much ever happens here—the trains go through. When they were building this track the workmen rested here on Valentine's Day. Mrs. Kelly, the postmaster, comes out each morning to raise the flag. On Valentine's Day people come from near and far to buy homemade Valentines and have Mrs. Kelly personally stamp them. She hand-stamped about 6,000 valentines last year. David Dick, CBS News— Happy Valentine's Day from Valentine, Texas.

February 27. To New Mexico and the Acoma Reservation to do a Pueblo pottery story for *Sunday Morning. I watched Lucy, an eighty-year-old woman, as her sturdy but sensitive and sure fingers laid down the coils of moist clay she was shaping into a large pot. When finished it might command a price of three thousand dollars. The Indians go to what they call a secret mine of gray clay, bring it home chunk-size in buckets, break it into fragments, dry it in the sun, add broken shards to it, which are the remnants of pots made by ancestors, then begin molding it into the new creations. There follow much polishing by hand, the graceful painting done with colors taken from natural materials, and the firing done outside on the ground using the largest cow pies I've ever seen.*

March 5. The announcement from the University of Kentucky Board of Trustees that I've been named associate professor of journalism is a great honor. The University of Kentucky opened my mind and taught me to listen, not only to myself but to others in the world around me. It laid the foundation for a career in broadcast journalism by teaching me the importance of the humanities. I'm coming home with my wife and small child to Kentucky to spend the best years of my life.

Later that day I was on my way to West Texas to do "Spring Comes to the Big Bend." *We found bluebonnets, budding yuccas, canyon wrens, a hawk, a bright and shining stream, a setting sun, the rising full moon.*

We drove up and over into the Chisos Mountains and from there we made a long looping drive to the Santa Elena overlook—the Rio Grande cuts through canyon walls that rise almost two thousand feet. We returned to our beginning, our base of operations, where there's a spectacular view called "the Window," a V shaped opening in the mountain giving a view of the desert floor with the sun setting through it.

March 8. Boat trip on the Rio Grande. Destination: up the river to the head of the Colorado Canyon, where we put in with two large rubber-inflated boats. It was a day-long excursion from the head of the canyon to the end of it at "the Big Hill." We saw widgeons (ducks) and a herd of wild horses, and we went over rapids. I did an on-camera with the Rio Grande and Colorado Canyon in the background. We pulled in near a little cave and went for a cold swim. The water came up to my chest, which was a very good thing, because I didn't have the strength to swim against the current.

The immensity of the canyon walls puts a man's ego into extreme perspective. Unless you are irreconcilably stubborn, you will be stripped bare of all your minuscule worries, your endless attempts to immortalize yourself, all your hurt feelings, your most favorite petty considerations. If you go to Big Bend and turn loose all those fiercely, frantically held notions about yourself, you will be taken body and soul into the warmth of the Great Creator. But let us suppose you are stubborn to the end. If you remain that way long enough you most assuredly will become a ghost town, and finally even the last vestige of you will be covered over, will be sealed up in the dust of your inevitable dissolution.

March 20. To Arkansas to do a story on the state's education association.

March 21. Interviewed Gov. Bill Clinton. *He's thirty-eight years old in his first term. He certainly looks like a young Democrat on the make, on the ladder to national office, maybe president.*

April 23. The packers arrive. *In a few hours our little house will be stripped bare and the bits and pieces we've collected over the years will be*

271

put into boxes and crates for our move to our old Kentucky home. It's a time for looking ahead, walking up and putting our arms around the future.

April 27. We are temporarily back in Kentucky, bringing more things from Dallas. *It is 5:30, our first morning in Camelot, and the most wonderful rain is falling, steadily with a fine quality about it. No wind, the rain soft. The sky all around is like pure ash. Scarlett said it was like pearl gray cotton.*

May 17. *The last day. On the* CBS Morning News, *Bill Kurtis announced my retirement. On the daily conference call with the Broadcast Center in New York, Evening News executive producer Lane Vanardos said, "Good luck to David." And that was about all Moses heard from the mountaintop.*

May 18. My CBS retirement party. Vice-President David Buksbaum and national assignment editor David Fitzpatrick came from New York. Buksbaum said Rather had wanted to make a surprise appearance but was prevented from doing so by an illness in his family. Dan spoke on the eighteen-minute tape paying tribute to my career and mentioned my "marching to a different drummer." Phyllis George said if I ever needed any "Brown sugar" I could stop by her Cave Hill home in Lexington. Kathy Moore gave me a framed picture of the Dallas bureau staff. There was a large floral display from N.S. Bienstock talent agency in New York, and a personal letter from Executive Vice-President Sauter: "I want to express my appreciation for all you have done over the years to bring such distinction to CBS News. Your dedication and journalism will be missed." CBS gave me a clock from Tiffany's—the inscription didn't mention my batting average. It read "Pace Yourself," the mantra I invoked throughout my CBS career.

May 19. *We left Dallas behind without a tear, without an emotional word. It happened smoothly, as naturally as breathing. We were happy, we three, as we made our way across east Texas for the last time. Never again would I have to live in dread of covering a tornado, a hurricane, a plane crash, a presidential campaign, a hotel fire, a boating disaster, a funeral, a grieving human being, a mass murder, a Central American massacre, an idiotic jerk-around request from New York for a quick and dirty interview. Never again would I have to suffer the humiliation and indignity of having to work with some certified asses. Never again would I have to live in constant fear of having to appear live on national television and not being able to talk, the constant fear of losing composure. Never again would I have to pour my heart and soul into a script and have a producer in New York turn it upside down and inside out.*

July 1, 2002. Regrets? maybe one—Plum Lick Farm should have become Plum Lick Publishing Company sooner than it did and books ought to have become our main crops from the beginning. But we still live on the farm in the house my great-grandfather's brother built about 1850, and the view from Plum Lick is toward the world of letters rather than plowing and forcing another dollar from a disenchanted soil. In 2002 the bottom line has noticeably improved: a new road leading in, a new roof on the slightly leaning house, new septic system, new furnace and air conditioner, and new front porch.

From 1985 to 2002, Quixote came to grips with many important lessons: eleven years of teaching (1985-1996) at any university is enough to shake the soul of Job; publishing a local newspaper, *The Bourbon Times* (1988-1991) can kidnap your sanity and cause you to lose friends; owning and operating a farm (1985 and forever after) can rob you of every penny in your pocket.

You see, several funny things happened on the way to farm fantasies: foot rot and coyotes ate the sheep; wobbling cycles of market prices sealed the fate of cows and calves; and the labor force decided it didn't want to work in the tobacco patch at any price. "Alternative" crops, ballyhooed as saviors of agriculture—peppers and alfalfa—lasted about as long as snowflakes on our hot country stove. We drew the line at artichokes and ostriches.

We grow a small garden and have started an even smaller grape arbor (strictly for table consumption in our own home—we'll not be competing with California). There's one knobby pear tree and recently we discovered a small but promising asparagus bed that had been sleeping on the edge of the garden before we arrived in 1985. Now that I've reached age seventy-two I find relaxation in mowing grass and watching a wagon wheel of jonquils bloom each spring. I cut just

273

enough firewood for our bedroom fireplace—one winter at a time—and I try to stay calm about my prostate cancer, which refuses to die without me. I'm hopeful the pernicious cells and I will go together into the great goodnight about the year 2030, but there's no certainty. In 1993, I underwent surgery to determine how far my cancer had spread. It hadn't made it to the lymph system. Nine years later, after radiation, the prognosis remains—one day, one bone scan, and one positive thought at a time. My internist listens to my heart and tells me, "We're thinking a healthy hundred." My urologist says, "The die is cast," which can mean anything. My reply is, "Our die was cast the second we were born. We're all terminally ill or healthy, depending on whether the glass is half full or half empty." As Shakespeare said: "...death, a necessary end, will come when it will come."

During eleven years of teaching at the University of Kentucky, I was director of the School of Journalism, University Orator, and a member of the University of Kentucky Hall of Distinguished Alumni. I was inducted into the Kentucky Journalism Hall of Fame and received honorary doctorates from Cumberland College and Eastern Kentucky University. But none of this convinced me that I should stay in academe—there were too many convoluted faculty meetings and too many students who wanted A's for doing as little as possible. I decided it was time for me to go to Plum Lick and concentrate on writing about the people and things I knew best.

For twelve years I've written the monthly backpage column, "The View from Plum Lick," for *Kentucky Living* magazine, and I'm a regular columnist for *Appalachian Life* magazine. For seven years I've been a featured speaker for the Kentucky Humanities Council.

For six years Lalie has written a regular column, "Kentucky Women," for the Kentucky Farm Bureau's newspaper *All Around Kentucky*. She is a chalice bearer at St. Peter's Episcopal Church in Paris, Kentucky. When Ravy is home from the University of Kentucky she and her mother sing side by side in the choir—they are high sopranos.

Rose Casale Dick is a devoted grandmother and Roman Catholic communicant in Atlanta, Georgia. I wish for her a long life filled with the joys of quiet, untroubled days.

Sam Dick is anchorman at the CBS television affiliate in Lexington, Kentucky, and the father of a son and two daughters. I pray that Sam will never have to cover a Jonestown or a Beirut.

Deborah Dick Farr is a successful businesswoman in Salt Lake City, and she deserves the richest of new opportunities.

Catherine Dick O'Shields is the mother of two sons in Atlanta. Her oldest, Jay David, is named in part for me, and her youngest, Joshua, is named for his great-great-great-great grandfather, who came to Plum Lick in 1799.

Nell Dick Blankenship is a nurse in the cardiac unit of St. Joseph's Hospital in Lexington and the mother of a son and a daughter. Nell, named for her great-grandmother Nellie, is a quiet and patient caregiver.

I call upon each of my children and their children's children to remember me who can sometimes be found sitting in his rocking chair on his front porch overlooking Plum Lick Creek—he who read not only books but of himself...read of the sky, the light and the dark of the moon and its effect on humans, animals, and gardens...he who read of the early morning, the high noon, and the coming of evening...he who read of the rain, wind, and snow.

Now read of yourself. Return to your own Plum Lick whenever you feel the need. Grip the ends of the arms of a rocking chair and feel where other hands have touched.

With Lalie, I found my "peace at the center" in the old house alongside Plum Lick Creek—we call it home sweet Kentucky—where there are no committees, consultants, or circular firing squads. We've had a good life, and we pray there's more to come.

Our fear of dying has greatly diminished. Last year I became chairman of the board of the North Middletown cemetery, and Lalie is one of the volunteer workers. We enjoy mowing the grass around the monuments of Lucile and Samuel, William B. and Laura Neal Crouch, and the Rev. Coleman and Nellie Cralle Dick. James and Catherine Neal, my great-grandparents, also receive our careful attention. From time to time, we speak to them. Lalie and I have picked out the places where we too will sleep in eternity. But until that day of reckoning comes, we're dedicating ourselves to the best and fullest of lives.

It's been a long way circling around the mountain, but we've come home. I did not become an Edward R. Murrow, an Eric Sevareid, a Walter Cronkite, a Dan Rather, a Roger Mudd, a Charles Kuralt, a Bob Schieffer, or a John Roberts. What is more important, I believe, is that through it all I have remained David Dick and, with Lalie's help, I've come home to Kentucky.

The Beginning.